A
Girl's Guide
to Taking Over
the World

Writings from the Girl Zine Revolution

A Girl's Guide to Taking Over the World

Edited by

Karen Green and
Tristan Taormino

St. Martin's Griffin | New York

Design and page layout: Jaye Zimet
Editor: Mikel Wadewitz
Production editor: Mary Louise Mooney
Title page photo courtesy of Belle Iskowitz

Library of Congress Cataloging-in-publication Data

A girl's guide to taking over the world : writings from the girl zine revolution / edited by
    Karen Green and Tristan Taormino.
        p. cm.
    ISBN 0-312-15535-2
    1. American prose literature—Women authors. 2. Young women—United States—Social life and customs. 3. Young Women—United States—Literary Collections. 4. Underground press publications—United States. 5. Feminism—United States—Literary Collections. 6. American prose literature—20th century. 7. Feminism—United States. 8. Women—United States. I. Taormino, Tristan, 1971– . II. Green, Karen.
    PS647.W6G57 1997
    813.008′ 0352042—dc21   96-40528
                                                                          CIP

First St. Martin's Griffin Edition: July 1997

10 9 8 7 6 5 4 3 2 1

Table of Contents

Slumber Party   friends secrets sex

Mirror, Mirror   body image health

The Parent Trap   `parents siblings family`

Princess Phone   gossip letters technology

Runaway Daughters and Rebel Girls   politics anger power

Acknowledgments

Karen and Tristan wish to acknowledge the following people and their contributions to this project: Charlotte Abbott, Frédérique Delacoste, David Groff, and Felice Newman, for their early support of the idea and for extremely helpful suggestions; Rachel Pepper, for her overwhelming generosity and the use of her zine collection; Kate Lambert, Christine Doza, and J. M. Beazer, for diligently collecting zines and then lending them for research; R. Seth Friedman for his wisdom and advice and for being a "zine hero"; Leah Lilith Albrecht-Samarasinha, Tammy Rae Carland, Lisa Crystal Carver, Darby, Sarah Dyer, Diana Morrow, and Sabrina Sandata for their visions, their courage, and the thoughtful, honest stories they share in this book; Hillary Carlip for her book *Girl Power* and her assistance with the introduction; Michelle Duff for her smile, her love, and all her hard work on this book; Kate Bornstein, Sandra Lee Golvin, Gerry Gomez Pearlberg and Heather Lewis for their insight, advice, and friendship; D. Travers Scott and David Eckard for living a parallel life; the contributors, subscribers, and supporters of *Pucker Up*; Meow Mix Bar and the 1996 New York City Riot Grrrl Convention; Karen Finley; Adam Parfrey and Feral Press; Laura Antoniou; Kim Cooper; Ron Lieber; Dr. Ducky DooLittle; Kathy Acker and Kathe Izzo for their incredible love and support; and Ann Magnuson for all her inspiration and hard work.

Extra thanks to Mikel Wadewitz and Keith Kahla, two of the smartest editors and the best guys in the world to work with.

Karen would like to express her love and worship for Tristan, who is the most incredible partner and lover she's found on this planet. She would also like to thank the following people: Colleen Nagle and Pete Weiss, for their abundant creative energy, support, and ideas; Sarah Schulman, for her patience and love; Steve McDonough, for his enduring loyalty; Kate Lambert, for her fabulous brain; Michelley Cartaya, for all her lessons; and Laure Leber and Charles Wing, for their encouragement. As well, she thanks her mom, Van, Sal, Aunt Anna, and Joshua for their love and inspiration. Finally, Karen would like to thank her dad, Roland Brophy, for all his love and support.

Tristan would first and foremost like to thank Karen who is just about the smartest, most wonderful woman she's ever met. Tristan would also like to thank the following people: Kate Lambert for her true love of zines; Audrey Prins-Patt for still being a guardian angel; Anna Lisa and Scott McMorrow for all their contributions; Roman Altman and Jill Muir Sukenick for keeping her sane; the memory of her father, Bill Taormino, her grandfather, Thomas Pynchon, and her grandmother, Catherine Pynchon, who all made a tremendous mark on her life and who passed away during the completion of this book; and finally, to her mother, Judith Pynchon, who is the first feminist Tristan ever met and a terrific role model.

Extra special thanks and the dedication of this book to all the contributors, everyone who sent their zines, and all the girls who do zines, put their heart and soul into them, share them, and make the world a better place for other girls.

Foreword:
Zinestresses of the World Unite!
Notes on Girls Taking Over the World

by Karen Green and Tristan Taormino

"Sometimes paper is the only thing that will listen to you."
—"Jennifer" from Girl Power

Definition of a zine: "a small, handmade amateur publication done purely out of passion, rarely making a profit or breaking even."

—Factsheet Five

Girls (and boys) have been creating and circulating zines for over a decade. In the nineties, zines have exploded into an immense underground culture complete with major media coverage, zine conferences, and magazines dedicated to reviewing new zines. These zines, ranging anywhere from Xeroxed handwritten rants and cut-and-paste collages to professional design and offset printing, possess some of the most intelligent, political, and outrageous writing today. We define "girl zines" as do-it-yourself publications made primarily by and for girls and women.

As more publications for women attract high-price corporate advertising, girl zines often skip high production values and wide distribution to focus on a grassroots approach to publishing. Without the pressures of the high-powered publishing world or advertising money, zines have become forums for uncensored, underground writing on the edge. The writing in girl zines tackles important issues for girls, like body image, sexuality and violence; it also pushes the boundaries of genre, mixing personal stories, fiction, rants, poetry, essays, and journalism.

While the mainstream press centers around major urban areas, girl zines are being produced everywhere from Austin to Memphis to Minneapolis. From the deep South, the Heartland, and the Pacific Northwest, these are voices of a new generation of women writers debating feminism, politics, sex, culture, and the media. *A Girl's Guide to Taking Over the World* showcases these new (primarily young) female writers and artists, explores the power of this form of communication, illustrates

how these zines represent some of the new voices of women in America, and provides a great resource guide.

Women have historically had limited access to channels of communication, and, ultimately, to
power. We don't have to reassess statistics of unequal salaries, gender discrimination, and patriarchal
double standards; we know it's out there. We also know that there are fewer mainstream avenues
for women to articulate the injustices and the inequalities. As our capitalist society co-opts the radical energy of counterculture movements, and processes it (thus watering it down) through the media, we get only a semblance of feminist activism. However, women are still struggling to make their
way in the world.

We began this project based on the notion that zines were a growing forum of communication
for women, but we could not have predicted the overwhelming responses we received: 500 copies
of about 300 different zines. We've corresponded with so many women and girls who have thrilled
us with good spirit and provocative creations. We devoured these zines, trying to figure out just how
we could make final selections for this book. Regrettably, we don't have more room, because really,
we could fill *several* books with the material we received. We have tried, however, to compile a representative sample of the work that's out there. We have chosen what we consider to be some of
the best writing and creative work, and have tried to capture the varied flavor of the girl zine movement.

Needless to say, we've learned a great deal from the zines we have poured through. Primarily,
we've gotten an amazing overview of the major issues facing girls and women today. It is difficult to
define or generalize about the girl zine movement. Like *Ms.* Magazine Managing Editor Barbara Findlen says in her introduction to *Listen Up: Voices from the Next Feminist Generation*, "Generation X, thir-
teenth generation, twentysomething—whatever package you buy this age group in—one of the
characteristics we're known for is our disunity. Maybe we're not as unified as the generation that
preceded us. Maybe we're just not as categorizable."

Girl zines cover just about anything that concerns the girls who create them. Their incredible
creative and meaningful titles—*Alien, Not Your Bitch, Princess Charming, My Life and Sex Thrive in the J.
Crew Catalogue, Hot Snot Pot, Angry Young Woman, You Might As Well Live, Spilt Milk, Indignant Gingham,
Everything I Do Turns to Shit and Garbage, Hungry Girl, Diabolical Clits, Fierce Vagina*—represent the wide
range of zines out there. Some zines have a political nature, focusing on feminist issues, such as race,
gender, and class. Some are strictly personal, with revelations about self-esteem, relationships,
growth, and pain. Some focus on taboo issues of incest, rape, violence, sexual abuse, and mental illness with an intense emotional range. Then there are zines that are fun, that mock society, or that
focus on the nostalgia of childhood. And yet there are still more zines about being in high school, going to rock shows or worshipping particular personalities like Amy Carter, Chelsea Clinton, Joan
Jett, Audre Lorde, and Lydia Lunch. In fact, certain music icons—like Bikini Kill, Tribe 8, Liz Phair, and
Tori Amos—are featured in dozens of zines and are clearly important role models for girls.

What threads these zines together is that they are all very real and very much from the heart. They don't have advertisers to please, and they weren't created for financial success. They originate from a need for expression, a need girls have to discover and create the truth about themselves and their lives. Through zines, we can see young women uncensored and free to discuss their realities.

We know firsthand that self-publishing can be a difficult and demanding process. We publish a 68-page quarterly zine and it does drain our energy and our pockets. There is little, if any, monetary benefit from zines. On top of that, distributing your work, getting your zines out into the public eye, can be grueling, if not impossible. Most of the zines we received have a circulation under 1000, many are under 500. You may ask, "Why bother? Maybe a handful of people will read it."

But, the truth is, many of these girls and women tell us they don't do their zines for an audience necessarily. Many of them have a need to express themselves creatively and do their zines for themselves. For some, when they put their work out there, the reward is finding that their friends and other girls are touched by their stories, identify with them, and are inspired to tell *their* stories.

That's why it is so vital that we continue to support this form of communication, and why this book is so important. If we listen, maybe we can begin to understand women a little more intimately. We could learn, perhaps, what a strong and vocal group of individuals are developing in this culture. If we listen, we can hear the voices of our mothers, our daughters, our sisters, and our friends telling us their needs, their thoughts, and their emotions. We could learn more about our own families and how to grow and change without hurting each other so often. If we listen hard enough, we might begin to hear that what women really need is to be taken seriously, to be esteemed and valued, even to be worshipped, for the powerful creatures we are.

In the past decade, zines have flourished. You can find them in bookstores, in coffee shops, in record stores. People collect them or swap them or give them away on the subway. They are accessible, they are cheap or free, and they can reach people. This movement isn't one that is static, finished, or easily categorized and captured in a book. It's a vibrant, changing force that we expect will continue to develop. The groundwork has been laid for the next generation of girls and women to use these forums for expression. Schools, especially high schools, would do a great service to students if they would add zine making to their curriculum. Imagine the voice you are giving a child when you show them how to put together their thoughts, struggles, ideas, wishes and dreams in a small book.

The future holds many possibilities. Technology and the growing world of the Internet has grown vastly more accessible. Already, women and girls are putting themselves and their words and images onto the electronic landscape. Sites like Geek Girl, CyberGrrl, Gurl, and Fat Girl are just a small sample of the vastly growing arena of girls in cyberspace. (You'll notice some selections in this book from such on-line resources.) Eventually, you'll see a book or two on electronic zines (or e-zines), and how they impact our lives. E-zines will still take as much (if not more) energy and dollars, but they do provide a more colorful medium. Currently, home pages are relatively inexpensive, and the potential for wide national and international distribution is a lot more likely on the Internet.

But the proliferation of cyberspace and technology doesn't mean there will be a drop in print publishing anytime soon. A big part of the thrill in making zines is the manual work it takes to put them together. Most zine makers put a lot of effort into paste-up and often zines are full of collage-art. And from the many stickered, starred and sparkle-covered letters we received, we'd say these girls enjoy the physical labor. From our experience, this labor can be cathartic as well as inspiring.

This project has been fun and exciting for us. We reveled in all the wonderful mailings we received and in lugging home the many different zines that came to our little post office box. We've had the opportunity to see what is going on in some of the hearts and minds of women in America today. There was a lot to learn and a lot with which we identified. Some of the project, like some of the zines, was therapeutic. All of it was enlightening.

Because zines are generally personal and intimate works, they are simply about women's lives as they are lived on a daily basis. The writing tends to integrate information in a way we're not used to seeing. Among other things, zines are sites for communication, education, community, revolution, celebration, and self-expression. Historically, the titles of the sections we chose to organize the book—from the slumber party to the princess phone—are also sites for these activities. Our categories represent the spaces in women's lives where they communicate with each other and themselves. This is a personal approach, one that integrates static categories like race, class, and sexuality. Interestingly, all these spaces seem innocuous on the surface, but are actually quietly subversive; what goes on between women in these settings can be more dangerous than they appear.

Some of the things we found inside the pages of girl zines just might surprise you.

Other Voices, Other Wombs

"Pen to paper, Ann. Pen to paper."

Such were the words of a wise old therapist whenever I suffered from writers block which was, and regrettably is, often. I have always had trouble keeping a diary. But I never seem to have any problem stringing sentence after run-on sentence together whenever I'm on the phone with a sympathetic friend. Even when the friend is not so sympathetic or is clearly distracted by the television crackling on the other end of the line, the fact that someone is within earshot of my latest diatribe makes the words flow effortlessly. Knowing that someone is listening, or even just half listening, makes all the difference.

When I think of how much benefit my teenage self could have gained from the multitude of zines that have proliferated over the past decade, I weep for all the lost potential. Except for Joan of Arc and Anne Frank, the thoughts of teenage girls have rarely been taken seriously. Maybe I'm prejudiced, but this disregard seemed more pronounced during the seventies, when I was a teenager. Fueled by images of Jane Fonda straddling an anti-aircraft gun in Hanoi and Bella Abzug mouthing off under a wide brimmed hat in Washington, I yearned to storm the office of my high school newspaper and print a manifesto culled from all the anti-establishment ramblings exchanged with my fellow freaks over Kool menthol filters in the smoking area behind the gym.

Although I never took any hostages, I did manage to work my way up to senior editorial writer, where I lashed out at school authorities who forced us to attend the fascist pep rallies. I even had the audacity to play movie critic and pan Bertolucci's *Last Tango in Paris*. As a teenage girl, I was always creeped out by films where older men drooled over sweet young things. And yet, the only message that seemed to be playing over the airwaves was "Be Pretty, Be Sexy, Be Cute." All self-worth revolved around these concepts. If only I could regain the lost hours (weeks? months? years?) spent obsessing over flattening my stomach! But "fuckability" has always been promoted as a woman's most important trait. Even the "underground comics," which were supposed to be championing a new way of thinking, said the same thing. R. Crumb gave me my first glimpse of sex, and, for all its countercultured hipness, the message didn't seem much more radical than Dad's copies of *Playboy* hidden on the back shelf of his closet. And yet I didn't (or couldn't) articulate my discomfort with it all. The opinions of girls were either dismissed or vilified until, of course, those girls began to fill out their bra cups. Then those opinions would be patiently tolerated in hopes of reaching the pot of gold that lay at the end of every young hippie chick's rainbow-colored hip-huggers.

It may always be a motherfuckin' man's world, but it sure seemed more so back then. Before my self-esteem took the adolescent plunge, I had attempted to put the democratic system to a test. I called for free elections in my home to allow a rotation of power beginning with each family member having equal time sitting at the head of the dinner table. My lobbying was promptly squelched by dear ol' disapproving Dad. My first political act, defeated by the patriarchial state.

Where in this media-driven society was a young militant in a training bra to go? In the 1990s she can go to a Bikini Kill concert and realize that self-expression is just a power chord away. Or fire up the PC and spew out her rage on a website full of like minded misfits. Or pick up any one of the countless zines circulating on a given day and realize that she is not the only one feeling suffocated by the Barbie conspiracy. Or she can put pen to paper and start her own media empire.

But in the early seventies? Oh sure, we had *Ms.* magazine, but to a thirteen-year-old girl who wanted to enjoy being a girl, *Ms.* seemed too "old"; too "stodgy." It lacked the irreverent humor I loved reading in *National Lampoon* or the glamour of *Star,* the first (and only) magazine that covered the misadventures of the jailbait groupies on the glitter rock scene. Still, life for a junior miss back in the 1970s seemed to fall in one of two categories—the cock-rock world mythologized in *Rolling Stone* or the pimple-free, mini-padded cell wallpapered with the squeaky-clean pages of *Glamour* and *Seventeen.*

Fortunately, for me, there was a world of subversion right in the heart of small-town America. It was called The Library. There I stumbled upon the autobiography of Isadora Duncan. Armed with that book and Patti Smith's debut album, I eventually found the courage to move to New York City, where I was soon elected president of the Ladies Auxilliary of the Lower East Side. Formed from a coven of suburban refugee art students and born-and-raised Noo Yawk rock chicks, we met once a week to engage in a potluck ritual that simultaneously mocked and celebrated the Junior League.

We organized events such as the Stay Free Mini Prom where all the losers who were never asked to dance at their proms the first time around could rise, Carrie-like, from the ashes. We tested our Amazonian prowess as we faced each other in the ring on Ladies Wrestling Night. We invited a Mary Kay cosmetic representative (and *his* bodybuilder "assistant") into our inner sanctum and wreaked havoc with their powder puffs. We created a Secret Boy File, listing the pros and cons of each scenester it had been our pleasure (or displeasure) to date.

This last activity seemed to empower us more than any of the others, and it became clear that by joining forces (and comparing notes) nothing and no one could stop us.

One member whose day job came with a word processor and free photocopying suggested we consolidate the minutes from each meeting into a newsletter. I suppose we could have called it a zine. Each week we added names to our Hall of Fame (Ellie Mae Clampett—for her culinary skills; Betty Page—for her grace under pressure); voted on the Creep Of the Week (always male); and printed progress reports on the worthwhile charity work we engaged in (such as setting up a Fund for Anita Pallenberg, whose glorious former self as Barbarella's lesbian vixen lover we watched metamorphose over at everyone's favorite den of iniquity, the Mudd Club.)

But never had I seen the power of the press more powerful than when we decided to form an all-girl, all-percussive "orchestra" to play at our Rites of Spring Bacchanal. After Pulsallama's first gig we got a rave review in one of the first zines I ever saw, called *Short Newz*. This one page xerox sheet chronicled the latest on the downtown music scene. The effect it had on the "Ladies" was both awe-inspiring and terrifying.

With just a few assorted adjectives, conjunctions, and well-deserved exclamation points, the duality of woman was revealed. Suddenly, we were stars, and there wasn't enough lime in the limelight to go around. Though more gigs, more press, and even an EP were to come of it, jealousy and ambition did us in. It also ended the Ladies Auxillary.

But like the atom, the enormous energy of Eve and her descendants, when properly harnessed, can well exceed the power of a million sons. Though everyone in Pulsallama eventually became friends again, it was never to be the same. At one point, some of us even wanted to create our own magazine. We pooled our dues money, and I was sent to take a course at The New School called "Starting Your Own Magazine." It was taught by some guy who exuded a "been there/done that" world weariness that had no doubt been the result of his failure to become the next Rupert Murdoch. His enthusiasm was infectious. I had never been more discouraged in my life.

I returned to the group defeated. It would just take too much time and money to start a "real" magazine. Why we never thought to just scribble our opinions down and head to the nearest Kinko's eludes me. Maybe we were burnt out. Maybe it was time we all made some money. Maybe we figured no one was listening. Who knows?

From the Revolutionary rabble-rousing of Thomas Paine's pamphlets, to the Unabomber manifesto, Do-It-Yourself publication is as American as Mom's homemade pipe bomb. Even so, the DIY aesthetic that has fueled bohemias past and present can wear a person out. The energy I had when I was nine and hand printing copies of the *Sweetbrier Road Neighborhood News* served me well into my thirties. But I get down on my knees every night and thank the Goddess for all the fresh talent popping out of her womb every day that can grab the baton and fly like a bat out of hell into the future. So, after a long relaxing soak in a hot bath full of herbal-scented epsom salts, I can recharge my battery by leafing through my new issue of *Bust*—which never fails to inspire.

Maybe I didn't have all these great zines when I was a teen but that doesn't mean they can't work retroactively. Reading *A Girl's Guide to Taking Over the World*, I marvel at the choices offered to teenagers and young women today. Opinions! Unexpurged, unedited and unapologetic opinions that are no longer easy to dismiss. Why? Because the dots are being connected now and the audience is bigger than ever. And for any grrrl who is terrified of putting pen to paper, fear not. Someone is listening.

Actress, singer, writer, and recovering performance artist, Ann Magnuson moved to Los Angeles in the late eighties after years of performing in the downtown New York City art and music scene where she played den mother at the now infamous club 57. Most familiar to television audiences for her role as the eccentric magazine editor in *Anything but Love* (opposite Richard Lewis and Jamie Lee Curtis), she has also appeared in her own Cinemax comedy special, *Vandemonium*. Her other television appearances include *The John Laroquette Show, Caroline in the City, The Drew Carey Show*, and as Lily Munster in *The Munster's Scary Little Christmas*. Her film credits include *Clear and Present Danger, Making Mr. Right*, and *The Hunger*. She has performed on stages all over the world, including Off Broadway in *Four Dogs and a Bone* and in her critically acclaimed one-woman show, *You Could Be Home Now*, at The Public Theater. She has released five indie albums with the cult rock band Bongwater, and her solo debut, *The Luv Show*, was released on Geffen Records. Her writing has appeared in *Spin, Details, Vogue, Harper's Bazaar*, and *Conde Nast Traveler*. She can be found in cyberspace at http://sd.znet.com/~tkytoast/annpage/.

Slumber party

friends   secrets   sex

Slumber parties are notorious for their raucous laughter, their all-

night talking, and even the unmentionable, first sexual encounters. Like

the slumber party, the pieces in this section describe some of the most

intimate moments between friends. Here, zinemakers reveal some of

their secret desires, talk about their closest friends, and explore their

sexuality.

Tristan Taormino

Sticks and Stones May Break My Bones

By Leah Lilith Albrecht-Samarasinha,

editor of Patti Smith and Sticks & Stones

Patti Smith, my first zine, was named after Patti Smith (no shit), the woman/goddess/poet/performer who got me into punk rock and was a major influence on my writing. Y'see, I was a crazy, suicidal, arrogant, brilliant, mutt sixteen-year-old queer-power slut on scholarship to a bougie hell of a private school that didn't know where I came from but couldn't wait for me to go back. This, also, in a dying mill town with a boy-mosh-core punk scene with little politics other than the local chapters of the Hammer Skins. Patti made a lot of sense. The zine I named in her honor started out as a goth/surrealist kinda thing that also published all my friends who were good writers but couldn't get published by school lit rags because we were talking about sex and killing ourselves, and continued with me till college. *Patti Smith* published writing about sex and death, bulimia, being a teen queer, with a proto-grrrl aesthetic. Proto, 'cause when I started it I had no idea there were any other girls my age who identified as feminists the way I did—angry, slutty, rageful girls who took no shit. Even once I became aware of the existence of Riot Grrrl, I still felt like too much of a bitch to fully fit into the sweet, nice-nice "girly" attitude of a lot of grrrl zines I saw.

Sticks and Stones came out when I was nineteen, in December and January 1994–95. In *Sticks and Stones,* I published the rants about abuse in my family that I'd been writing in my journal since I'd got the hell out, but had never even shown my close friends. I also published pieces about being mixed-race and working class and connected all three—firsts all around for me. By then, I'd been living on my own in New York City for a year, had tried getting involved with Loisaida-style anarcho-punk, and was starting to leave it, as well as Riot Grrrl, behind. I was coming to realize that the reality of those groups was far less than their reputation, and much of the time they did not understand or respect my colored girl, leather-dyke, femme, survivor self. *Sticks and Stones* came out of my trying to stay in punk/Riot Grrrl youth culture and remake it with others along anti-racist and anti-classist lines 'cause it had meant so much to me. Riot Grrrl zines and music were homemade productions from other crazy girls that told me I was not crazy or horrible, a freak isolated from all the world. Grrrl zines like Erika

Reinstein's *Fantastic Fanzine,* Ananda La Vita's *Smile for Me,* Chandran's *Bloodline,* Christine Doza's *Upslut* and *Construction Paper* were more important than I can fucking say in my healing process. They all showed me that you could tell the truth about things you were never supposed to, and live.

I left Riot Grrrl behind because it could not grow with the questions we were asking of it. It was a movement founded in the ideas that girl love can save the world, that grrrl unity could conquer all—which it can't, and those of us who realized that ended up moving further out, creating our own new freak scenes. But I will always remain grateful to grrrl-punk and zine culture for teaching me to speak the truth, love my freakishness and make my own freedom. It started me on the journey.

was to be the cheese...

three dollars

Maxine

a literate companion for churlish girls and rakish women

ambi

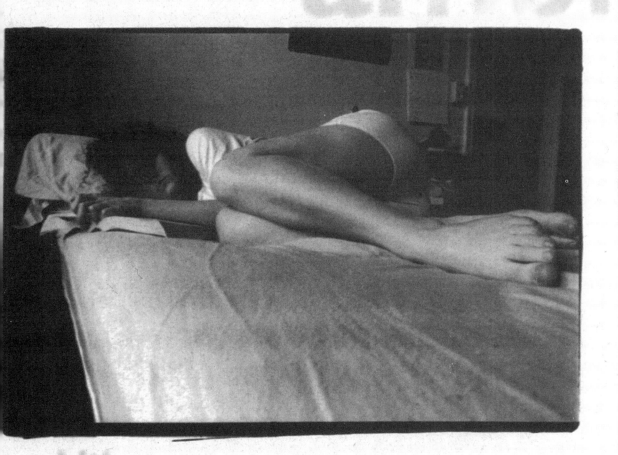

ambition

ambition

TORI MARLAN, MAXINE #2

Learning to Fuck

Sandra Lee Golvin (from <u>Diabolical Clits</u>)

On my forty-first birthday I learn how to fuck you. How it took so many years I cannot explain. I was not prepared for the place I went to as I moved that plasticene cock in and out of your cunt as it sucked for more. You did not tell me that I would be able to feel myself inside of you I mean all the way in the deep place tapping the far end of your pussy, feel myself all along the length of that dark wet place that wanted me I could tell. You are my butch lover, you wield the cock from behind sending me home sweet home. But you will lay on your back for me, dig the way I thrust into you, find the rhythm that sends you flying up that hot rod, my cock, over and over past the point of satiation so that it will never be enough for you or for me. Now I wake up every morning wanting to take you in that way, me standing by the side of the bed, you with legs bent, ass at the edge, cunt open and wet, waiting for me. There is a power in my hips that charges us when I strap on the black leather harness with the cock that wants you like a divining rod wants water. He takes me to you, finds the way in the dark and eases in, slowly, out, slowly, in, slowly, always slowly in this beginning time. As we find that rhythm, that salsa, that cha cha cha, I hear the smack of our cunt lips sucking wet and the sound makes me weak. I grab your ass and raise your steaming pussy up to meet me, driving my hot rod home. You have told me how watching this makes you crazy and now I know what you have meant, how the slipping in and out just sends me, explodes my brain as I lead with my hips, suck your toes, fuck you fuck you fuck you to another place. I hear myself whisper *"mi mujer, mi mujer."* And the words take me all the way to the knowledge, the first time knowledge, that in this moment I am not "she," but something else, and you, you my butch love, are my woman.

Jesus Kick

by Julene Snyder (from youtalkintame?)

He's hot. And, God forgive me, I want Him. He's hanging up there on the cross, all anguished and bleeding, just a winding scrap of loin-cloth that clings, hinting at coy shadows beneath. He's been through so much . . . but now I'm here to ease His pain.

Clearly, He wants me, too. He wants me bad.

I'll be going to Hell any minute now, because I want Him back. I'm in line waiting for communion, and that's the moment that the Lamb of God chooses—in all his omniscient wisdom—to hit me smack between the thighs.

Thanks a lot, Jeez, for this sticky, awkward moment—reeking of dripping panties and impure thoughts—as I wait for the wheezing priest to slime a host on top of my tongue. I sneak a look up Christ Our Lord's loincloth, but I can't see a fucking thing.

I curse—silently, but with great frustration—and walk slowly back to our pew, hands folded devoutly before me.

I'm eleven years old.

And I want the Son of God so bad it hurts.

I am definitely going straight to Hell.

I'm lying in bed, but I have no intention of going to sleep just now. I learned a long time ago, how—if I rubbed that one spot exactly hard enough, with just precisely the right motion—I can make stars blast straight from my crotch and clear across the bedroom ceiling.

Tonight, I have a new story to illustrate my nightly ritual, one that has to do with a certain nearly naked, ropy-muscled body, and a particular pair of crossed, neatly nailed feet.

Ohhhh yeah. Sweet Jesus.

The thing about Sunday is it comes every week, no matter how hard you pray. And the other thing about Sunday—if, that is, you're being raised as a Catholic this week—is you have to go to Confession.

Whoops. That part hadn't occurred to me earlier in the week—an extremely moist, passion-play-filled week—punctuated with nightly offerings to Christ Our Lord, followed by prayers for forgiveness and promises I'd never think of Him "that way" again.

Promises that I'd broken, without fail. Now, the jig was up. It was time to confess. Everything.

"Bless me father, for I have sinned."

I swallow.

"It has been one week since my last confession."

I pause. Swallow again.

"I . . . uh . . . I dishonored my mother this week. One time I whispered 'bitch' at her back because she wanted me to do the dishes and the *Banana Splits* were coming on."

I swallow. More of a gulp, really.

"I . . . uh . . . I lied, when I told my mother that my little brother had knocked over her Hummel figurine, even though I really did it. But it was an accident, I swear."

I try to swallow, but can't. Something's caught there. Something that feels much too large to fit down my throat.

I don't know how to say it, exactly.

Somehow, "Gee father, I've been beating off to the image of Jesus Christ every night for a week, and boy! does He get me off," doesn't seem quite right.

"Three Hail Mary's, my child," I hear him say.

And before I know it, I'm out the door of the confessional. Off the hook.

Except that God knows. He knows good and well that I haven't confessed all my sins. No wonder I feel so guilty.

When my mother comes out of her confessional, she finds one anguished penitent waiting for her.

"What? What is it, honey? Did that priest say something bad to you?" She looks so fierce it makes me wonder for a minute why she thinks a priest would be bad. Can't she tell that I'm the bad one? God sure knows. He knows all about my badness in the dark every night, right before I say those lying prayers, the ones that promise never to do it again.

"Can we go outside, please?" I'm snuffling, through hitching sobs. We walk for a long time around the parking lot of Our Lady of Grace Church, until, finally, I confess to Mom. Sometimes . . . sniffle . . . sob . . . sometimes . . . I . . . touch myself.

I know it's bad. I know I'm bad. And I haven't told any of this to the priest. So I won't be able to take Communion. I haven't made a Full Confession. I can't.

Finally, I look up, wipe snot away with one clenched fist. But she's not mad. She's not yelling. In fact, she's got a funny look on her face. She looks . . . well, she looks like she might be getting ready to laugh. Right out loud.

Then she sees the look on my face, and twists her mouth into a more mom-like expression.

"Oh, honey." She puts her arm on my shoulder, wipes a tear from my blotched face. "Don't be so sad. Everybody does what you've been doing at night. I bet even that priest does it sometimes."

I'm shocked. Everybody? Can that be true? Everybody thinks impure thoughts about Jesus Christ Our Lord? Then I remember. Oh. Yeah. I hadn't exactly told her that part. Mom takes me by the arm and walks me, gently, toward our Buick Elektra.

"Why don't we try that nice little Baptist church next week, sweetheart? You know, the one with that nice young reverend?"

Oh. Yeah.

I smile. Wipe the tears from my face. Pull my hair off my shoulders.

I remember the Reverend Tom Ray quite clearly. Maybe she's right. Could be he'd be just the ticket to get me off this Jesus kick once and for all.♥

GUYS YOU DON'T WANT TO MEET...

BY KIM'N'ANDRICE

i worry she might say something like "I Didn't Mean It."

by Karen Green (from Pucker Up)

You might call it a formula, but I call it a gift.

I always liked taking risks. Even at age twelve when I broke into neighbors' houses to steal laundry money for pinball. My ever-present need for quarters, for stimulation. When I got older, I moved on to bigger things—all still satisfying a certain consumptive need.

Did you ever grow up fat? Actually, any form of alienation at an early age will do.

It was a blistering hot day, and I was fat. I cut myself in the morning breaking into Megan's house. Her mother was insane and the house was a crawling sty. I had to watch out for dog and cat shit on the floor. Megan was a nerd and no one liked her but me. She read lots of books with titles like *Dragonslayer,* and she was mousy-looking. I liked her because she was smart and I knew at a future point in my life being smart would come in handy. Not a hoodlum, mind you, but a thief.

Thieves are very clever. That leads more or less to another reason I liked Megan. She played Dungeons and Dragons, which, at the time, seemed an ideal way of actualizing my fantasy of

becoming a thief. It took only one game for me to realize that it was a hoax, and that rolling dice was no way near as satisfying as prowling through the insulation-filled attics that connected the town houses in my housing complex. On these jaunts one had to be very careful because sometimes there was little support between rafters. There were also many bees. Touching insulation felt like instant cancer, so I avoided that, too.

Although I enjoyed scamming off Megan (yes, I went through my asshole days at a young age but I am better now), nothing pleased me more than visiting Tracy. She wasn't much taller than me, but she was thin and much more beautiful. Her skin was a dark tone and her hair and eyes were brown, quite like my own. Tracy and I hung out with pot-smoking, slimy boys in Levi's dungaree jackets and bandannas wrapped around various appendages. We all smoked Marlboro Reds. Have I set the scene enough? Of course the music was AC/DC and Blue Oyster Cult. There was roller skating and lots of pizza. Tracy always had a boyfriend, but because I was fat, no one really paid me much attention. I tried to be a boy instead. That didn't always work, though, cause sometimes a boy would approach me and ask me to skate. I would get my hopes up and skate, but it wasn't long before he was trying to feel me up or get me to suck his dick. This is when I contracted the belief that all men would ever want from me was sex and that they were incapable of feelings.

One evening Tracy and I were hanging out at one of our forts in the woods near the dump. We'd just seen a dog's head in the pile of trash and were reeling with disgust. We were also drunk and high, chain smoking, and binging on Doritos and Reese's Peanut Butter Cups. (I was already well on my way down the path of self-hatred.) Tracy's thin frame and B-cups obsessed me; I wanted to possess her body—move my spirit from this chunky frame into her aesthetically pleasing form. I looked up from my wallowing self-pity and realized Tracy was staring at me.

"You ever kiss a girl?" she asked.

"Huh?"

"I just thought you were a lesbo or something, you always dress like a boy."

"Uh."

I didn't have many words yet, but I felt like I was watching some romantic scene from *Superman*. She walked over to my log and straddled me. She kissed me softly. We started making out, and soon I was tasting those B-cup breasts. I began to regret for the first time my lack of a penis. She took off all her clothes and lay back on the log, spread her legs.

"Eat me."

My drunken state prevented, luckily, any paralysis, and I placed my face on her pussy and found her clit. I was only licking at her for a few minutes and she said, "Put your finger in my ass. Don't fuck me though, I'm still a virgin." I licked my finger and entered her ass, which was at first resistant and then voracious. Her body convulsed and I sat up savoring the stickiness around my mouth. She got up and quickly dressed, kissed me and said she would call the next day. She didn't.

I WON'T PLAY GIRL TO YOUR BOY NO MORE

SABRINA SANDATA, *BAMBOO GIRL*

Pinnacle

by Sarah Zoe Mondt (from *Charm Booklette*)

I

It's all so dreamy and she loves to nod and scratch her ear. It is a lot like a lovely pale shade of shell. The world is in a brand new shade of pale-ease today. Everything tingles and she rubs her body, ears, nose, cheeks, neck, chin, stomach, under her breasts, above her crotch, only stopping to turn over her cassette, to wonder why couldn't her name be Candy? She presses her lips together—hard. She rubs around, but not on them, so as not to fuck her lipstick. She sticks her hand down her thermals to scratch her inner-thigh, vaguely considering getting up to scratch, no, not scratch, to wash her face so she can rub her lips all she wants. She thinks of Javier and is startled by a shadow.

When Lily opened her eyes in the warm darkness of this morning, a feeling of dread came over her. Well, not dread, exactly. More like immobility, or fear of change. She wanted only to turn back over into the comfort of the deep gray of her bedroom and the weight of Magdalen's arm (protecting me? holding me back?) across her chest. But then, sitting on the airplane, it all seemed like an old dream, a scene from a cooling TV set—picture fades to black.

Magdalen wondered how Lily could guess where she was going, when where she came from was so unclear.

"I don't need to know. I will be walking, wandering, unafraid." They crossed the Mississippi on a bridge, on their feet. Hot winds, the backwash of semi-trucks threatened to blow them into the dark, creamy, brown river, and then, fainting from heat by the side of the road, the gravel road, they sang, shouted poetry, dreamt of dewy forests and cool paths. Magdalen said these are the magic pastures of youth, these are the crystalline moments to gaze upon in dreams.

Lily said she felt strange and confused and Magdalen talked to her and Lily said, "You say the nicest things," and Magdalen told her she was the nicest girl and that she loved her, too. And all across this great country, seventeen-year-old girls are reading Kerouac for the first time, turning on to try and burn. But when it doesn't happen, who's next, who is it that relieves loneliness so great even bestiality seems close at hand, no longer obscure?

Sitting in the sky on the Air-fone they say— "It was cool talking to you"—and—"Yeah"—after hours of nonstop verbal searching. And, after they say goodbye, Lily hears her whisper—"I love you"—quickly, softly, and then hang up. But she goes anyway, she's got to go anyway, and the descent begins at sunrise. Orange stripes hang above massive expanses of black water. She remembers the detachable rafts she read about in her safety manual, looks down on New York and its impossibly bright shores. It's not even the city, but millions of tiny lights are burning—all of them green. There's no stopping from here on out.

Later, her Cuban taxi-driver softly croons "Dream a Little Dream for Me," and almost gets into about five accidents. An angry bicycle messenger pounds on her window as they gently bump into him amid the slowly-milling ocean of yellow cabs and black sedans.

"Imagine a girl, contrasted by me, this song, this city, sitting by a campfire at night, in the woods,"—dream a little dream of me—"She's thinking of me, but I, chin upturned, look ahead at busy crowds, flashing signs and think only of the future." But her words are lost on the cabby as he swerves to miss a pedestrian.

The trees grow darker, closer together, they are a throbbing black mass—each one indistinguishable from the next. Dream a little dream for me.

II

Clanking steel doors slam closed with a deafening crash, a wood gate is added protection. The old freight elevator sets off with a jerk and Lily snaps her gum. The Boy waits outside in his Scirocco with the sheepskin-covered steering wheel and tinted windows, eating out of some hapless customer's take-out box. Lily only agreed to deliver these stupid cardboard cartons to get the fuck out of that smelly can. "I don't know what I'm doing with that kid anyway," she thinks. They'd spent the last three days together, ever since he'd caught her trying to steal his guitar. They were on the subway when Lily casually picked up the battered case and wandered off with it, wandered through graffiti-splashed walls with her new guitar, looking for a sign of life. It was nearly two stops later when The Boy noticed it was gone. Lily hadn't gone too far, instead deciding to find herself a spot to try and make enough change for the ride back into Manhattan and a phone. He found her muddling her way through "Hang on Sloopy" and chewing on her lip. "Whatever," Lily had shrugged, dropping the guitar and standing up when The Boy confronted her.

"Hey, hand me that box, will you Jane?" he asks in that annoying voice of his every so often. "Could you open it too?" Lily thinks he's so gross as he sticks shiny fingers into a grease-spotted box, lifts them back out, shoving more than a mouthful of someone else's Beef Lo Mein into his already working jaws. Lily sees them careening over the cracked pavement, two cartoon idiots foolishly outrunning death at every turn. The Boy arches his eyebrows at her, holding up a fingerful of oily noodles. Lily almost starts to cry or puke because she wants to run and run and instead she can only sit there and remind him that she is a vegetarian.

The radio is playing "Wild Horses" by The Rolling Stones and Lily thinks she remembers someone playing it for her once, and then she remembers it was she who had played it for a tiny girl late one night and made her cry. "You'll never love me the way I love you, Lily, you can't love anyone. You think love is giving up everything for one grand gesture, one word that will be the proof of everything." Lily had told her that she couldn't prove anything worth proving and that she was making her tired.

These are the thoughts that everyone has. Someday everyone will know you are a fraud. Lily thinks it is the best thing when she is alone, alone to piss by that old road, wind and moss whispering through her legs. Lily says she doesn't need another to show her the beauty in this stupid world, she's probably seen the best of it already. Magdalen used to straddle one of her legs and kiss her on the mouth when she was

playing the guitar and looking away. Sometimes Lily would play "Space Cowboy" just to piss her off. But Magdalen never got pissed, she usually got hurt. "I want to be with someone by myself," Lily would say.

"Man, I've been snorting too much speed," The Boy says after his third trip to the bathroom at All-American Burger. "Or maybe it's that valium from last night. I feel shaky." They go out and get into his car to head back for another delivery. He drives like a maniac, and Lily doesn't even laugh at him when he thinks that a fire hydrant is

a midget. She feels bored. She's not that mad when he asks her to make the last delivery for him, he just can't climb those fucking stairs again tonight. The old studio building on Broadway looks pretty shitty, but the seedy side of life has always been appealing.

Lily always used to say she didn't want to forget any of the words she'd ever said. She used to say, "If only I could give a certain something so I could save, retain, a moment or interaction, so I could hear things I missed, record something I otherwise wouldn't know existed." But the echoes through these halls could fill anybody with complacency. The concrete ceiling, infinite, cracked. Rectangular, fluorescent light tubes buzz and glare. A heavy door slams behind her.

Lily says she can tell right away when a man wants something from her. She can always read the predatory look they get, it's not too hard to ignore. The man who opens the door for his Chinese has that look, he has a really big smile. Lily wonders if anything can disappoint her anymore and she doesn't have to think twice when the Steven-man invites her in.

"Have some food, Jane. Or, actually, you must be sick to death of this food by now," he laughs amiably. He isn't embarrassed to eat in front of her. He has blue eyes. Lily tells him that blue eyes remind her of a broken ashtray and he looks at her with a protective sort of fatherly lust. Lily makes up a story about a boyfriend she used to have with blue eyes, who threw a cigarette-filled ashtray against a cement wall when she refused to go to New Orleans with him. Steven looks like he really likes the story, but instead of his face, Lily can only see salmon-colored chunks of ceramic bouncing and breaking into powder on the floor.

Magdalen used to tell her, "You fuck me up," and Lily would say, "No, I fuck you," and "You're pretty. Fucked up." She would ask her who she thought she was, and feel stupid when Magdalen wouldn't say anything, just pick at her unraveling sweater.

Lily tells Steven stories about her mother and her cat, Oprah. As she talks, Steven keeps this really earnest look on his face and tries to appear intense. "I went to a couple of hippie boarding schools, got fed up, toured around for awhile with some assholes in an Oldsmobile until the peyote ran out and I split."

Steven smiles an enduring sort of smile at her, one that says I'm glad I asked you in, that is better than *The New Yorker*. Lily thinks, he's the type of man that you meet at an opening, and he acts like you're so charming he just has to say, "Let's Go Somewhere To Talk." He's exactly that man. He's a boring type, but it doesn't really matter. Lily likes to tell stories and she says the thrill is in herself. Later, Steven looks sad and laments the fact that she is from California and is leaving in two days. He barely blinks when she tells him her name isn't really Jane.

Lily says she didn't always used to be this way. She used to be straight up. It was that boy who fucked her up. The things she used to do for that boy, things she was too smart for, things that were too big of a gamble, too big of a risk. Lily says the prize isn't worth the game. But she loved him. He's no motherfucker, and wasn't it sincerity that echoed in his voice when he *sincerely* thanked or pled or said good-bye. (My girlfriend's here . . .) But what the fuck. All false idols hit the dirt someday. They all fall someday. Lily says he was just her first bad influence and that everybody has one.

Gray-eyed girls are always double-edged, she thinks, and drags her finger across the centerfold's lips, decides for the third time that tonight she's leaving while Steven is at his gallery. Lily slouches on his futon, sucking on Coffee-Nips and waiting for him to come back with her baba ganoosh. Until then, she stares at TV, smugly thinking that her own life is incredibly similar to a bad sitcom. She calls Magdalen's parents' house, planning on regaling her with exciting tales of the big city and demanding her clothes back. Magdalen's slow mother says that Magdalen has run off again to God-knows-where and sounds surprised that she's not with her. Lily slams down the phone and sits straight up, cracking her knuckles and shaking her hair out of her eyes. Lily looks around Steven's stupid studio and feels cheated. She stalks over to the lame children's book Steven is writing and illustrating, the one he described as "sort of out-there." He'd told her, "It gets really crazy, you know, everything the boy wishes for really does come true—like, the ground is the sky. Really wild." Lily sees herself ripping it to pieces and then burning the remains, like at a funeral.

She misses California, its bright waves that

expand her eyes, clearing them out, putting them back in her head. When she was in California she used to think that when someone loved her, they would do anything for her, they would know exactly what to do. If she had a cut would he flick away the dried blood with his tongue? If it was on the instep of her foot the way it was so many times when she was three and four, would he smooth the flap of skin back into place as he lovingly licked it clean? Lapped it pure? She wanted to have beautiful shoulders. She wanted him to love her in the glassy waves and the warm sand. She wanted to make him happy.

Girl Picnic

by Elissa Nelson (from Hope)

When we went to the cemetery that afternoon I wasn't going to do anything. She said things we could do to each other but I didn't want to. I thought it was gross. It was just later she told everyone differently. But she was *lying*. I never really wanted to do any of that. She wanted to do it. Then later she made it seem like it had been all my idea. My fault.

Well, okay. I did want to kiss her. I really liked her. It's totally innocent, kissing someone. But she stuck her tongue in my mouth, and that woke up all the other ideas I didn't know were there, of things you can do to someone. She started it, kissing me, and then she started touching me, and then I just touched her back. I don't know. But she liked it, she totally liked it. It wasn't like she said later. She loved it, the whole time.

I was sleeping over at her house. I didn't really understand why she'd invited me. We weren't really friends in school, I didn't have enough of anything to be her friend. Maybe she'd heard about how I liked her. It seemed weird that she would have invited me over, especially if she knew I liked her, because all her friends who

knew how I felt, they just called me names. To them, there was nothing good about it at all. And I didn't even *do* anything about liking her, I just liked her. I mean I didn't giggle, or pass notes, or even talk about it; just once someone asked me if I liked her and I said yes. I don't know, it was a crazy, hopeful moment, it was dumb. But the girl who I told, told everyone else. I just shouldn't have said anything.

But I couldn't have said no; that would have been a betrayal to everything I felt. It was a big crush. She was in my gym class and all the girls changed together; I never really looked on purpose, and it wasn't like I was checking her out, she's just—her body is so long, and she looks solid, but she moves like there's water under her skin instead of muscle. I love watching her in gym, especially playing soccer. When she kicks the ball it's her whole body that does it. Even her head bends forward and back on her neck like a flower, and her hair swings forward and then falls back. It's blond, and short. It shines like the sun's on it, even when she's indoors, and it smells really good. If you sit next to her in math class you can smell it. You get little waves of her smell when she moves her head.

I wish I could explain her, about how, when she stands in the line in the cafeteria, she doesn't hold her tray like it's a tray, she holds it carelessly, in one hand, and sometimes she bangs it against her thigh as she waits. And she laughs so loud, in the lunchroom, in the halls, and even during Monday morning assembly. She is never afraid to laugh loud, no matter where she is. When she walks, her arms swing and her chin is so high. She is the tallest eighth-grader, taller even than any of the boys. She's like a tree, walking down the hallway, and the rest of us are shrubs. Everything about her is as though she is the only one, the rest of the world can be there or not, and she will be the same. That's why she's so popular, I think, because she just doesn't care. She does whatever she wants. Except, I guess she thought this is something she couldn't get away with.

Nobody else was there, in the cemetery. I guess that's why we met. We'd been at her house trying to think of something to do and we decided to go on a picnic. So there we were. It was just me and her. It was late March, sort of cold and soggy, and the snow had melted but the grass was dead and brown, with no green anywhere yet. I hate that time of year in cemeteries because the only color is on the little American flags and on the plastic flowers. It makes me sad. She'd brought a blanket, a gray wool one from when her grandfather was in the army, and we laid down behind a row of gravestones on the

Carpet Muncher Beaver Patrol Clam Digger Muff Diver Let's Be Friends And Go Homo

hill, where it wasn't as wet. The hill is the rich section, where the gravestones are really tall, and we were hidden by them. This was a make-out place for the older kids, but not for us, two little eighth-grade girls. I didn't want to think about what would happen if anyone saw us. I could barely think about that anyway—I couldn't think about anything because I was there with her. We sat on her grandfather's scratchy old blanket and I had my back up against a big statue of Jesus on the cross, on the other side from where Jesus was. Behind her was a marble angel six feet tall and his arms were out, like he was about to fly off, or had just landed. Maybe he was protecting us, or maybe it was a warning. You couldn't tell anything from the expression on his face—he was just one of those patient angels, not really affectionate or angry. I guess if you're an angel in a cemetery your best bet is to be patient.

The food was still in the basket we'd brought. We were lying on the blanket. I felt like we *were* the picnic. Especially me. I was sort of stuck, I'd leaned up against the back-side of that crucifix, cold marble, and I couldn't move anywhere. I was trying to be far away from her. I didn't want her to think I was going to do anything. I didn't want her to think that I wanted to do anything. I was so stiff. Later I had bruises on my shoulder blades from forcing them so hard into that cross behind me.

I just sat there, for a really long time, and I was shaking and frozen, although it had nothing to do with the weather. She was all of it. She was talking, but it was just her voice that I heard, not her words. Her voice, sort of loud, like she was proving she wasn't scared or feeling weird, but she also sounded as nervous as a girl in charge can sound. She talked for a while, and then she was quiet for a while. Then, she moved over from the far edge of that blanket, tentatively but still deliberately, like a queen, like she did everything, and it took a hundred years. I knew she was going to do something. It might have looked like a picnic because of the blanket, but it wasn't.

But I was clinging to that idea in case anyone came. A picnic. Picnic picnic picnic with her, the most beautiful girl, a girl who didn't speak to me in school but here she was, and maybe almost in love with me back. Or something. She finally made it across that blanket and she sat on my lap. One leg on each side of my hips, right there. Long legs, and I held all her weight. It felt perfect, like holding her made me strong, too. She kissed me. I thought I was going to die. I didn't know if it would happen right then, or tomorrow when she told her friends, but I knew sooner or later someone would strike me down.

But I didn't care about getting struck by lightning or beaten up after school, I didn't care about anything, I just kissed her back. Of course I kissed her back. This was her. My big crush, my first kiss, this was the girl. She was sitting on my lap and I felt her weight and smelled her hair up close, and I touched it.

Then we did other stuff, a lot of other stuff, things I'd never thought of, but I guess she had.

And when she brought them up, I mean, started doing them, they were definitely a good idea. She kissed me on the mouth and used her tongue, and that would have been enough to last me for the next three years, but she kept going. She took off her bra and put my hands under her shirt, and then she did it to me and put her mouth there. I couldn't even tell you. My body shook for real, like when you're in the car and you go over a bump and your stomach just drops out. And I really wondered why I'd never thought of this before.

She just kept going, she kept going, and there we were between Jesus and that angel and I was on my back looking up at the old angel with the crazy wings, and I was lying on a blanket that itched and smelled like her basement, like laundry detergent and dust, and nobody was ever gonna buy the picnic story at this point. There I was with her and no clothes on. I was cold and excited and scared and my body and mind were both very confused, but I wouldn't have moved away for anything. I couldn't have. I was like the frog in biology class, stretched to the corners and pinned down. I guess she's the kind of girl who squeals at the frog at first and won't touch it, but then, by the end of the dissection unit, she's throwing the poor thing around the classroom, at all her friends. I wouldn't have thought she was like that, but that's how it's turning out.

She told one of her friends what had happened, and of course they all found out after that. She's the princess, though—somehow she made herself look innocent, like I'd done everything. No one in school will talk to me now. And the walls in the girls' bathroom say stuff about me, mostly just that I'm a lesbo. Somebody wrote not to let me in the bathroom because I'm not a real girl. I change in the toilet for gym now because it is too awful otherwise. They act like I would rape them or something if I saw them naked. Everything eventually got back to our homeroom teacher and she made me go see the school counselor. Nothing even happened to the other girl because she acted like such a victim. She cried when my teacher tried to talk to us both. She cried, this girl who is the strongest, who never gave up anything like that, who never let that guard down. And even when she cried, especially when she cried, she didn't show who she was—crying about this, about me, about what I'd done to her, like she hadn't liked it as much as I had. So I was the only one who had to go see the counselor, and he was going to call my mom. So that's when I cried too,

and I said that none of it had happened, the girl was mad at me for something else and, ick, I said, did he really think I'd touch another *girl* like that? I wore a dress of my sister's the day I had to talk to the counselor, and cherry chapstick. I guess I fooled him.

But it's not true what I said to him, I can't be sorry it happened. Being with her was the best feeling in my whole life, no matter that I was scared to death. Of course, now there are the worst feelings in my whole life every day in school, but they don't even balance it out. I think that when I'm older and gone away from this school and these people, I'll probably find another girl—not a popular girl, not a queen this time, but just a normal, pretty, quiet girl— and I'll do it all again, forever. So maybe they are right about me. And you know, I think I'm mostly glad.

Mirror, Mirror

The reflection of the self is one of the most volatile experiences in the

life of women. It's a struggle for most women to build or maintain a

positive self-image. This section illustrates both the painful and glorious

vision that women have of themselves, their bodies, and their mental

and physical health. In this section, you'll find women loving and hating

themselves. But mostly, you'll discover how women are learning to

create and redefine their self-image.

Read It and Weep (or Laugh)

by Tammy Rae Carland

editor of I ♥ Amy Carter and J.T.O.

When I started working on the first issue of I ♥ Amy Carter, I was attempting to reach out and connect with something that I was afraid of losing because I was moving far away from everyone I loved. I was afraid of losing my frequent contact with my girl friends—something that has been essential to the quality and continuity of my life. Basically, I started this zine in a state of isolation, and it ended up broadening my pool of friends and narrowing my scope of isolation.

Not so consciously, I was also afraid of losing control of these intricate and solid emotional floodgates that I had spent years building up inside of me. These floodgates became an internal self-editing machine that prevent me from revealing too much, too soon, to the wrong people. Sounds healthy enough, doesn't it? Except, for me, it was all about keeping sheltered things I needed to be liberated from. So, in fact, when I was seemingly protecting others from being uncomfortable, I was making myself almost exclusively disassociated (and therefore extremely uncomfortable and invisible) in most social or intimate situations.

When I started I ♥ Amy Carter, I was starting to crack—in the best sense of the word. What I'm talking about is how I needed to get to this place where I could let all the dirty and complicated things touch each other. So I started making this zine where I could flaunt my love of the torrid (and maybe true) lesbian clips from the National Inquirer along side of worldwide statistics about ritualized wife-killing. I could also let myself write from a place I had avoided in the past. That place was unrehearsed, without spellcheck and no editing (okay, maybe a little editing). It was also a place of personal identity which, for me, would be a dyke from a welfare family who experienced an enormous amount of violence and sexual abuse. I made it safe and important to talk about poverty and incest in the same sentence without worrying about backward readings of one equaling the other. Perhaps starting the public conversations about class was the hardest thing I've ever done, and am still trying to do. I tried to do all this with very little rhyme or reason. I would just write and cut and paste until it was done. I also think I ♥ Amy Carter was a rather funny zine. It had a sense of humor without being self-humiliating. And, oh yeah, most importantly, it was completely made for and by women and girls.

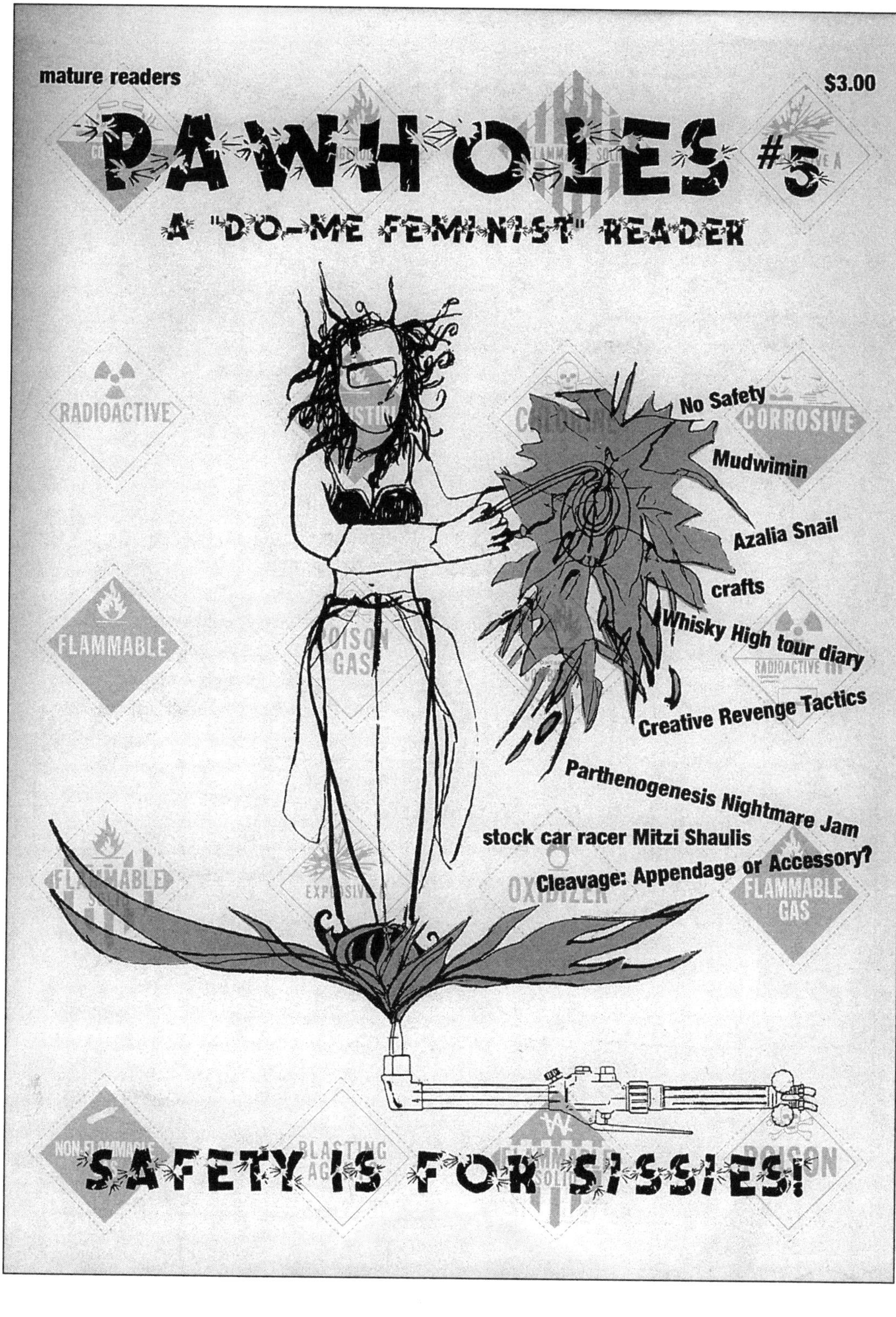

mature readers
$3.00
PAWHOLES #5
A "DO-ME FEMINIST" READER
No Safety
Mudwimin
Azalia Snail
crafts
Whisky High tour diary
Creative Revenge Tactics
Parthenogenesis Nightmare Jam
stock car racer Mitzi Shaulis
Cleavage: Appendage or Accessory?
RADIOACTIVE
CORROSIVE
FLAMMABLE
POISON GAS
FLAMMABLE GAS
OXIDIZER
SAFETY IS FOR SISSIES!

The Double Blue Line
(When the Positive Pregnancy Test Brings No Joy)

by Jennifer Kosta (from hip Mama)

She stood in front of the bathroom sink and watched the double blue line become more visible. She walked out of the bathroom and into the bedroom, and sat down on the edge of the bed and cried. Cried because she didn't know what to do or how to feel. Cried. She didn't feel the pleasure of a woman who wanted children, and she didn't feel the fear of one who couldn't possibly be ready. She felt somewhere in between.

She phoned him at work and could only say two words—it's positive. She sat in a state of calm for a time, the sun coming through the window warming her neck. The couch felt comfortable. It cradled her. Soft around her thighs and hips. *What do I do?* Those words were like a toy train on its circular track going round and round in her head.

He came through the door, his eyes on her until his body reached her. He leaned down and kissed her long and soft on the lips. *I'm going to be a Dad,* he said. And they sat beside each other and laughed. A soft laugh that soothed her from the inside out. She will never let this moment go. She knows it won't last. A sudden chill ran through her body, reminding her and warning her of the storm that would come.

That same night he wants to destroy the life they made. She thought he loved her. She cried herself to sleep that night and the many that followed.

Pain. What is causing the pain? They went to the emergency room. So many tests and examinations. All of them causing more pain. He was sitting next to her, but she felt alone. Tears streamed down her face as the nurse inserted the catheter. She wanted her mother. She wanted someone who could feel what she felt. Who could comfort her. He didn't know how. She told him to leave, but he didn't. Maybe it would be different during the ultrasound. *Maybe when he sees the tiny baby, he will love me,* she thought. No. It scared him more. None of the tests showed anything to worry about. Everything would be fine.

They left the hospital walking miles apart. He slept on the couch that night.

Their arguments were about everything and nothing. Every day there was a threat to end the relationship. Every other day they fell back in love.

Still, they don't know. She loves him—not for who he is now, but for who he was. He feels the same. It's as though for a short while they walked hand in hand down a lovely road, but each took different paths when they reached the fork. Even as they continue down their separate paths, they call out to each other, hoping to find the love they lost.

Menarche Hell

by Sarah-Katherine (from *Pasty*)

t's ten or so, and I'm sitting here sipping hot Ovaltine and bleeding quietly into the tampon that is tucked up inside me, snug as a bug in a rug. It's comforting: the hot, sweet Ovaltine, and the tug in my lower belly. Both sensations seem inevitable.

Three more hours and it's time to pull the little string that's dangling between my legs and draw out the pungent, wilted cotton plug. I'm new enough to tampons that the idea of doing this is notable—not quite daunting (I've done it before), but still, something to think about doing well before actually performing the act. Pull the string—slowly and smoothly, until the tampon pops out of my vagina, slimy; like a second-term miscarriage. Flush it away. Replace with a fresh, dry tampon, which will pull against my insides unpleasantly until I push it high enough. In a moment, its presence will be unnoticed. Then, hands washed of any residual clots of tissue, I will be able to enjoy six more hours of secret bleeding.

I guess this is no big deal to most of you girls out there, right? I mean, you've probably been doing this since sixth grade. I haven't—oh, yeah, sure I've been bleeding, but this tampon thing is brand-new to me. I always used to wear pads, because I basically thought it was gross to jam cotton up your snatch and just let it sit in there, getting smellier and bloodier by the hour. My idea about periods was that that blood was *supposed* to come out, not just stay up inside. Actually, I still believe that. It's probably a million times better for your body to just let the blood run out freely into a pad.

Another reason I wouldn't wear tampons is because (don't laugh) I thought they would stretch me out. Can you imagine? Some guy's pumping away and going, "Am I in yet? I can't feel a thing!" All because of those fucking Super Absorbent Plus jobs the size of D batteries.

But now, I guess, I'm a tampon girl. I finally got fed up with walking around in a saggy, stinky pad. I got sick of the feel of old blood in my butt crack after a night's sleep on my back. I couldn't take that pubic hair crust any more—you girls know what I mean. In short, I was sick of feeling (as the TV says) "not-so-fresh."

So now, I'm just a walking, talking, plugged-up orifice—yee-ha!

My first period, since I'm on the subject, was absolutely horrifying. I was eleven or twelve, and I knew all about periods—technically. I wasn't prepared to pull down my panties and see a stripe of brown in the cotton crotch. At first I thought it was shit, and was totally humiliated. Like, nice wiping, girl-friend. I wadded up about half a roll of toilet paper and wiped my butt until it was raw, then I changed into a nice clean pair of underwear. A couple hours later, when I had to pee again, I was mortified to see that the stripe was back—darker brown, too.

At this point I started to freak. I figured one of two things was happening down there: one, I had become suddenly incontinent, or two, GOD WAS PUNISHING ME BY MAKING MY PUSSY LEAK ICKY BROWN DISCHARGE. In the next few minutes, the incontinence theory was disproved by much frantic butt-wiping and checking. Which left only option two, that God had some kind of vendetta against me, and was causing me MAJOR female trouble. The worst, meanest part about His punishment, in my panicked opinion, was that eventually I'd be forced to tell somebody about my problem. Then maybe they'd want to SEE it! The anticipated shame of THAT, the telling and the examination, was unimaginable.

Hours passed. I wandered around the house, picking things up and putting them down, waiting for my mom to come home from work. And then what? I didn't know. I made and drank cup after cup of herbal tea. Every ten minutes or so, I'd duck into the bathroom and check out the crotch of my panties. Perhaps it would stop of its own accord. Maybe it was just a WARNING from God.

Now why, you might ask, would I be so convinced that God hated me enough to cause me such a miserable, embarrassing malady? Friends, I'll tell you what: I had been masturbating for as long as I could remember. Though nobody had ever told me not to, I knew that touching myself was a filthy, perverted pastime—one that normal, healthy people didn't do. So you see? It made perfect sense that God would choose to punish me in those parts—those parts I wouldn't leave alone.

So, not only would I have to tell a grownup about the brown stuff, I'd have to tell them about the touching—the cause of my shameful punishment. I was both mortified and mortally terrified.

I don't know when it finally clicked that what was happening was merely my first period, not the wrath of God. Maybe later that evening? I don't remember. I think what threw me off initially was that the blood was brown, not the cherry red I'd always expected. Years later, I read somewhere that a girl's first flow can range from red to brown to almost black. Can you imagine how crazed with fear I would have been to see a BLACK stripe in my panties? I'd probably be writing this in crayon from a state institution, not on a PC in my own cozy bedroom . . .

I wouldn't wear pads, that first time, for some reason. It just never occurred to me to do that. Instead, I changed panties about four times a day. On the third day or so, I told my mom. I was still apprehensive—it could still turn out to be censure from God—but maybe, just maybe, things were okay down there. Before the week was over, it had ended—the crotch of my underwear was again mercifully unsullied. How to explain how I felt? Light-headed, goofy, clean, and lovable again. Relieved. Redeemed.

Almost immediately, I went back to masturbating, my desperate pleas to God forgotten in my stealthy lust.

So that's the story of my transformation from girl to woman, complete with all the shame and horror that transition included. Girl to woman, pads to tampons. Furtive masturbator to, well . . . furtive masturbator. Some things never change.

issue no. 4

$2

for the mentally ilL

"wednesday night . . ."

by Witknee (from <u>Alien</u>)

Wednesday night i started experiencing the "usual" panic attack, mentally and physically, as always, i calm down emotionally after a couple of hours, although my body is still reacting—heart beating fast, trouble breathing, eyes darting back and forth, paranoia, etc. which is unusual. at work on thursday i leave early because it's getting bad again. the panic attack calms down, then gets worse in the evening. i contemplate going to the hospital. i go to the hospital. i'm scared shitless at the hospital. i get checked in and the nurse asks me various 'procedure' questions. "is there a chance you might be pregnant?" she asks. "definitely not," i reply. "are you sure?" "yes." "how can you be sure?" "i just know i'm not pregnant." (considering the fact i've never had intercourse with a man). i then go over to another desk and get my insurance verified. i'm in. i chicken out and want to leave, realizing no doctor can help me. it's ten o'clock at night and i'm in a strange place—it will be nearly impossible to open up to any psychiatrist. all the nurses console me and tell me i'll be okay. i start crying and think i'm crazy and i should check myself in for psychiatric care. and fuck, all i want to know is WHY THE FUCK IS MY BODY IN A PANIC ATTACK MODE FOR 36 HOURS? i guess they consider me to be an emergency cos after 30 minutes i see a doctor for a regular check up before i can see a shrink (the usual wait is one hour). during those thirty minutes i watch *ER*, contemplate running out of the place, and watch a family mourn over a relative's soon-to-be death. i see the doctor and get an EKG to measure my heartbeat. the doctor is nice and treats me with respect (that isn't often). finally i see "the" doctor, i.e. the psychiatrist/shrink/whatever (i prefer shrink). he is a HE. #1 problem. to make a long story really fucken short, he won't answer my one question and just keeps asking me useless lame questions that i already know the answer to. he asks me if i've ever done drugs. I answer him honestly, yes, i've smoked pot, done mushrooms, LSD, and cocaine; never alcohol, all recreational. he states the reason i have panic disorder is because of my one-time-only cocaine use and the reason why i suffer from severe depression is because i've smoked pot. i tell him that is not true, cos it's not. yes, say yes, i say no. i get real hostile, in which he probably assumes i'm a drug addict being defensive. i raise my voice and tell him i'm not a drug addict and none of these drugs that i used over one and a half years ago have to do with my current mental condition. he doesn't believe me, but says "okay" very condescendingly. after our forty-five-minute consultation he tells me i don't need to be committed. well, thank you sir, i didn't want to be committed, i just want to know why my body is doing this. in response to my question (to refresh your memory the question was why is my body reacting like i'm having a panic attack) he tells me he has come to the conclusion i'm not bipolar, but i do have panic disorder. he then tells me if i ever want to get better i should seek counseling FROM HIM and go back on medication. he doesn't answer my question, he never answers my question. i tell him i will never go on medication on a daily basis again and i don't want therapy. he looks at me with no hope and walks out of the room and talks shit about me to a nurse. i leave.

at first i thought i wanted to be committed . . . after an hour into the four-hour experience i realized i didn't. the shrink asked me if i ever have suicidal ideations. for the record, i still think about suicide, a lot. told him no. i lied to him. if i had said, yes, for the past thirty-six hours i have been thinking about swallowing my pills, and recently i've been thinking about death constantly, i would have been committed, with or without my consent. that is the law.

i could have mentioned my thoughts of suicide and nothing would have happened. it's okay to tell a shrink you're thinking of suicide. but i know i would have spilled my guts and told him exactly how i would kill myself, the details, the time, how, etc.—that's when they can commit you.

what i realized: the medical industry is fucked up. (like any of us didn't know that before.) i was treated with no respect, as a woman and as a minor/adult (i'm eighteen years old). of course doctors are always right so there's no way for me to prove them wrong. INfuckenCORRECT. they just don't like to be questioned (most of them anyway). i felt very degraded and violated mentally. before i went to the hospital i had always thought of it ('the hospital') as my 'last resort' and that it could always help me. i now know i am my own last resort and there is no way i will ever go to a hospital again for my mental health. granted, others have had positive experiences in hospitals. i don't care to take the risk again. at first i thought i could really benefit from this and maybe talk to a "professional" about my recent and past problems and SHE (note how i have a strict gender preference to shrinks) could help me. that obviously didn't happen, didn't even come close. i walked out of that hospital really confused and angry. it made me take a step into a do-it-yourself health care approach. i'm doing this on my own, all the way. no more shrinks or medications for me. i've started reading a lot of books, from herbal and diet remedies to mental health, and instead of talking to a shrink, i've been writing my problems and looking at it from a different perspective on my own. and it's helping. i've just had all this bad luck when i've sought out "professional" care and i can't afford it any more (financially and emotionally). i'm glad i refused that doctor's suggestion of counseling and medication. it showed me i'm stronger than i was in the past (one year ago i would have, without thought, immediately gone on medication). if anyone is going through the same thing or has gone through the same thing i'd really like to hear your story and how you are doing now.

another thing that doctor fuckface said that really bothered me was that he told me i'm not bipolar. i told him very little about myself, only my family problems and drug history and panic attacks. so i felt really insulted when he told me this. and i don't give a shit what he 'concludes to' but it made me realize how much i cling to that label. i wouldn't necessarily say it's unhealthy, but it's not healthy either. i sometimes use it as my identity, as a crutch—that's unhealthy. but acknowledging it and realizing that it is a problem is fine. as always, i have to find a medium for my extremist self. another thing i was thinking about was that he concluded, after a forty-five-minute consultation, a diagnosis of me; *i barely told him anything*. it took me sixteen years to determine what i have and how i can deal with it. i didn't even know this man. i don't know his background at all. is he homophobic? male supremacist? a republican? etc. etc. obviously, if he was a sexist racist homophobic classist gingrich admirer, i wouldn't take anything he said seriously. would you?

society determines our/my/your sanity. society is the court system, the government, the adults, the people who don't even know you. i have learned, through countless shrinks, that i will take in what they say and their advice, but i will make the final decision after i educate myself on it. you should do the same. (and this goes for physical illnesses as well).

"there is something horribly, terribly wrong . . ."

by Sarah F. (from Pisces Ladybug)

there is something horribly, terribly wrong when so many girls suffer from eating problems. i'm not talking about the clinically-diagnosed anorexics and bulimics—i'm referring to me, perhaps you, and i believe most middle and high school girls in this country who have made food our best friend and worst enemy. on several occasions, i have gathered with other girls in various situations, and, usually as part of a late-night bonding session, each girl relates her own eating disorder story. this is sick. i don't have to look hard for other girls who have abused food, we are everywhere.

i have this theory that every girl has one (or more) life issue(s) which we deal with our whole lives. this could be abuse, disability, sexuality, race, or a trillion other things. somehow, millions of girls abuse food to manipulate their problems—whether to gain attention, divert their energy, numb themselves, or to create more pain. society has sent out the message loud and clear that a woman's body is her most valuable asset. it should be no wonder then that one after one, million after million, girls' problems manifest themselves in the torture we inflict on our own bodies. if we can't control our bodies, then what else?

anorexics and bulimics that you see on *Oprah* and afterschool specials, who diet their way into the hospital and into the grave, are only a fraction of we who are afflicted. when i think back on my middle-school lunch table, it is shocking how many girls did not eat. even more still refuse to treat themselves to an ice cream or a second brownie. they do early morning exercises and skip meals the week before homecoming so that they can fit into their dresses, which, by the way, already fit. they read teen magazines and admire the flat tummies and sleek, airbrushed thighs. they are not in serious medical danger, but this is killing their spirit, diverting their wonderful discipline and power to a futile cause, and they are shelling out their money to the system that perpetuates the whole process.

Let the revolution begin

as girls, we can set each other free.

i used to be one of these girls. a look at my diary from seventh to ninth grade is truly frightening. on these pages, i ripped myself to

shreds, with stinging self-inflicted insults and pleas for "just ten more pounds" on every page. i played out my role as planned—i dealt with my problems by abusing food. i engaged in a battle that i could not possibly win so that everything would be my fault. my weight went up and down relatively little compared to how much effort i put into changing it —i attracted compliments more often than concern.

i've changed. once i dealt with the real root issue i was struggling with, my food problems absolutely vanished. i spent the summer before my sophomore year finding out who i was—and realized my value as a person is not weighed in pounds. and so now i have come full circle. talking about my eating disorder with other girls is a comforting thing because i can see how far i've come and how truly secure i now am. at the same time, it's just so sad that self-starvation is a common experience among girls. it's sick. there are so many of us. it is absolutely crazy.

i know that we can change things. talk to girls who are ten to fourteen years old. listen to them. we can help our younger sisters. we need to give each other positive reinforcement. we need to be active in the lives of preteen girls cos they look up to us. i don't know about you, but i would give anything to help a girl deal with her problems healthily, so she wouldn't have to go through what i've been though.

TAMMY RAE CARLAND, J.T.O.

Self-Hate

by Jean (from Scrawl)

veryone is guilty of this one. in fact most people i know surf quite frequently in the black waters of this little ocean. i want to know why that is. people aren't necessarily taught to hate themselves, but, then again, people aren't really taught how to love themselves, safely, either. my friend meredith used to have a theory that humankind naturally relishes in its own agony and thus instinctively covets the unattainable. i'm not entirely sure how or why that makes sense, but it seems to be pretty evident in the behavior of people these days. self-hate can be found at the root of everything, from ridiculous pride and ego-tism to self-image problems and eating disorders. but why is that? it's almost as if most people con-sider their self-hatred a form of honesty. in an attempt to be modest, they just end up over-critiquing themselves and underestimating themselves. i have a lot of friends who practice this wonderful self-destructive behavior and, as a result, can act like real assholes sometimes, because they've become so fucking cynical that they don't give a rat's ass about anything but (ironically enough) themselves. it's pitiful, annoying, and really very sad. not that i'm innocent of it myself, but i'm trying to get over it. i think maybe that's why we're all friends, because we can get through to each other like that, we all know what we feel, and even if we're feeling them at different times, we've all been there. yeah, i think one can trust one's friends to put up with one when s/he is being a self-pitying, self-hating, at-tention-hungry lunatic. i mean, hey what are friends for, right? but i digress, and i can't seem to come up with any sort of conclusion to this self-hate thing—it's beyond me. trying to figure something like this out in a single commentary would be like trying to watch a french movie with chinese subtitles: you can get the gist of it, but honestly, you really don't have a clue, do you now? so the only thing to do is just sort of deal with it, not to let it overwhelm you, because most people are as similar to each other as they are different. so it **should** be reassuring, to a degree, that there are at least 5 billion people (out of the 5.4 billion in the world) that are constantly hating themselves in one form or an-other. too bad it's not reassuring. oh well.

Tough Girls, Navel Girls, and Warrior Women
A Conversation About Body Modification

by Tristan Taormino (from <u>Pucker</u> <u>Up</u>)

P ower and energy are literally bouncing off the violet and black walls at the body (re)design palace, *VENUS MODERN BODY ARTS*. *PUCKER UP* had the opportunity to talk about body modification with two of the top women in their fields who call *VENUS* their home: piercer Maria Tashjian and tattoo artist Squid. I was struck by just how seriously they take their professions, as well as the historical, cultural, personal and political implications of their work. They had plenty of thoughtful things to say, including some insightful, inspiring ideas about aesthetics, identity, and power.

PUCKER UP What kinds of body modification do each of you do and how long have you been doing it?

Squid I tattoo . . . and I've been tattooing for about three years professionally.

Maria I do *comprehensive* body piercing, and I've been doing it for about four years.

PU So how did each of you get into piercing and tattooing?

M I should have this answer practiced by now. I've always liked the look; like back in high school, [I liked the look] of multiple earlobe and cartilage piercings, and nostril piercings. I would do some [piercing]—what I consider "hack stuff" now—on my friends and myself, kind of experimenting at that time. Eventually, I started getting into tattoos and going to conventions, and I saw a lot of piercing that was going on and found some literature, etc. I hooked up with my partner, who was tattooing, and I was doing a little bit of piercing out of my apartment in Manhattan. We decided together that we'd join forces, advertise, and work out of his studio apartment; so, we started doing that, and we got a lot more of a regular clientele. Then we both went to study in California under Fakir Musafar, and I basically fine-turned some of my skills. We were working out of the apartment for a couple of years. Then, we decided to quit our full-time jobs and open up this retail space about twenty-one months ago.

PU How did you hook up with Fakir?

M I called him up, basically.

S How did you find about about him?

M Through his *Body Play* magazine and also through friends. I went to a seminar by Raelyn Gallina, who's a person who does branding and scarification. She's good friends with Fakir and I got caught up in that network.

PU Squid?

S A lot of my friends were tattooed. Actually, when I was thirteen years old, I went to get a tattoo with my sister who was sixteen. I went to Marguerite, this woman who's excellent. She had tattooed some friends of mine, and she was *very* nice. It's kind of interesting . . . I wanted to go to her because she was a woman. What I wanted was this very simple tattoo, but I went to her anyway just because I knew she was cool and she'd be patient with me. I try to carry that over. I do a lot of tattoos on people that have never been tattooed before; I still remember what it was like to be in that position. You're nervous and you really don't understand anything about it. So many shops have such an attitude—big attitude—and are almost downright nasty to the people that they're tattooing because they're bitter, I guess, about what they're doing . . . My first tattoo experience is something that I reflect on now, in later years, when I'm dealing with customers. I ended up hooking up and becoming friends with some really good artists, and I was hooked! I was just getting tattooed and tattooed and tattooed, hanging out at shops everywhere, and just being around it a lot. [Steve Ferguson who owns the Ink Spot] took me under his wing and wanted to teach me the business. I started out answering phones, and I ended up apprenticing with him . . . He was really great to me; he gave me a gift that is hard to come by. A lot of people would give their left thumb to learn how to tattoo properly . . . And I haven't waitressed since. Thanks, Steve!

PU Most of the people who work at Venus, I've noticed, have a countercultural aesthetic. What do you think is the connection between all of those other expressions—whether it's blue hair or their clothes—and piercing and tattooing?

M Well, piercing, tattooing, branding, and scarification are all different ways to modify yourself. Personally, I have a "vision" (for lack of a better word) of what I can see myself looking like, and I slowly . . . work there.

S There are some examples of people who really have totally modified themselves just into their own creatures; it's incredible. It really, *really* is an amazing thing to see.

M That's exactly it. . . . I personally feel extremely fortunate that I can look how I want to look, create that vision, *and* impose my aesthetic with jewelry and everything else on the general public. And they seem to enjoy it! I do a little bit of the jewelry manufacturing, and I get really excited when I make something. Other people get excited about it, and then we put it in their bodies to become part of them. It's awesome.

PU How do you feel about your role? If someone walks through that door who has a vision like

that, of how they want their body to look, and how they want to change it, you're the person who makes that happen.

M We can tell them what we feel will work and what won't work with their body. For example, sometimes people come in and say, "I want to get a bunch of surface piercings up and down my arm." We might say, "Well, in our experience, that type of piercing has an 80–90% rejection rate, so you might want to consider this instead." Or: "You will be left with scars in all likelihood." So, we work *with* them. It's really fun; it's like designing your body . . . It's wonderful to work with people and get them excited about changing their bodies.

S It's a big responsibility, too.

M *Oh yeah.*

S It does hit you that this person will never be exactly the same as God made them after they come to see you. The thing that really gets me, almost beyond anything else, is that sometimes I think, "Who the hell am I to be playing God with people's skin?" But, at the same time, I see so much butcher work, so much bad work (and I know Maria does too, sees bad piercings) by people that don't know what they're doing who are fucking themselves up, fucking other people up because they don't have the proper skills. That really makes you want to go on and keep doing your work and make sure that people . . . get what they want, are safely taken care of and . . . are not being mutilated or hurt in any way.

PU How do you feel about the power you have? You have to get pretty intimate with every person who walks through the door. Sometimes it's just on a physical level, but it also may be on an emotional or spiritual level, too, depending on the person and what the piercing or the tattoo means to them. How intimate do you get with people?

M That's a good question.

S In a way, it is very intimate. I am personally incredibly picky about the people I will go to . . . It's a power play, kind of . . . it's about assuming responsibility for this individual who's put all their trust in you. . . . I feel like I am in control of my room and the surroundings; if sometimes there's something weird about the person, I can feel that. I can feel if they're struggling with me about just the fact that I'm in control. I'm taking care of them; they really don't have much to say about it. For me to do my job, do it well and give them what they want, they need to abide by my rules and do what I'm asking them. It's not that different, I guess, than . . .

PU . . .Than giving your body over to someone for something else?

S Yeah, that's what I'm saying . . . It isn't all that different than what a dominatrix does, except that it doesn't have anything to do with sex whatsoever. So, it's not intimate in any sort of sexual way, but it is intimate in a way like a mother takes care of her child or anybody who's caring for somebody else and is putting all their attention and concern into another person.

M When you go in the room with someone and you're going to pierce them, you empathize to a certain extent, but at the same time you do have some distance. You have to because this person is paying you to execute a piercing, quickly and with the best skill and accuracy that you possibly can. If they're extremely anxious, you don't want to empathize to the point where you're all riled up and you're not capable of doing a quick and efficient piercing. I noticed that when I first started piercing, I would empathize more and definitely get more anxious, feed off of their emotions. Now, I try to get them into a state where they'll be more relaxed . . . so I can work as quickly and efficiently as possible. Of course, you commiserate to a certain extent if someone's really anxious. The example that comes to mind is this woman, I pierced her clitoris recently. It took her an hour before she would drop her pants. I sat there with her, and, of course, I knew my mother was waiting downstairs for me, but I didn't rush her or anything like that. After we talked about it for a long time, she mellowed out, then we went for it. It was great. It's really important to take your time with people and understand where they're coming from, but, at the same time, you have to keep your composure so that you can do what they're paying you for to the best of your ability. It's a little bit of both—empathy and distance.

S Definitely.

PU What was the most intense or meaningful body-modification experience you have each had?

S My own tattoos. Getting tattooed is a very intense experience, depending on where and how big the piece is. It is not something to be taken lightly. I don't mean to say that all tattoos are that painful because most small tattoos are relatively painless, like tattoos on your arm. People never describe it as pain to me; they describe it as annoying. But if you're very serious about getting work, and you're getting large pieces, it can be very intense. There's nothing quite like it. I can't say that any experience that I've had working on someone else—even though a lot of the pieces are very exciting to do—was quite as exciting as having my own body modified in such a permanent way.

PU Maria, do you agree?

M In terms of myself, it's a hard question. I was thinking about the piece I got from Bernie which is like the longest I've ever sat for—six and a half hours. That was . . . a personal thing, to see how long I could last. I was determined to sit there for the entire thing. It was really rewarding, watching this image appear . . . It was about stamina and trust, and that was my most intense experience. In terms of piercing, Fakir did my hood, and that was good. I felt very honored. The first clitoral piercing I did myself was probably also one of my more intense experiences.

PU Did you know the person?

M No, but we were totally hugging and everything afterwards—it was awesome. She said, "Now I expect every orgasm to feel like that!" It was cool; I was really happy for her that she could go away with it and have this embellish her life.

PU Do you feel like the field of body modification is dominated by men in general? What about specifically at Venus?

S *Any more or less than the rest of the world and any other business?* I still get reactions from people like, "Oh you're the one who does the tattoos?" They don't expect a female to be the tattooer. Anyone who knows anything about the history of tattooing knows that there have always been some women in tattooing, not nearly as many as men, but there always have been women. There are a lot more today than there ever have been. But, there still is an extra challenge; although that's the case in just about anything that you do that isn't a "typically female" thing to do. People react to it.

M I think people still react more strongly to women who are heavily tattooed more so than men who are heavily tattooed. I think they [the tattoos] are seen as more of a butch thing than jewelry is. Jewelry can be seen easier as an extension of fashion, whereas tattooing is seen more as a grueling rite of passage and a permanent mark.

PU So you think that the idea alone that you're covered with tattoos signifies to them . . .

M Tough girl.

PU . . . You sat for all this work, and you are tough. It marks you as a different kind of a woman.

S And more than a tough girl, it's also the mark of a woman that isn't really concerned about how most men perceive her or how anyone perceives her. I mean, you're making an obvious statement that (pause) "You can go fuck yourself if you don't like it!" (everyone laughs) It's pretty obvious.

M Tattooing is extremely popular, and so is piercing, but a piercing you can always take out. Like I said, I do think that a lot more people contemplate a piercing over a tattoo, although people get more freaked out for a piercing than they do for a tattoo, which I still, personally don't understand . . .

PU Do you notice a difference between men and women, as clients or as practitioners of body modification? Do you feel like there are different issues for people who are coming to be pierced or tattooed that have to do with gender?

M There are definitely more men than women involved in piercing, but that's changing . . . I'm not sure why it is. At Venus, there are more men that have stayed longer. We've had a couple of females besides myself, but they haven't stayed for too long.

S We have the best guys in the world . . . working here.

M Definitely.

PU Does anyone do cutting and branding and other kinds of scarification here?

M Yeah, we do branding. We don't do scarification, basically because we haven't studied it enough. It's not to the level where we could perform it on the public, but on each other, well that's another thing . . .

S Yeah, they dabble . . .

PU I get the sense that you all dabble on each other.

M But we don't offer scarification as a retail service. Branding is a very serious thing that's gotten a lot of press lately; the media's jumped on it like, "this is the new thing now that piercing is mainstream"—which I don't necessarily agree with. I don't think all piercings are mainstream.

PU MTV, speaking of mainstream, did this story about this guy in some Midwestern town who was a high school student who was expelled for having his nose pierced.

S Yeah. I saw that.

PU What do you think it is about piercing and tattooing that causes so much anxiety?

M Fear of the unknown. People say, "Oh my God, what size is that hole in your ear? Oh, that must hurt!"

S The biggest reaction is: "Doesn't that hurt?" That's what I hear in every little town from here to California. My friend has a labret ring, and she gets twice as much shit . . .

M It's the pain factor. They think that piercings and tattoos involve an extraordinary amount of pain. Just a comment about the thing we were talking about before. It doesn't bother me that lots of different kinds of people are into this or that mall chicks or "navel girls," as we refer to them, come in and want to get their navels pierced. It doesn't bother me at all. It doesn't make my navel piercing less significant or important to me because I did it at a certain time, with a certain person. In fact, this "navel girl" is trusting you with her body. I generally don't judge the people. I think maybe they'll come back. I always plant the seed of their next piercing: "So, what are we doing next time you come back? Want to do your hood?"

PU And if they have a great experience with you, they will come back.

M Definitely . . . These are the masses that are coming to you and you have the power to impose your aesthetic, and make a living at it.

PU What do you think are the politics of all this? Piercing and tattooing are practiced in cultures that tend to be Third World and now there are white, middle class Americans . . .

S First of all, they found the Arctic man with his tattoos. It has come from so many different places, it's hard to pinpoint where it began. In Japan, tattooing was the traditional body suit for the Japanese mafia. It was a sign of austerity, power, wealth, warriorism, a type of responsibility to their unit. It was like you got your stripes and that's the way I think of it . . . I think of it as a luxury, but it's more than an expensive gift, it's something that you really earned. It doesn't matter what you paid for it, you *earned* it, you went through the process of it . . . You have to want that, you have to be serious about it. I feel almost like I've earned a certain respect for myself, and there's something important about being finished, about it being completed, and feeling complete. It's a real respect thing. In America, it's totally different; it comes from the real working class . . . but then it's not just blue collar . . .

M I think also the fact that all these different countries and cultures throughout history have been doing tattooing and piercing shows that it's something more basic, instinctual, very human and universal. All these people, all these cultures, individual of each other, stretch their piercings, got tattoos; what does that suggest? That it's something very basic, something primordial, a human instinct.

PU So, it transgresses cultural and historical boundaries?

M Yes, I truly believe that. Tutankhamen, an Egyptian pharoah, had three-quarter inch plugs in his ear. That's being erased from coloring books and stuff like that. You don't see depictions of the plugs or anything else like that, but these things have been going on for so long. I definitely think it's a sign of something very human, transcendent of culture and time.

S In many cultures, it has to do with austerity, a rite of passage of manhood.

PU The thing that you said before about power and respect . . . I think for women, especially, whose bodies are touched, poked, penetrated, marked, beaten, cut, bruised, and scarred without their permission . . . for women to take control of it and say, "I want you to mark my body in this way," and then have it done, is incredibly powerful.

lezzie
SMUT

September 1993
Volume One, Issue One

**Lots and lots
of very interesting
things inside, take a look...**

$10.

The Fat Truth

by Max Airborne (from FaT GiRL)

thought I was over it. *FaT GiRL* was going to be a celebration of fat dykes, a place to see ourselves in print, a place to bitch and moan, a place to organize. I had no idea what I was getting into. I knew it'd be a lot of work, and collectives could be difficult. But nobody told me what it would really be like; that I'd have to look at myself in ways I had never imagined, deal with feelings I didn't even know existed. There was no sign saying WARNING: DEEP SHIT AHEAD. Perhaps some part of me knew, but I dove in head first, deluding myself enough to do so innocently.

My eyes opened as the collective struggled to define fat. How could we determine who was fat enough to be part of *FaT GiRL*? We went around and around and around. Nobody ever really defined it, but the tension and fear seemed insurmountable. Everyone had feelings about it, most of us held back. I was afraid to admit I thought the line started with me, afraid to think about my place in the fat spectrum. If women much smaller than me are fat, what does that make me? Super fat? No, the proper euphemism is "supersized," I discovered. And what the hell is the line for that? Who's deciding anyway? I started feeling like there was no way someone who weighed a hundred pounds less than me could possibly share my experience of being fat. If they claimed the label for themselves, my feelings were being invalidated, my experience being whitewashed. "Hey, I want control over my *own* identity. And yours, too, so you don't knock over the walls surrounding my fragile sense of self." Ick. What a scared and nasty me I discovered. The whole process continues to be painful, and I haven't really spoken about it until now.

Fat Sensory Overload Like the sudden deep clarity of an LSD trip, all the thoughts and feelings I've always had about my body are now shouting at me full blast. The voices have existed forever, but I used to turn down the volume so their controlling effect was subliminal. (The killer part of the story comes when I simply realize the voices are in fact my own, and I control them. Ha! I guess I'll have to write another chapter when I reach that part in the plot. It'd be easy to write then, after the fact.)

I silenced my inner reality for most of my life. Not that I didn't have opportunities to listen. There was the time I started seeing a therapist (willingly for the first time) because I wanted to stop feeling suicidal, and needed help dealing with the memories and effects of my past sexual abuse. During the intake interview, the therapist asked me how I felt about my body size. I said, "Oh, I've worked very hard to accept myself. Yeah, I've dealt with that." I saw her for a year and a half, and didn't bring it up once. I think I actually believed myself. But the truth was I couldn't handle going that deep. Now it makes sense, because the depth of the fear and self-hatred that I am uncovering seems infinite. I guess I have enough moments of being OK at this stage in my life that I can handle it.

My intellect and my psyche have been at war forever over the fat truth. The first time I got angry about my childhood lifetime of forced diets, I was nineteen. It was the day before I moved as far away from my family as I could get. My dad asked me—for the last time—when I was going to lose weight. I had spent my life in terror of this man for the violence he'd committed, but that question fueled all the fear I ever felt into unstoppable projected flame. I screamed, nearly out of control, that I didn't ever want to hear another word about my weight from him ever again, that he had fucked up my whole life by making me hate myself. I reminded him how he behaved with me when I was four, going away on a trip and having me promise that I'd be skinny for him when he returned. "What kind of creep would do that?" I demanded to know. He was in shock, and denied everything. How easily we forget! We never spoke of it again, and a few years later I cut him out of my life completely. I wish that fire had pushed me out of my *own* fat-hatred. Instead, the flame retreated and I went on with my life, feigning ignorance.

A year later, I went to Nicaragua to help build a school. I became quite ill from parasites, and had bad diarrhea for most of my two months there. I secretly rejoiced that I was afflicted with something that would make me lose weight. The family I stayed with had no mirrors, and I became obsessed with the idea that I wouldn't look at myself until I returned to the US, looking completely different (thinner). My political consciousness was determined not to diet, but there I was, relieved and excited to be ill enough to lose weight against my will.

The Volume of Compliance

It has always been like that: My decision not to diet wasn't made out of self-love, but one of desperate rebellion and psychic survival (which I guess is a twisted, oppressed form of self-love). It has been a virtual "Fuck You" to the assholes who've tried to kill me all my life. Unfortunately, it doesn't address the fact that I have continued doing their work for them. And, like most of life, knocking on the door is only the beginning. I've barely stepped through, and it's clear that most of my work lies ahead.

Now that I'm listening, my sense of my fat self is acute; every thought and action presents itself to me undeniably. It's much more difficult than just turning down the volume, but I can't go back. I need to find a way to address the voices, but I often feel like I'm hovering above everything, looking down at myself; seeing it all clearly, but unable to participate.

This awareness of my size comprises a good portion of my everyday brain activity. It always has. It's amazing to me that I was unaware for so long. Now I can't help but see how many things I do and don't do because I am fat. I sit down with a group of friends and I'm only comfortable if I sit on the outside, partly because I need more space than most people, but mostly because I can't stand to be in a position where, in order for me to get out, I have to ask someone else to move to make room for me. It's too painful to call that much attention to my size.

I have cut most of my biological family out of my life for long periods of time. Even when we do talk, I don't want to see them. I say it's because they were abusive to me, which is true, but what I don't say is that I am still ashamed of myself for being fat, and don't want *them* to see *me*.

Each morning, I get to work around the same time as another fat woman who works in the building. I watch her take the long way around, avoiding the stairs at the back entrance. And I watch myself ascend those stairs each morning, determined not to look like I can't, determined not to show that I am out of breath when I reach the top. Desperately trying to convince myself that it's OK to be fat, that fat doesn't equal disabled. I tell myself that I'm out of breath for lack of exercise, but the truth is I don't exercise because I am afraid to find out. I see fat women who have a hard time walking, or don't walk at all, and it becomes all I can see. I forget about the women I know who are fatter than me who exercise and are in good shape. My fears take over, and as I get older and fatter, my fears grow. The longer I go, the harder it gets. I'm only twenty-eight. I am terrified of my future.

Redrawing the Battle Lines Finding employment as a fat butch dyke in a city where I don't know anyone is close to impossible. I can dazzle anyone with my impressive resume, but when they see me in person for the first time I'm just too much for them. I see myself starting to feel paralyzed by my dependence on my already-established network of friends for employment. When I have to look for work I hear the voice of my father, who warned me nobody would hire me if I was fat. I desperately want to prove him wrong, but the reality is that employers *do* discriminate against fat people. The real challenge for me is not proving him wrong, but realizing that just because he was right doesn't mean I am to blame for fulfilling the prophecy. I need to love myself anyway, despite the fat-hating world.

Friends say their first impression of me is that I am secure and self-confident. They're surprised when I tell them it isn't true. I'm amazed to know that a fat girl can hide so well. I guess I've had to— can't let the enemy know you're down! My entire life is a war. How can anybody not see that? How could anyone not see what I do just to survive each day? I can't continue to allow such ignorance of my reality and the reality of every fat person in my culture. It may be all I talk about for the rest of my life, but I will not shut up until fat girls start growing up with the self-respect we deserve.

Girl Talk

by Tammy Rae Carland (from I ♥ Amy Carter)

I've been thinking about how I think about my body. Or rather how I don't think about my body. About how I was taught not to consider my body as a site for pleasure and/or resistance. It was the place where I stored memory and secrets, and it was the thing that attracted unwanted attention. In other words, it was an awkward container. There has been a considerable amount of work done on the representation of female bodies but not nearly enough work done on the self-representation of women's bodies. I've been talking with women about this lately and I've heard all kinds of different stories. One of the ongoing themes of these conversations has been the issue of fear. The vagina is a simultaneous site of lust/desire and fear/disgust. And this dichotomy is internalized as much as it is an external construction. These stories are about women who have never seen their own vagina, women who have been afraid to sleep with another woman the first time because they thought they wouldn't know what to do. And another story is an all to common experience of women being afraid of feeling too intense and emotionally vulnerable with a body that was 'like' theirs. All these symptoms of self-loathing and self-deprivation really need to be addressed. Within the critique of representation, we also have to foster a dialogue amongst ourselves about how this affects women's relationships to their own bodies. Most importantly, we have to be there for one another—for instance, as friends and/or lovers of women, we must stick through it when the person we love begins to touch or express the pain that has been acted out on her. Even if that pain mirrors something in us that we aren't ready to touch or remember, or something that we feel like we can't quite relate to.

The Parent Trap

parents

siblings

family

Zines often represent the major issues in the lives of girls and women

today. Family plays a big role in everyone's lives, for better or for worse.

In this section, you'll find discussion on different aspects of family life.

This section explores what family means for many girls and women in

America today.

THE PARENTING ZINE

hip Mama

#9, THE BIRTH ISSUE
$3.95 U.S./$4.95 CANADA

A Spy in the House of Hate: California's GOP Convention

Born to be Wild: Labor & Birth Stories

Family Law Emergency? Quick Help is Here

Plus Fiction, Poetry, Queer Midwives, Mumia Abu-Jamal on Mother Love, A Refugee Experience, March to Fight the Right, and Way More

Sassy Ladies in Leotards Flying Like Angels

by Lisa Crystal
Carver, editor of
Rollerderby

My mother, who raised me all alone while my father was busy off being in jail for most of my youth, was always very open about sex—to an abnormal degree, maybe—except about one thing . . . homosexuals. It came up when I saw two men having some sort of love problems on *Starsky and Hutch*. My queries were answered with only a firm "I'll tell you when you're older"—the first and only time I heard that phrase from her, and then I was sent in to take a steamy bath. My imagination gnashed on what might possibly happen between two same-sex members. The reason Mom wouldn't tell me is that her biggest fear was that I, her only offspring, would grow up to be a lesbian and not give her any grandchildren. But being kept in the dark only inflamed my imaginings. When I saw on TV sassy ladies in leotards flying like angels around the roller rink, elbowing each other viciously out of the way *(Roller Derby)*, I thought that's what lesbians did with each other. I thought, "That's what *I* want to do when I grow up!"

Unfortunately, by the time I was grown, *Roller Derby* was out of fashion—but that didn't stop me from seeking out its spirit or naming my magazine after it.

I started *Rollerderby* in 1990, and I'm not sure why. When magazine editors are asked what their influences were, they usually list a bunch of other magazines. But, as far as I know, there were no magazines like *Rollerderby* before *Rollerderby*. My influences are just being female (thus, I am confessional, plain-speaking, nosy, laugh hysterically much more often than a man would, and have a hard time sticking to one topic) and being fortunate enough to be the rulingest sign on the zodiac—the sneaky, sex-obsessed, bossy Scorpio.

I should mention that I started the touring operatic troupe Suckdog in 1987 or 1988. Yes, it was opera! Quit calling it performance art— that's when two people tie their hair together and don't say anything for seventy-two hours to prove some point. *We* were much busier than that, what with writing and memorizing rhyming songs and choreographing dances. And our shows always had lots of rape, murder and revolution—that's pretty operatic!

Suckdog released three albums, including *Drugs Are Nice*. Vale from *Re/Search* described our music as "funny, weird, sexy, perverted, uninhibited, and above all, FUNNY." It's strange that I chose to become a singer because everyone had always made a big deal out of what a bad voice I had. At age eight I became the only person in the history of my grandmother's church forbidden to sing the hymns. At thirteen I was kicked off the cheerleading squad because the captain—a snotty fifteen-year-old—said I was trying to get all the attention by cheering so loud and doing my kicks so wildly (that was basically what had nixed my right to sing in church five years earlier). I took two singing lessons, but the instructor grew so frustrated at my complete lack of ability to do what he said that I ran away in tears, determined to just do it my own way. Which is what I did.

I faced similar hardships with *Rollerderby* in its first few years. *Rollerderby* has been kicked out of two copy shops and five printing presses for being "not the type of material our staff wants to deal with," but that never upset me; I just gave my money to some other printer instead. What does get my goat is when high-minded folks ridicule *Rollerderby* for having no substance and for being just about me and my friends and my cats. But screw the high-minded folks, 'cause now I'm rich from talking about me and my friends and my cats, and what do *they* do all day long to make a living? As Dame Darcy would say, "BAH, HAH, HAH!"

("Sassy Ladies in Leotards Flying Like Angels" is an excerpt from the introduction to Lisa Carver's book, Rollerderby *(Portland, Oregon: Feral Press, 1996), and is reprinted with permission of the author and publisher.)*

In Retrospect

What were my parents like when they were my age? Would they have hung out with somebody like me?

by Zoë Miller

(from Girlie Jones)

I like picturing what my parents were like when they first met. My mother a smart, rational girl going to graduate school at Berkeley; my dad an intellectual college drop-out who drifted West. San Francisco in the '60s with the Grateful Dead playing in the street, not yet a big deal. I try to imagine what they had in common—a love for the same music, Dylan, Fleetwood Mac, a frustrating family life. Did they think of each other as hot? Did they get butterflies the first time they kissed?

My dad has told me the story more than once. "I heard a foxy lady had moved in." Cat in hand, he knocked on her door, feigning a concern that the cat was lost. Was it hers? What did they talk about? Was it awkward? I wonder, I am not looking for clues to my future romances, I want to know what they were like at my age.

In 1970, my Dad was only twenty-three, the age I am now, and they had a brand-new baby. I try to imagine what he knew and I don't. And wonder if it's true what they say, "We wanted a baby." They left San Francisco for Indiana in 1969, the Summer of Love. They left the place everybody was flocking to—the music, the scene—to live on a commune. I can hardly fathom leaving all my friends at age twenty-six (my mother) and pregnant. That is nothing like the life I live. I go to sleep alone each night, not involved, with my baby (my cat) beside me.

My life seems safe and mundane compared to theirs. I try to picture what they would have thought of someone like me. Would we have gotten along? Me and my parents? My Dad and I might have lingered by the buffet at a party stuffing our faces and cracking goofy jokes, talking in silly voices. My mom would have been good to talk to—to the excess. Someone I could trust. I would have thought they were brave, leaving their families behind to find themselves. I wonder how the risks they took then have made me into the cautious person I am. My mother told me at eighteen and again at twenty, "You're more mature than I was at your age." My Dad tells me about the good friends they had, friends long out of touch. Their lives seem too anchorless to the homebody I have become. They say they're glad I stayed, but the more I think about it the more I feel I would have seemed square to them, never really leaving home.

I am more similar to the people they are now than the people they were then, I am grounded and unspontaneous. Maybe we are living our lives in reverse. Maybe our lives are nothing alike at all.

Why Do You Think They Call It JEWelry?

by Barbara (from *Plotz*)

My sister works in a jewelry shop. It's a nice jewelry shop with nice and friendly people working there.

One day a woman came in and asked for my sister's help. And my sister, being a kind and helpful worker, did just that. It seems that the woman had a ring that she wanted to get appraised. It was a big chunky amethyst ring, and when she showed it to my sister, this is what she said: "I FOUND THIS RING IN MIAMI. I'M BETTING THAT IT USED TO BELONG TO SOME BIG OL' JEW WITH BIG OL' HAIR."

Flabbergasted (my sister is much more the coquette than myself), she found herself just repeating: *"Some big ol' Jew, eh?"* The woman left the store and my sister relayed this startling information to her boss, an Israeli man, who in turn promptly said to her: "You'd better call your sister, this sounds like *Plotz* material!"

A Woman's Place

Zairian Refugee Maika Tshimbalanga

Struggles to Find Her Place as a Single

Mom and Business Woman in America

by Lauren Barack

(from hip Mama)

On the corner of 18th and Lapidge in San Francisco's Mission District lives a technicolor vision of the future in a mural on the Edificio de Mujures—the "Women's Building."

On the left, an older Latina woman cradles waves of white-crested water in her wrinkled hands, while the younger woman on the right grasps the element of fire. Her cobalt-blue hair snakes along a fire escape, towards more images: a Black doctor, a White mother, and a Brown healer laying hands on another woman's dark brown hair.

On this wall, in this painted world, all the women are successful, happy and co-exist equally. But for Maika Tshimbalanga, 41, who works within the brick walls, it is a world she finds hard to believe.

A single mother, former businesswoman, and now a refugee, Maika came to the United States four years ago, when she was seven months pregnant with her daughter, Mwanza. Eager to leave the increasing strife in her native Zaire, Maika hoped to build a more stable life for herself and her unborn child. Instead, she traded one struggle for another.

"The kind of things Americans value are not as valued in other places," says Maika, her French accent muffled as she nibbles her vegetarian sandwich at Café Beano, a nearby sandwich shop filled with camellia trees and spider plants.

She eats slowly, careful not to drop anything on her jeans or blue sweater. Her dark hair is tied in a neat ponytail accenting a canvas of bare cocoa skin, deep almond-shaped eyes and small gold earrings.

Fluent in six languages, including French, English, Swahili and Tshiluba, Maika was educated in Belgium and Zaire, and earned her Master's degree with a scholarship from the Canadian government. Before immigrating to America four years ago, she managed import and export for an oil company in Zaire.

But it took Maika two years of sending out applications and faxing hundreds of resumes to find a job in California.

"Some didn't bother answering," she says, her voice still containing disappointment. "Or they said we don't have anything with your qualifications but when we do we'll call. Of course, I know what that means."

Finding a job can be hard for anyone, but Maika knows her accent and skin color didn't help. A world traveler, Maika has encountered racism, but not to the extent she found in the United States. Even her daughter, now four, is not immune.

Just last year, Mwanza came home from day care and told her mom that other children were saying she wasn't beautiful because she was Black. Then, while picking her up one afternoon, Maika heard two children say, "I hate Blacks."

"This word 'hate', this is not part of my vocabulary," said Maika. "I knew my daughter would be confronted with this someday, but not this early. I don't want her to internalize that she's less beautiful, less smart. She will have less chances. It's too early." These incidents never would have happened in Zaire, but the home Maika speaks of wistfully is a home she cannot return to.

Riots in her hometown of Kinshasa, Zaire's capital, spurned Maika's decision to leave in 1991. Independence from Belgium in 1960 had brought freedom but also adversity to the former Belgian Congo. By 1965, military control of Zaire had been seized by Mobutu Sese Soko, a right-wing dictator who, with the support of the United States government, declared himself President for life.

"The situation had become so bad, they de-stroyed everything," Maika said of the uprising that broke out in Kinshasa the month she left. "The military started it. [Mobutu] thought he could control it to show how powerful he was, but it got out of hand and everything was destroyed."

The closing of the schools, already shut down by the government in 1990, had forced Maika to send her eldest son, Luya, then 14, to live with family in Canada. But now stores and hospitals were also closed, and Maika fled to the San Francisco Bay Area to live with a cousin.

"At first I just considered it maternity leave," Maika said, wryly. But when word came from Zaire that the political situation was only getting worse and members of her tribe, the Baluba people, were being killed by the military, Petaluma, California became her new home.

Fifty miles north of San Francisco, verdant farms dot the landscape along Highway 101. Just past Novato, a faded green sign advertises for Arabian horses. Take the first Petaluma exit, and the road winds past open fields and an occasional gas station. Within a couple of miles, the town appears.

Wide store front windows display bathing suits and hunting gear. Colossal trees shade the sidewalk in front of the corner ice cream shop during summer days.

Very few refugees from Zaire live in her neighborhood, but Maika slowly met people—

single mothers from her daughter's day care, and friends of her cousin.

"In a sense, those other people became my village," she says while making lunch for her daughter at their apartment. Although it's a Monday, and her office is open, it's also President's Day, and Mwanza's day care is closed. Without someone to watch her daughter, Maika has to stay home, losing a day of work and a day's pay.

As Maika fries eggs, sweet potatoes, and other vegetables, Mwanza darts between the kitchen and living room, eating slices of pear and dancing to the blur of children's shows on television.

"Mommy! I'm hungry!" Mwanza cries, as she runs her sticky hands along the table.

"C'est tres chaud," Maika warns her daughter as she places steaming slices of sweet potato on a paper napkin.

The child quickly pops a slice into her mouth, and immediately spits it out onto the red plastic tablecloth. Mwanza grabs her tongue with her hand, and looks up at her mother with large eyes.

"See?" Maika smiles, and begins to blow softly over the potato.

Mwanza has never seen Zaire, nor met her grandmother. Given the political instability and the $3,000 it would cost to visit, a trip home doesn't seem likely.

After the $200-a-month Maika spends getting to and from her job in San Francisco on the bus, and the $600-a-month for Mwanza's day care, she is left with little from her salary as an administrative coordinator with the nonprofit Women's Foundation.

So Maika recreates Zaire by speaking French at home, instilling the values in her daughter that she learned as a child, but it isn't easy. "Here, the ego is so strong. They value the individual, the person as the center," she says, as Mwanza interrupts to ask for another slice of potato. "Sharing is important to me, and she knows that."

Sheltering her daughter is also important to Maika, especially after the incidents at Mwanza's day care. Maika fondly remembers her own "spoiled" childhood spent on long river trips on her family's boat and lounging at the local yacht club. "I was cocooned," says Maika, emphatically. "It has its bad side, being too naive, but it has its good side too. You can learn things slowly."

Since coming to the United States, that cocoon has burst, along with many of her dreams. Her hope of running her own company has been dimmed as she watches even American women struggle to find grants at her job.

"In Zaire, I had a language that I knew, a culture that I knew and a certain level of achievement," she says. "I had a lot of dreams I thought I would realize. I used to take things for granted, maybe because I was lucky. But now I question everything. I don't have the same confidence anymore."

But she keeps dreaming, she says, to keep her spirits up.

"Without dreams there is no way we can make it," she says smiling. "It's not necessarily easy, but I'm laughing today because it helps."

The Relatives

Up North

by Goddess of Venus

(from provo-CAT-ive)

This past week my parents and I drove to Pennsylvania to drop off all my stuff for college. In September I will just take a plane to school. We stayed one night with my grandmother and grandfather. I was bored, so I decided to watch my foolish relatives' actions while keeping a close log of what happened.

My grandfather and father were comparing their "war wounds" of the surgeries they had undergone. (Sick!) My grandmother and great aunt were sitting off quoting dates when people in our family had died. (It's a sad time when you begin to remember people's death dates over their birth dates.)

I also observed my grandmother's strange obsession of saving paper towels. You might be thinking, what on Earth was she doing?!? Well, my grandmother is a very caring, thoughtful person. When she finds a towel that reads a cheesy message like, HOME IS WHERE THE HEART IS, she saves them to give to the people who the sayings remind her of. (I wonder if they print napkins that say, I HAVE DEEP OBSESSION WITH BLOOD. FORGIVE ME, so that axe-murderers with sweet consciences can leave their victims nice little notes.)

My grandfather also smokes (a lot!). I asked him how many he cigarettes he smoked a day. He began the count: One . . . two . . . three . . . (heave, cough) . . . thirty-six! I sat out on the porch with him while he smoked. We began talking and he reminisced about when he was a teenager. He remembers he first started really heavily smoking when he was sixteen. He told me he really wished he had never started. He told me it was hard for him to walk from one side of the trailer to the other without getting out of breath.

He then began to tell me stories of what he and his friends used to do. On an average Saturday night, he and his buds would go down to the pool hall to shoot some pool. Of course, the girls would know the guys were there and they would sit outside and watch them. My grandfather told me about his cool car being a great girl-attractor. This is all he would say on the subject, but I know the unedited version tells how many girls he grubbed with in the back seat. I think it's neat that my grandfather can still remember those times so easily. By the time I get to be his age (let's see, in about sixty-five years), I will be talking to my grandkids about how many of my friends died of AIDS when they were young (back, of course, before they had a cure), and how many were murdered and how many committed suicide. Just this week, a girl in Little Auburn, Alabama, was strangled to death. This world is getting crazy, and it really scares me. I hope I make it until I graduate from college. I am really scared of getting hit by a stray bullet. WOW! The 90s sure are depressing.

The Electra Company

by Lotta Gal

(from Bust)

My father ruined me. No—not that way. It's just that, well, he's such a great guy, and, much to my dismay, far greater than most of the men I've dated. This is a problem. It's becoming more and more of a problem as I zero in on The One. Or attempt to. Unsuccessfully, I might add.

Growing up, my self-employed dad was usually home to receive and counsel me on whatever load of pubescent misery I'd dragged home from school that day (check where it says: present and available). He was sensitive way before a nation of 80s quiche-eaters adopted "listening" as a snare to get the snatch (check off: attentive and loves a good chat). He grew up with a divorcée mother and a sister, then managed to marry a woman with only sisters and spawn only daughters himself. This is one man who knows women. Knows how to talk to them. Knows how to appreciate them. Knows them (note: intuitive and a deft complimentor). And, if that don't beat all, he's an artist. La piece de la resistance: he adores music, dancing, museums, good books and movies, as well as architecture, travel, and fashion (check everything remaining). Now, I know what you're thinking. He's not gay. He happens to also adore women. All this and straight too? What a bargain.

Well, he is and he isn't. He happens to be simultaneously the most selfless and self-absorbed man I have ever known. He is an artist, after all. There are times when I'm both thoroughly impressed and confounded that my mom has put up with him for all these years. But on the whole, he's an amazing catch. For a father. Just a father, thank you very much. Oh, and did I mention that they're still married? To each other. That is correct. The last of the nearly extinct "Happily Married" Species Domesticus in captivity. Plunging me ever deeper into the minority.

So, where does this bitch get off listing her prodigious patriarch as a dating liability? She's gotta lotta nerve. And when so many other women have suffered through so much blah, blah, blah-di blah . . . I know. I know. But look, this is my own personal reality. This is all I know. Stumbling across a man who treats me as well as my father does simply isn't as g'damn easy as you would think it should be. Especially while living up to my expectations, however, warped, of how a successful marriage continues to defy planetary logic. When I stumble through a dance at a wedding reception with a guy who's holding me as if I were his mom and not The Girl He's Fucking, I long to be effortlessly led around the floor by the

confident grasp of my father. When I'm wide awake and trembling from menstrual torture and my fella asks me if he can "get me anything" as he rolls over, I can't help but think of how my father gently rubbed my tummy-in-turmoil until I fell asleep on the living room couch. When I oblige to help my beau bury his cat in Central Park and he meets me at the animal hospital an hour and ten minutes late, I am reminded of my dad, who, in over a kabillion years of picking me up from Girl Scouts, band practices, keg parties and airports, was never late.

When I have occasion to say, "Badges . . . we don't need no stinkin' badges . . ." and my date looks at me as if I've lost it, I have. I've lost the will to date. I want to scream, "Why can't you be a younger, taller, version of my dad . . . but not my dad? He's wittier than you, he's more conscientious than you and he can discuss Wagner *and* Vonnegut, Gaudi *and* Gaultier, Anais Nin *and* NIN!" OK, so maybe he doesn't know much about Trent, but he's open to suggestions. No gap.

Perhaps it's not exclusively a My Dad Thang. Perhaps it's all men of his generation. They knew how to dance. Saw their dates safely home at

3AM to Avenue C. Chewed with their mouths closed. Hmm. Come to think of it, they also treated women, for the most part, like shit. So, what am I left with. That I'm spoiled? After countless childhood lectures, spankings, and groundings? Maybe. But he doesn't patronize me. I am not Daddy's Little Girl. He supports me. Not with credit cards. With respect. Through all the jobs, all the careers, all the schmucks who were Doing His Daughter, he has supported me. "Follow your heart" he says, when I can't decide whether or not to let a boy into my life. My loins. "Follow your gut." He has welcomed every last of the dregs of guys that I have paraded through my bed with the same genuine warmth of a man meeting his son-in-law. And he has held me without admonishment at every tearful and drama-packed break-up. Poor Dad. Who would have thought that being a good father could turn out to be damaging? I have been criticized by men on more than one occasion for having survived the wreckage of puberty with only a few nicks and scrapes. It seems this makes me less tenacious, less dysfunctional and therefore less . . . interesting. Fuck you very much.

I've discussed this with my sisters. My grown-up, unmarried sisters. They agree. Why should a man hang out with us when they could hang out with a woman who was treated like shit by her father? She expects less. The barest necessities of kindness will provide heaps more than what she's used to. And I can only surmise that from his point of view, marrying a woman who grew up in a fucked-up home is a lot less daunting. Fewer expectations.

No, that's not fair. I take it back. I've had it good. Too many women have not.

So, do we all win or do we all lose? Well, none of us should compromise. We've heard that before. We should all have high expectations. Regardless. We should all be appreciated, respected, and adored. My dad is a man who, by example, has taught me how a woman—a truly loved woman—might be treated. Should be treated. If your example sucks, you're welcome to borrow mine.

Baby, Don't Do It!

by Missy Bean

(from _Easy_)

Lately, I've been noticing a trend developing among the girls in my school. This is not just some new style of clothing or a new hair fad, but oh, how I wish it were. No, this is something far more permanent, something that cannot be undone . . . PREGNANCY. More and more girls are having babies now. High school moms still living with their moms, usually holding a part-time job for minimum wage (if they have a job at all). Those who have made the decision to continue coming to school often miss days on account of a sick baby, or their mom (God forbid) has got something to do other than watch their irresponsible kid's baby.

I've been pondering the problem of teen pregnancy for quite some time now and a question comes to mind: What could possibly make a girl decide to have a baby? This question only brings on more. Does the girl actually _decide_ to have a baby or does she just think that it can't happen to her?

Some ideas have come about as a result of these questions. Mostly they stem back to the small town in which I live. Granted, there is not much to do for a girl my age here, but really, do you honestly believe that a good fuck will remedy your boredom? If that's what it takes to amuse you, my dear, I feel awfully sorry for you. My next theory leads me right back to this little town. There is a really bad drinking problem here, not just on an individual basis, but as an entire community. Again, since there's nothing else to do, some girls will go get drunk and fuck some guy. This type of girl, sadly, makes up the majority of the high school population. My only other theory leads me to the conclusion that these girls have little or no self-esteem, which really upsets me. I wonder though, can I really blame this epidemic on the town I live in? Can those pregnant girls blame this town? I don't think so. I live here and I'm not pregnant. I just can't understand it. Honestly girls, just because there's nothing to do, that's no reason to go and have some meaningless sex with a guy who will most likely be out the door the second he sees the little "plus" sign on your pregnancy test.

So where are the girls left? Probably living with their moms until they go on welfare and are forced to live in a crappy apartment with their loser husbands/boyfriends and the baby. Who is going to buy the diapers? How about the formula? The hospital bills? Probably the new baby's grandparents. Now there's gratitude for you. Some of these girls think that an engagement will fix everything. The marriage will create some kind of instant family complete with instant family values, right? . . . WRONG! Nice try, honey, those "family values" flew out the window the second egg and sperm were joined.

What bothers me the most is that these girls used to be my friends. We used to have goals. I still have many of the same goals. I've achieved some of them already. I'll be going to college in the fall and getting my own place. These girls will probably still be living with their mom in three-generation families. They have thrown all their opportunities away for an orgasm . . . I just wonder, was it worth it?

Hey, I've Got a Comment!!!

by J-me (from Easy)

'm not saying I think being a teen mother is the best idea, but this is a personal thing that you can't really understand unless you've been there. These get-drunk-and-fuck girls aren't the only girls who get pregnant. A girl in a teenage romance, long-term, monogamous relationship can get pregnant, too. So can an unmarried girl in a serious, long-term relationship. Responsible girls using one or more methods of birth control can (and do!) get pregnant. Being on the pill is no magical guarantee—trust me on this one.

Any girl having sex can get pregnant (no, *really?*), so the problem, at least for me, goes beyond living in a small town where there's little Any girl having sex can get pregnant (no, *really?*), so the problem, at least for me, goes

beyond living in a small town where there's little to do but drink too much and do stupid, irresponsible things. Everyone (EVERYONE) deep down *does* think it can't happen to them—but sometimes it does, and then you have to deal with it.

Whether or not to keep an unplanned child is an impossibly difficult decision if you're not already 100% sure what your decision is. I respect any girl who has the guts and strength to go through with bringing a child into what might not be an ideal situation, but only if she is making an enormous effort to make the situation the best it can be. I would *never* condemn anyone who decides not to bring a child into a situation they feel could not be improved or dealt with in any way. This is a hard fucking thing to deal with.

farewell, father

by girl (from Bust)

My father is dying. Or I guess he is slowly disintegrating, dissolving into an ever simpler form of life, his body gradually letting go as his million tiny veins give way one by one, clotting and popping, failing him as he fails us. I am angry but he never really did anything to me, not like some. The story is confusing: we were a good family, we are good people; we were a disaster area. He was a good man, a good dad; he was not even there.

The man is giving way now to a feeble child, clutching onto the tail of his existence with grim strength concentrated all in the gripping, and my dad is along for the last ride. Reduced, pared down and clean. Erased. This slow loss preoccupies me more in terms of the difficult symbolic legacy he endowed upon us—our archetype of what is a man—than of the loss I have yet to endure. He has already left it to us because, in life, he has left the hard shell behind.

I thought I had forgiven him but maybe not yet for that.

My oldest friend was irked by a self-help ad calling out to those damaged by pervasive absence, by the workaholic, distant, ungiving patriarch:

"Did you have an emotionally unavailable father?" "Duh," she said, "I mean, come on, hello? Were you raised in America in the '50s, '60s or '70s?" She grew up across the street from me. I guess I always thought her father was there for her. He took us for rides in his MG, he told spooky stories at slumber parties, he laughed and teased and stood around waving his Bloody Mary while watering flowers with the garden hose. He crashed their marriage and got up unbloodied to walk away from the scene, from the wreck, didn't look back.

My father clings tightly to my mother after fifty-three years of union as she helps him to the table. How could I not learn something good from this image of absolute symbiosis, interdependence, commitment? I don't know. How to lose yourself inside?

But how will I ever find myself in a relationship, in a partnership, when my role-model mate was an ultimately absent, angry, uninterpretable man; a huge and empty shape, a clenched knot of forehead and grim jaw, now gentle with oblivion as his mind drifts toward pure present. Now no past, no future, without his pain and his fear. Freed from them, he is a sweet presence, light and childlike, almost demure. Even the harsh lines of his hard skull are softened like a baby's, all soft spots, gelatinous, bruised. His essential humility and vulnerability shine out. This man is not the one I grew up with. I can't hold anything against him. But what did he give me to expect, what did he teach me about men?

I seem to find bright, charming men who turn out to be brooding and dark, who need me to spell it all out for them—what I am feeling, what they are feeling, that their actions signify, that feelings have repercussions, that things connect. This is the way of my father, this unawareness, groping blind in the thrall of an emotional context. Not even groping, just standing there numb and dumb. Is it just more of the same old, same old, universal late Victorian twentieth-century manhood? Is it just the same old he said/she said gender-gap crap? Do women whose fathers actually talked with them find mates who can communicate? (Oh, man, what I woulda gived to have been Eddie's Father's daughter.)

Goddess knows I don't wish to whine about how my dear old dad wrecked me for other men by alternately ignoring and raging blindly at me, through us, at the world. But, as he lays dying, this is what I'm mad at: when he's gone and there's no longer any chance to reconcile the man with the symbol, I will be sorry. I don't have much time.

I have five big brothers. One of them went and lost himself in Vietnam, but the others all seem to be survivors. The older ones are more tightly wrapped, rigid; the younger have gained more sense of humor and accessibility, being farther out of orbit in the family solar system, my father the silent center. I am the farthest out, and maybe I have the farthest to come back.

All my brothers, I believe, admire our father; they are uncritical, and have essentially based the pattern of their lives on his. (We are, all of us, people who do the right thing; we believe in making a contribution. We are all good citizens like he showed us how to be.) It's in reflection on the inner life that my father's blankness penetrates us, his lack of self-knowledge, passive, void, frozen. We are all carriers. And now he has permanently lost the gift of speech he never really knew how to use. I honestly don't think the others ever saw or understood how much I hated our father. How could they? He was basically a nice man, hardworking, eager to please, shy, repressed. Stern, guilty, unhappy. Fucked up. Angry.

I love my dad now. I know how to see the person inside the father. I can be his daughter. In the panic and chaos of facing this primal pain and unimaginable loss, I am trying to find a way to make connection. (Once, I was mad at my dad for existing, now I guess I'm mad at him for leaving.) The eradication of the foundations of my known cosmos, from which I have always tried to escape, is showing me how deep and permanent the bonds are. I have to learn how to lose and find myself inside the cycle. The source is incessantly collapsing back in on itself and I have no choice; it's sink or swim.

Destiny

Trip

by Destiny Itano,

as told to Darby

(from Ben Is Dead)

It happened long, long ago, when I was a little, little girl. I was two and my parents and I were living in a truck, kind of commune hopping . . . My parents were twenty-four at the time. . . . We were traveling around in our truck.

The Untimely Pit Stop A friend of my parents was pregnant, but she didn't really remember when she got pregnant, she was not sure how far along she was. My mother, who was a nurse, and this other midwife, were taking turns staying with her over a two month period. They figured she would probably have the baby in this block of time.

So, at this time, we were staying at her place in northern California, in the Redwood Forest, probably a thirty to forty-five minute drive from the nearest town. There were a couple of houses next to each other near a river.

Destiny Pops a Button It was only the second day of our stay. Sometime in the morn-

ing, my dad went out to chop some wood, and I was playing in the button box upstairs. My mom came in and saw me put something in my mouth, and figured that it was probably a button. She said, "Give it to me." I was at that age when, if my mom said that, I would just swallow it . . . and that's what I did. She didn't really think anything of it until a couple of hours later when I was lying on the couch, practically comatose—limp as a doll—with my eyes open. I was just staring straight ahead, not responding to anything. My mom didn't really know what was going on, she just thought I had gotten sick or something. My dad came in and my mom told him she thought there was something wrong with me. My dad came over to me and said, "Hi Destiny," and I didn't do anything, didn't blink. They were waving their hands in front of my eyes; nothing. My dad said, "I think she's stoned. What did she do, eat some hash or something?" And my mom said, "Well, I don't know; she was in the button box. She ate something that was in the button box." So they asked the pregnant lady, and she said, "Oh, no, there wasn't anything in there. I don't think so." A half hour later—she was a real spacey woman—she said, "Oh, you know, there were two hits of Osley purple acid in there." And my parents ran up the stairs, dumped the entire box out onto the floor and found there was only one hit of acid in it. I don't know how I ended up picking that little piece of paper to stick in my mouth.

This is a Two-Year-Old on Drugs So, my parents had a brief, freaked-out discussion about what they should do. They were really freaked out, shitting their pants, wondering if my brain was fried and thinking that I was probably going to stare straight at the ceiling for the rest of my life. They figured that it was too late, that it was obviously throughout my system. There was nothing they could do. They were going to be as cool as possible and try to keep me from having a bad trip.

They went around and told everybody at the other houses not to come to our house unless they had to. My parents explained that I had accidently taken drugs, and that they didn't want to freak me out. My dad said he played solitaire, very deliberately, for a very long time at that point.

Later he tried picking me up and carrying me around and stuff. It was raining a lot, and while he was carrying me, he was staring out the window at the river. I remember looking at the river for a couple of seconds and then my eyes got really big, and I just wanted to get away from the window. The river was really freaking me out. It turned out that the river flooded the road later that day.

Is It Cool? I didn't really do much of anything for a long time after that. They would sit me up on the couch and I would slide down, and then just fall over. They had the fire going and I was just lying there in front of the couch. This went on for about five hours. The woman who was pregnant had another kid. He had been out all day, and didn't know what was going on when he came in about sundown. He came running in and everyone said "No, no! Be quiet. Destiny took some drugs and we need to stay quiet." They told him to be cool, and of course he wasn't cool. Typical seven-year-old. He came

over—ran over—and stuck his face into my face and said, "Is it cool? Is it cool?" My eyes went "boink," and as they chased him out the door, I sat up. That was what woke me up. And there was this gradual thing where I was sitting there staring, and then I would just giggle for a couple of seconds, and then I started laughing, hysterically. Anytime someone would look at me, I would just laugh.

Just a Really Stoned, Normal Kid

Then I settled down; I wasn't running around so much, but I was talking—a lot. They tried to feed me, and my dad said I acted pretty much like any stoned person does. "No, that sounds terrible"—until I tasted the food, and then it was like, "Great!" I did that for awhile. And then they asked me if I remembered lying on the couch. I said, "Yeah," and they asked me if I remembered what I was doing. I said, "I was looking at the fire. The fire was so beautiful." And then I said, "The elephants were really nice! I was dancing with the elephants on the ceiling. They were really nice." That's what I was doing the whole time I was on the couch. They thought my brain was frying but I was just dancing on the ceiling . . . with the elephants. I think they were too freaked out to analyze it. They weren't thinking, oh, wow, this is really cool and we want to know all about it. They were just too freaked out to be thinking like that. They were just really glad that I was acting like a normal kid again; just a really stoned, normal kid.

After a while, I got up and started walking around—before this I was just learning to walk. I bumped into somebody, and I started laughing. So I started running, and running into people, and laughing. I did that for about two hours. Run, bonk, ha, ha, ha. Run, bonk, ha, ha, ha.

Speak English with One Easy Lesson

What's funny is that somebody noticed that I had never spoken in complete sentences until then. And after that, I never stopped using complete sentences. I think it was like a trigger; all of a sudden I had all of these things I wanted to say. They would try to get me to quiet down. By this time it was late at night. I started telling them about all the different rooms I had slept in since I was born, which was really intense for them, because they didn't even remember them that well. I was telling them that I had this really nice bed that had a brown blanket, and there was this big window next to it, with blue shavings on the side and a nice curtain, and outside there was a big tree. But I mostly told them about the bedroom. My dad said I was talking about really detailed stuff, like I would talk for an hour about the bed, and then twenty minutes or so about the walls. I remembered all the way back to the house where I was born, and we only lived there a couple of months.

I was describing the little minute details until about the time I crashed. And then, that same night, that woman had her baby. My dad said she went into labor about a half an hour to an hour after I went to sleep.

The End of a Wonder Evening

My parents hadn't even slept . . . they were up all this time, and then this woman had a really complicated birth. She had a prolapsed cord. My mom looked it up and all the book said was, "prolapsed cord: hospital emergency." Nothing else. So they had to get her to the hospital, and the road was flooded out. They had to walk her . . . they had her on a stretcher, and it was really dark, and my father was banging on the side of this house trying to wake the people up so he could use the phone because we didn't have a phone where we lived. They called an ambulance, and the person told them that they had to send a police officer first, because there was only one ambulance and that they had to verify that it was an emergency. My parents were waiting, and my mom had her hand inside, holding the baby back, because if a baby comes out with the cord first, the baby will be strangled. They have to do a C-section.

I can't even imagine dealing with the birth by itself, or a two-year-old on acid by itself, but both of those at the same time . . .

We don't know how the baby is doing these days but Destiny is fine and well and is currently a really cool chick living in Los Angeles. Wonder what Dr. Leary would think about this?

Pregnant at the Glass Slipper

by "June"

(from hip Mama)

I worry about stretch marks because I have to. I worry about them in between worrying about why Tara doesn't crawl yet, the teeth poking painfully through her gums, her refusal to eat, her need to always be held, the wet diapers, Governor Weld, the cold weather, the laundry I haven't done, and the bad taste in my mouth.

Secretly, I love the marks on my breasts. I watched them form with more wonder than dread. They are like an intricate tattoo, a testament to our mother-and-daughter relationship. I often rub the deeper ones with my finger while I nurse Tara. I like the thick impression that they have left on my skin. It's beautiful.

I love my pot-belly, too. It's rounded, small, just the right shape.

I exercise, but not because I want to.

I exercise because I have to prepare my body for display. It's ironic that the first time in my life I truly love my body, I mean, really respect and adore my body, it won't be acceptable in the club.

I feel that I must always be ready for the stage. The threat of welfare closing its doors on me before I'm ready, or a factory job being forced on me and my Bachelor's degree in English, keeps me doing stomach crunches during those beloved nap times.

I was an excellent dancer. I worked through the early months of my pregnancy. I made a lot of money. But I had hoped that part of my life was over.

I no longer crave the stage.

For a long time I was addicted to the smell of sweat, money, and cheap cigarettes. The stage was a place where, not quite eighteen, I learned about being a chameleon. I could seduce a credit card from a bum. I was like a shapeshifter. Any man could look at me and see whatever shape he wanted most. I was an airhead, an intellectual, a dog, a mistress. I was every kind of pervert and dominatrix and girl-next-door he could imagine. I could slide and spin on the stage and ultimately have the whole room, women and men, in a trance, in love.

I thought I was learning about being a woman.

Even more than the stage, I loved the dressing room. In that tiny, sweaty little space full of mirrors and cigarette smoke, women in all stages of costume and non-costume made love to one another. Well, we didn't literally make love (usually), but that's the way I see it in my memory. We flirted. We were naked. We were beautiful. Some of the women were really in love with each other. I loved them all in some way. For me, each of them represented a little piece of reality. And for a small-town middle-class white girl, their realness was enough to leave me smitten for life.

I thought, in that tiny, smoky dressing room, that I was learning not to be a girl anymore. I was learning about being a woman.

I even loved Paloma the night she came running off the stage and into the dressing room where I sat, five months pregnant. She was holding a knife and screaming "And you just sat there and let them do it to me," with lipstick colors streaming down her chin. That, in or out of love, was my last night of work.

*   *   *

When I was laying in bed, sometime after that night, I heard a funny sort of click and felt an internal shift.

Suddenly I was lying in a puddle. Water was pouring out of me and onto the bed. And when the contractions started, I was finally all woman.

I was all woman in the hospital later when my mother and my girlfriend held me and I gave birth to Tara. And now when I see my breasts, as I pull them out to feed my child, I don't think "I've got to save up for those implants."

I'm all woman—tiny, sagging, stretched breasts and all. And if Governor Weld and his welfare reform forces me back to the club someday before I finish my teaching credential, they'll go with me just the way they are.

Dear Diary

A girl's diary has always been the place where she records her experiences, her feelings, her wishes, and her secrets. This section reflects the more personal expressions we have found within girl zines.

These pieces contain true stories and accounts of various aspects of the lives of the zinemakers, as well as some of their innermost feelings and thoughts.

Ben Is Dead Is Born

by Darby, editor of <u>Ben Is Dead</u>

W hen I started *Ben Is Dead* in 1988 I hadn't a clue what a "zine" was—there weren't many. I was just looking for a forum and escape, and without any background in writing or editing—or reading other "zines"—I found myself creating a magazine of my own. No one said I couldn't . . . and the few that noted how horrible the first issue was, I used as inspiration—to make the next issues better. The zine became a tool for me to move around in the world. A signpost marking time so I could see where I was at, and where I might want to go. And a great excuse to do the stupidest things I might otherwise have been too scared to do. And it eventually taught me how to write and edit (not "proper" English, mind you)—with the help of other contributors *and* readers. Each issue is a mirror to my life, even if it doesn't always reflect it on a directly personal level. And when the issue comes out I am able to move on, to the next stage. And because we use themes, my otherwise scattered brain is able to focus on a subject and discover within it. The various people who have contributed over the years—mostly girls—have been able to utilize it to their own means, both personal and otherwise. *Ben Is Dead,* regardless of what people think about its contents and as corny as it sounds, has always been about discovery, expression, accomplishing goals, and creating new worlds for oneself. It's about not agreeing to all the rules and therefore not agreeing to all the limitations. It's about being what you make fun of as an effort to change. And it's about knowing enough to not take yourself too seriously especially when someone asks you to write a short essay about your zine . . . and I'll learn how to do that too, someday.

"i like things to be small. . ."

by Cindy O. (from <u>Doris</u>)

i like things to be small, to fit in my pockets. magazines, paperback books, strings and rocks, gum and photographs. i want this thing here to be smaller, maybe you could fold it twice and it would fit snug in the back of your blue jeans like doris number one did, getting dirty and ratty and torn.

i was on the bart train the other day and there were these four girls, high school girls. three of them looked just like TV, long hair that they would brush back with their fingers. all four had practiced facial expressions, small noses, lines drawn around their eyes. but one girl, she was too tall and gangly and it looked like she just got her braces off, the way she kept feeling her teeth with her tongue. her backpack had paintings of suns and moons and flowers that you could tell she painted on there, and you could tell her friends made fun of it behind her back. she was the one i watched. her backpack was unzipped part way and i snuck doris number one in. number one, full of my secrets. i couldn't hand it to her because i knew she wouldn't take it, not with her friends watching. i snuck it into her life for her to find later, alone, in her bedroom. the people on the train who saw me do it glared at me, mean and suspicious, like i'd stolen something from that girl, and maybe i had. i got off at the next stop.

but the truth is, i don't hand it out like i used to: watching people on the train, on buses, on the street—handing one to this girl who is laughing with her friend, one to that girl sad and alone on the last train of the night, the girl with the red boots, the one sitting on the wet curb, the boy who pulled his hair in front of his eyes and chewed on the ends. i still want the same things. to break—with this one small gesture—the crazy things we are taught; to keep distant and distrustful, alienated, lonely, and safe. i still want to know stories whispered and yelled and coughed out between too much laughing. but i live in these cities now and i know too many people, all half-way and california style. and i never got winter, cold sun, and thick blankets of snow. a warm room to hibernate in. time to sleep and read and swim around inside my head. this place is not condusive to that and i still spend my days running around like crazy. every day feels like ten. sometimes i say to my friends, "god, i havent seen you in weeks"; and then i realize it's only been two days. everything is changing faster than i can follow. my sister is leaving. leaving.

i was evicted from my home away from home. i have all my things packed in milk crates and boxes. i've climbed fences and got drunk in the abandoned school yard. i sat out on the grill outside the train station with a broken heart in me and a broken heart drawn on the sidewalk with chalk. i rode my pink double bike, wobbling and laughing. i rode the bicycle built for two all alone, feeling shitty and beautiful and lonely and good, filling up the front tire at every gas station and walking it when the gas stations were too far apart. i set up office hours in a coffee shop so far out of the way i knew no one would come visit me there. i pound on things and pretend to sing. i've found short cuts that take twice as long. i've made this city mine.

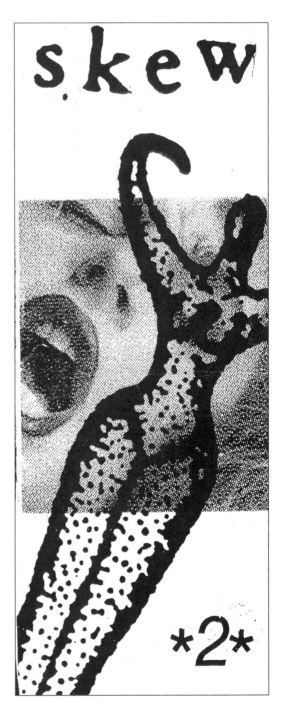

What Does "Sassy" Mean to You?

by Jennie Boddy, with intro by Darby

(from <u>Ben Is Dead</u>)

*I*t's pop culture, alternative/underground culture, sometimes even homosexual culture, right but usually left-sided politics, fiction, girls, boys, zits and lotsa cool clothes and Fluevog shoes. "So, who cares, what's so big about that?" you wanna know. Well, the thing that's big about this is that it is all dedicated to the young, who am I, where am I, growing-up girl. And before Sassy came along, girls without a cooler older sister to show them what was up had to learn from the whorably insipid, complacent teen magazines like Mademoiselle, Teen, Seventeen, and Young Miss (God forbid). Today that doesn't seem as bad, but until Sassy showed these other magazines what was up, they never really catered much to the oddball, unique, fringe-culture type of stuff. Sassy has affected that. Instead of just beauty tips and fashion and good-little-girl concepts, Sassy compiles many controversial topics and provides opposing views and options. Sure, sometimes it falls short. Sometimes you wonder, why can't they get some real-looking models for the fashion section (though, sure, they're more real than any of the other teen-girl mags). Or, you wonder what these writers would be saying if the publishers didn't have conservative advertisers' money to worry about (though they do come up with some insightful critiques that push the boundaries: "Reforming Teenage Murderers, Should We Bother?", "How's That Drug War Going, Guys?", "A Night in the Life of a Junkie," "Poor, Poor Little Tori Spelling," and "What It's Like to Have Big Breasts.") You wonder, why aren't they even more daring, less trendy? I guess you have to consider the magazine's true intended audience—teenage girls. I don't know, maybe a mainstream teen magazine which young girls can actually relate to sounds like no big deal to you, but it was something I really yearned for when I was younger. Sassy may not have been the all-enlightening experience but, instead of drugs, Sassy could have been the thing to push me to seek different ideas and directions.—Darby

I'll get burned for this one, but I think the *Sassy* phenomena is pretty beat. I wish I *did* like *Sassy* more, but you know the saying, *glad to see ya, wouldn't want to be ya?* What is it anyway: a socially-relevant, girl-affirmative, eye-opener for teens? *People* magazine for hip adolescents? *People* magazine for the staff and friends? Fashionably smart? Cute? Cool?

Well, Kool thing, what about the girl who has to shop at JC Penney's, or uses the modesty shower in gym class or loves Simon and Garfunkel? Oh, no no no no, that will not do. *Sassy* says so—be an individual, individual like all of us. If they were really so cool, they wouldn't have to tell people what's cool and how cool they are. What if everyone was "Sassy"? No one would bowl, no kids would ever hang out at 7-Elevens, the socker-rocker bi-level cut would be declared illegal, and everyone would talk funny.

Mainly, I think the magazine has good intentions, but missed the mark and became superficial and contradicting. I'm looking at eighteen past issues here (my overly-interested voyeur friend, Tammy, age twenty-five, keeps them), and on every cover is a darling girl, most of whom are actually young, I'll grant. Then you open the magazine to, oh, an article on why not to get a nose job. Well, OK, that's awesome, so then if you believe in what you preach, stop being mouthpieces for what everyone knows is correct to say, and (gasp) maybe one day adorn one of those monthly fashion spreads with a big snout—or, better yet, put a big-noser on the cover—and Blossom doesn't count because she's famous. You know Sally-average just isn't going to cut it: every issue is chock full of the cute and gorgeous, dressed to enter a 90210 set (harsh—a call I think both *Sassy* and *Ben Is Dead* would revile). Or, *Sassy* runs a great, self-affirming article on how destructive boy-obsession can be, but, my God, they positively gloat over Evan Dando or Keanu Reeves (dorky Jane Pratt, that one) until you want to barf. Not even because you intensely dislike either one of these two celebrated people, but, *man* (woman? womyn?)—it gets almost dogmatic. The sycophant quotient is about as high as it can get, with irking staff comments like how the cute boy next to one of them on the plane, who looked just like Matthew Sweet, turned out to actually be Matthew Sweet! Nauseating (at least Mike goes nuts over the Ramones, but that's not the point, I guess). The worst is Jane Pratt, the plastered-up, cake makeup phony with the brown hair and choker, the one with the cancelled TV show who writes things like "kiss" and "hon." You know, I don't really *care* that there she *is* in the REM video

WHAT DOES "SASSY" (THE MAGAZINE/THE WORD) MEAN TO YOU: • "The cutting edge of the new twentysomething journalism age that was." –**Matt Tyranauer, Vanity Fair** • "Cameltoe." –**Sean de Lear, Glue** • "It's about little girls with little pussies that aren't afraid to use them." –**G.G. Allin** • "We want a zit-rockers version called '*Stunky.*'" –**Seaweed** • "I suppose it has it's place; there's a lot of people who need to know what is cool and what's not. But I don't think they'll ever find out by reading *Sassy*." –**Brian Brannon JFA/Thrasher magazine** • "They are passing themselves off as more progressive than they really are. They simply have a lot of the same elements as *Seventeen* or *Mademoissele,* represented in a different style. They are still judgemental and holier-than-thou, telling young women how to look and act. Their writing style is ultra-swarmy and full of slang, if I might cite 1940s hip cat talk." –**Jean Smith, Mecca Normal** • "My girl friends are sassy" –**Mike, Steel Pole Bath Tub** • "Sexy awesome seductive salacious and young. –**Bix Jordan, B.W.P.A.** • "In the seventies there was a magazine put out by Peterson Publishing called *Star* and all the girls in there were foxes." –**Rodney Bingenheimer** • "Frank Thorpe" –**Mike Wolf, Am-Rep** • "Lisa Bonet" –**Mark Lightcap, Acetone** • "A bunch of women in their thirties writing a magazine for women in their twenties, who wanna be pre-teens." –**Jennifer Finch, L-7** • "Young, lots of frizzy hair, spunky and bright colors." –**Adam, Condomania** • "Skeptical, positive, self-respecting, it's being wise and able to see beneath the surface." –**Mike, senior editor, Sassy** • "Free-thinking, funny, follow your own impulses." –**Margie, senior writer, Sassy** • "Sassy is trying your hardest to look like a Barbie Doll, bleach blond locks, starvation diet, silicon, walking around with a perpetual smile while spitting in peoples faces." –**Kari French, performance artist.** • When Jessy barged into **Bob Dylan**'s recording session asking "What does Sassy mean to you?", Bob responded "Insolence."

(or backstage at a show or whatever it was, I can't remember now, it was so important) telling us how cute her dress is. If I was fourteen I honestly still do not think I would care. Her slant on the magazine—she is editor-in-chief—is turning it farther and farther away from things like yeast infections and gay/lesbian couples, and closer and closer toward self-promoting spin doctors for fashion trends and bandwagon-jumping. Why isn't Christina Kelly "editor-in-chief," surly as she seems to be? [I can always imagine her clucking her tongue in disgust at things]. She does write all the good features, like on topless dancers or street harassment, and I notice she seems to opt out on most of the lame stories. And by things like "Zine of the Month," at least she's trying to get some underground stuff into mainstream pop culture. Jane just doesn't have a clue.

Alas, the definite chord running through *Sassy* is its obsession with types, which in itself is fine, if they'd cop to it. Of course, it is *way* better than *Seventeen* or *Tiger Beat,* etc. [duh, like "Sesame Street" rules over "Barney"]. But if you are bone-headed enough to go buy *Seventeen* or *Tiger Beat* or the *Weekly World News,* for that matter, at least you know what bone-headed things will be in them. Instead, they think of themselves as innovative and radical, which is like *Playboy* actually thinking people buy them for the articles. My favorite thing they ever did was put *Poison Idea* in the Cute Band Alert—partially because it's funny, partially because they were a great punk band, and partially because it veered away from their K Records, Simple Machines, Juliana Hatfield obsession (and I *like* K and Simple Machines). While I'm giving examples, though, here's a few others: The person giving the movie *Singles* a five-star review said she really "related" to it; saying an album called *Every Good Boy Deserves Fudge* has a sexist title [duh, chord progression mantra, Blue Oyster Cult reference]; and, as a friend pointed out, asking a sociopath like J. Mascis to do an advice column for lovelorn teens (the guy who used to sit in the college cafeteria and put food in his hair, who gets cultural stimuli from soap operas, God love him); tattling on anyone smoking. . . .

But the thing is, any magazine can write about whatever it wants, and *Sassy* has affirmative and insightful articles that others of the genre don't. Actually, you can't even say there are others in their genre, because their peers never veer anywhere *close* to the issues *Sassy* writes about. So I tried to be nice, then thought fuck it. Like I said, I never meant to hate *Sassy,* and I don't (how can you really hate a magazine, anyway?). And what's a girl supposed to read, say, one who lives in an area where she doesn't get *Girljock* or *Fantagraphics Comics*? Definitely *Sassy*. What would I want my little sister to read? *Sassy*. And what of my peer group—what to read for kicks? Whatever the hell you want, be it *Mondo 2000* or *Wagons of Steel* (a zine dedicated to station wagons). Or *Sassy,* if it floats your boat. It just bugs *me,* which, as you know, doesn't mean a hoot, because, at twenty-eight, I'm not exactly their target audience. So now they all hate me and I'll never be their best friends. Damn!

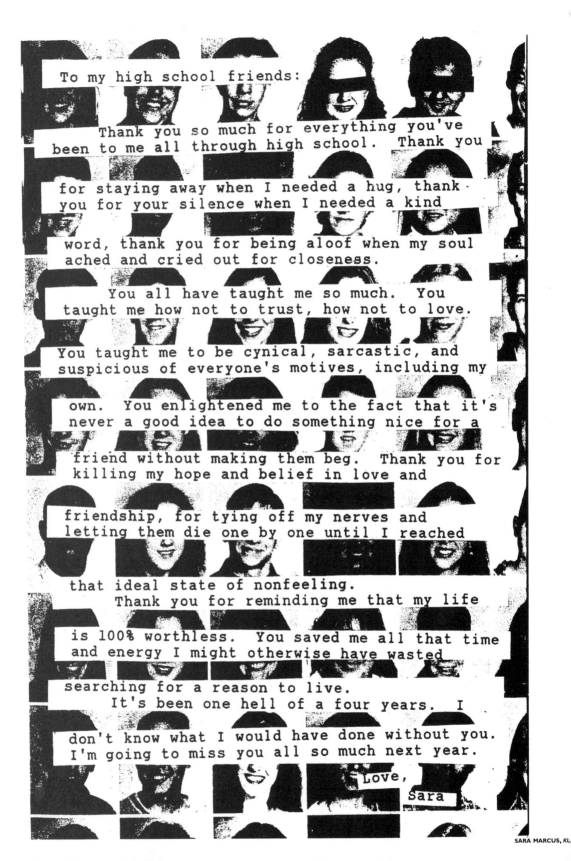

To my high school friends:

Thank you so much for everything you've been to me all through high school. Thank you for staying away when I needed a hug, thank you for your silence when I needed a kind word, thank you for being aloof when my soul ached and cried out for closeness.

You all have taught me so much. You taught me how not to trust, how not to love. You taught me to be cynical, sarcastic, and suspicious of everyone's motives, including my own. You enlightened me to the fact that it's never a good idea to do something nice for a friend without making them beg. Thank you for killing my hope and belief in love and friendship, for tying off my nerves and letting them die one by one until I reached that ideal state of nonfeeling.

Thank you for reminding me that my life is 100% worthless. You saved me all that time and energy I might otherwise have wasted searching for a reason to live.

It's been one hell of a four years. I don't know what I would have done without you. I'm going to miss you all so much next year.

Love,

Sara

Lusty Lady

by Erika Langley (from Blue Stocking)

The Lusty Lady doesn't look like a comforting place, a place to find yourself or harness your power. It looks like a peep show, a funk-scented, creepy, dark hallway where men wait, eyes wild as dogs. They wait their turn to stand in a tiny booth, feeding quarters, to watch naked women dance behind glass. Often, they masturbate. Muffled jukebox songs, the slam of doors and *whoooosssshkink,* of the change machines are the sounds that hang in the darkness.

There are no venues like this for women, this intersection of public sex and fast food, so I felt a little out of place there, but I was wildly curious. I had been working as a newspaper photographer, and my idea was to propose a documentary about The Lusty Lady. I'd heard it was run by women, and I liked the snappy slogans on their marquee: EXPOSE YOURSELF TO ART, etc.

Kathy, the show director, shook my hand warmly. She squeezed inside a booth with me and began feeding quarters. A door rose above the coin slot to reveal a square window. Behind the glass, five naked women danced in a mirrored, pink-carpeted room.

One was on the carpet with her legs over her head, another was doing splits vertically against the mirror, making use of the handles on the wall. The faces of men in windows were reflected in the mirror.

Kathy pointed to one dancer, who wore a fragment of a long-sleeved shirt, partially covering a large tattoo of a tree on her shoulder blade. "She has to keep movin' that shirt around," Kathy said, "so that her breasts and genitals are exposed at all times."

I proposed my project, and was sent to talk to June, the general manager. "We like your ideas, but if you want to understand this, you'll have to dance here," she told me.

I set out to become one of my subjects, to really learn about a much-judged, little-understood group of women from the inside. These women are shunned both by society and by many feminists, yet their stories, I quickly learned, are of ambition, courage, survival, and economic freedom.

Exploitation, objectification of women? Or, instead, is it a feminist thing to take charge of one's sexual power and brandish it: *I own this!* I was familiar with both arguments. I had to see what it was all about.

Of course, I never thought I was that kind of girl. My roommate in college was an aspiring model, selected for me by dorm lottery. We fancied that our very differences made us get along. I was never a threat to her spotlight, living in the darkroom, while she swirled in head shots, flowers, and men.

We threw this party one time, but only two guys showed up, friends of hers. They had the good sense to bring wine. We made short work of the wine, contemplating our failed bash, while these guys compared the two of us. They decided that I was the Virgin Mary and she was Mary Magdalene.

Both ex-Catholics, we knew the difference. "You're the one to marry, but she's the one you wanna hang out with," one of these guys explained to me.

I never knew I could be otherwise. I didn't own any high heels or short skirts or even a lipstick, and I had a disdain for what I called a Professional Girl: a girl who was so good at having lacquered nails and sprayed hair she could be called a pro.

I prided myself on my unprofessionalism.

I'm not blond, or stacked. I didn't think that just anyone, let alone me, could put on sexual power as easily as a skirt, and then put it away until I felt like the high priestess again, whirling myself into an erotic trance so I could talk to the spirits.

The audition was scary—trial by fire. I wobbled on my eight-dollar heels from the cheap shoe source. I was grateful for the presence of the other dancers, who smiled at me and were high-spirited, laughing and butt-slapping. I knew what men did in peep shows, but I didn't think we could actually see it! Half of the booths are one-way glass, but the other six aren't, and I could barely contain my open-mouthed astonishment to see men jacking off.

At art school, I took figure drawing. First day of class, we had to draw a naked woman. Everyone was terrified. By the second week, the model was like a still life in the drawing studio, and we all sharpened our pencils and chatted nonchalantly. Her nakedness was as expected and familiar as a piece of furniture. Similarly, the nakedness of the customers, my coworkers, and myself is demystified to the point where I feel like I work at a car wash, or a hamburger stand.

I've learned that in a mirrored room there's no place to hide. Being naked is a great equalizer. There is little bickering among the dancers; everyone's salaried, so there's no competition. There is no reason to lie.

I have spent so much time looking at my body that I've gone from critique to acceptance. Sometimes I see myself out of the corner of my eye in the mirror and I think I'm looking at someone else. What does it mean to be good at this? I can't determine if I was fatter when I started, or if my body image has changed, metabolizing rolls of flesh off the hips of my subconscious, my taut, hard belly like a drum.

I look at the other bodies, amazed by variety. Breasts crinkly from childbirth, nipples dark and large, sucked dry by babies; long legs, the curve of a tiny butt, nipples that stand up like bullets.

Imperfections are rampant if you look closely, though a woman sees these most in herself. Some of the hottest performers have butts and bellies, which suggests to me it's about confidence, not perfection.

For me, the Virgin Mary, the real value is being allowed to find my own power out there. I'm addicted to the glamour now, and my costumes are many: shiny long gloves like a Vegas showgirl, thigh-high stockings with a seam up the back. Frivolous! Improbable! Where else could I wear these things?

I can play slutty dress-up with no ramifications here. I have been naked long enough to accept my body and like it. Vanity is a drug to me now, and I'll fuck those mirrors all night long.

It took me awhile to be comfortable showing my affection for the other women. The first time a dancer with big boobs hugged me, I was startled by the naked softness and warmth of her body. I thought I was a very straight girl.

Now when Aviva gives me a big lipstick smooch on my belly, I wear it all day like a badge. Candy Girl runs her long nails down my back. Camille can spank my butt, but I'll spank hers. In the company of women, we cuddle and touch. It's not sex, not pressure, but comfort and affection. It's a lucky thing to have found.

On the other side of the glass, we see every age and demographic in our customers. In the mornings, there are lots of old guys, and blue-collar guys with their names on their shirts. Good morning, Bob, Larry, Jim!

Lunchtime, it's the parade of suits, all the financial district businessmen. In my estimation, these are the rudest customers of all. Perhaps their fast-food mentality is to be expected; it's their lunchtime. They want pussy, right now. Don't wanna see you smile, don't want the slow seduction. They want a Big Mac, not waitress service and a five-course meal. Basic politeness is a rarity among the suits.

In the event of extreme rudeness, we are empowered to police the customer. This is one of the pluses of being women-run, this idea that the customer is not always right. If they are ordering you around, or manifesting abusive behavior, they can be handily bounced. The support staff is swift and effective.

As the night wears on, the carnival ensues. Frat boys, belligerent drunks, biker types, bums, and even the trench-coat types you'd expect in a place like this. I like nights the best, when the men have shed their morning guilt and lunchtime attitude with their ties.

As long as they're nice, I try to be kind. I smile, looking them in the eye. I pretend to kiss 'em through the glass, my breath fogging their face into a blur. I see myself as a social worker, healing, gentle. I try not to have undue contempt for the customer, unless they're rude. This is about need, and they want to be treated like humans.

It helps to have a healthy man in my personal life to keep my perspective. I tell him stories from work, which he interprets with humor and reason. When I have a bad day, he reminds me that working in any customer-service job will expose you to a few assholes, not to be taken personally.

I'm always asked if I hate men from working in this business. I can't, having been given this crash course in their frailties and fetishes, for in the moments of faux intimacy we share at work, they are profoundly human and vulnerable, and my compassion is real.

It's been two and a half years now. People ask, don't I have enough pictures? I never seem to run out of powerful women to photograph, and I'm still learning things about myself, and the woman I can be, now that I know all things are possible.

Late at night, when the bosses are away, our spirits are high. Desiree can keep the drunks in line. "Gentlemen! For the price of a phone call, do you think you get to boss the naked lady around? Telling us what to do is like trying to teach your dog to drive. It's very time-consuming and it doesn't work!"

For the rest of the night, it is a surrealist joke; the first group of belligerent boys gone, another unwitting drunk is reminded:

"Remember the driving dog!"

We all collapse with laughter and start howling at the moon. *Barrrrrrrooooooo!!!*

As I leave, a janitor asks me, "I heard you all barking. What was going on?" But there is no explaining the deep significance of the driving dog; the caged primal wolf howl of naked women, late at night, amid eleven windows.

KATE EVANS, FROM *GIRL FRENZY*, REPRINTED IN *FaT G*

The Daily Grind

by Anonymous (from Pawholes)

It's 9 PM on a Wednesday night, and we night girls are just beginning our shift, while the afternoon girls are leaving. There are four of us sitting under the sallow lights of this dressing room—one, a notoriously wild entertainer, pulls snug black pants up over her ass. Another presses a pastie to her left breast, and stares ahead at nothing. I notice the skin of her belly looks pinched, and I can tell she's had a child. The other, an elusive girl who says nearly nothing, pulls a pair of dirty Keds onto her bare feet and slings a duffel bag over her shoulder. "See ya later," she says, and is gone. The wild girl in her tight black pants asks me, "Do you party?" "What kind of party?" I ask. "Blow," she says. "No," I say. "I'm not really into coke. Thanks though." "Yeah, well, I'm drunk, and it sobers me up," she explains. She snorts a line up her straight Cherokee nose. The other girl sits ignored. She is new and her costumes look cheap so no one talks to her. "I'll go up first," she tells me, in a thin voice that craves approval. "Sure," I say, not wanting to make her uncomfortable. I was new not two months ago and as I watch her leave I know she feels awkward . . .

So now I'm left with this gorgeous veteran stripper. "You're beautiful," she says, very straight-forward. "I don't tell anyone that," she adds. I'm so flattered, but at the same time I want to run away or at least cover my face with my hands. Next to her, with her slanty gray eyes, huge burgundy mouth, and skin the color of sandalwood, I feel pale and flaccid and unwomanly. Her hair is voluminous, waist-length copper. I watch its rusty glow as she leaves, a motorcycle helmet under her arm . . .

Alone in the dressing room, I sit in a black vinyl chair and breathe in the smell of my co-workers—baby powder, musk, sweat, and mildew. The carpet is damp and cool under my bare feet. A stray gold pastie gleams alone in the corner.

When the new girl returns from the stage, I'm pulling on a pair of obscenely short cut-offs and cramming my feet into four-inch black pumps. "You're up," she says, her face beaded with sweat and her hair separated into clumpy dishwater blond strands. She throws a wad of ones in her duffel bag and drops into a chair and exhales.

I teeter out of the dressing room and onto the stage. My stomach feels raw, 'cause my first set is always rough. I'm stiff and self-conscious and it is much easier for me to become the fantasy if I empty my brain, forget my identity, and pretend it is a dream. It is easier than you would think—with smoke drifting through the air and the lights casting red and green on my body and these rapt faces looming in front of me, it is very dreamlike anyhow. I become the "other girl"—the one without a boyfriend or a family or rules. It is a part of my existence that I savor—the freedom to be alone and admired and somewhat of a star for a few moments. It is a departure from the anonymous routine of my everyday life.

Tonight there are about ten men in the bar. Two are shooting pool, another two are throwing darts. The rest are dispersed around the bar and at the end of the stage. One in particular is perched on the edge of his bar stool, a stack of ones on his acid-washed, denim-clad knee. His eyes are perky and expectant. A queer little grin reveals protruding teeth. *Can't get laid to save his life,* I find myself thinking. *Loser.* Then I feel sorry for him.

At one corner of the stage, Jerry waits for me. He's wearing a smooth white and peach pin-striped shirt with creased charcoal trousers. His hair, dusky brown, lies thin and quiet over his bald spot. His hands are at his sides, harmless, pale instruments. There's a look of mild pleasure on his pinkish face. He is one of my most loyal regulars. I can't help but appreciate him. "Hey," I say, sliding up to him. "How are you this week?" he asks. "Oh fine." I say. *Yeah, right,* I think to myself. *I'm a grand in debt, my boyfriend is leaving me, and I'm failing in school.* But I'd never say that to one of my customers. I'm sort of a vessel for their troubles—they speak in low tones to me about their sadness, and pass me dollar bills while they are doing so. Jerry doesn't love his wife—that's his trouble. "You look as great as ever," he tells me. I swallow his compliment and thank him. "I can't stay. It's family night," he says in a light, scornful voice. He presses a twenty into my hand. "Bye." He strides tensely out the door.

With Jerry gone, I must move on to another man. I lock eyes with the acid-wash loser and move like satin toward him. He jumps off his bar stool and meets me at the edge of the stage. "How ya doin'?" I ask. "Great, now!" he exclaims. *How typical,* I think. How terribly typical. I keep undulating, keep that soft, pleased smile on my lips. "God, you're hot," he breathes. "Ya make me wanna cream, ya know?" And I can't help myself—I just start to laugh. What an asshole. I always get the last laugh.

Welcome to

MY LIFE AND
MY SEX THRIVE in the J. CREW CATALOGUE

numero deux.

One day I'm sprinting to no definite finish line,
but just to have a ball exhausting myself, and
nighteen days later I can fake a torn ligament
and take a long look at my an

ana fondly recall where i've sprained
them. Okee dokee, this is my zine.
all drawings, doodles are mostly
mine, AND all of the photographs are
not. i've tried my luck with cartooning;
the one, In The Car, summarizes the
realationship between my mom and i-this.
year. you'll understand me you get there.
the computer was occupied by other family units
these past fun months, so my typewriter came back for
an encore, and so did my pen. Brilliant thanks to
everyone who wrote... there are so many people i'll
never know in this world, who will live alongs with
me in the same era— Anyone out there who hasn't, any old
memo or telegram (do those still exist) will do. But if you feel
compelled to write please go ahead. my addres is on
the cover. 'GUILTLESS BLACK BEAN DIP' is primo.
delish.

leora

BONJOUR!

Temporary Insanity

by Heidi Pollock (from h2so4)

Your mind always wanders as you ride in an elevator. You've never quite figured out why, but you think it might have something to do with the paradoxical nature of motion implicit in elevator travel. You are moving, and yet you are not moving. So, are you moving or aren't you? Is travel motion? Does motion imply relocation? Of course your body doesn't move in the elevator. It can't. It's trapped behind a poorly cut, navy-blue polyester pinstripe. But yet you are traveling. And frankly, it's not as if this paradox is that unusual. After all, you were more or less stationary as the subway conveyed you uptown to 49th street. But that was different; you can see the outside of a subway. You never really get to see the outside of an elevator. You can only see the inside of the box. An elevator is really only a little, wall-to-wall-to-ceiling carpeted box with a lot of destinations from which to choose. Just a little box inside a big box, moving all day long but never really going anywhere. A horrible, creeping metaphor begins to edge its way into your conscious mind, but luckily you are saved from dwelling on this as you focus on the physical act of fighting your way through the small, motionless throng of humans, out onto the 32nd floor and towards the Securities department.

And there it is: The Glass Bubble. The Cylinder. The ultimate, fabulous, perfect emblem of a secure Securities floor. The Cylinder consists in part of revolving doors of solid glass, which might seem normal, only there's no metal encasing them and no convenient handbars to push against—just four smooth sheets of glass inside a clear glass cylinder. The more traditionally configured doors flanking both sides of The Cylinder are similarly comprised—of glass only—and set into a glass wall (See Fig. 1). The entire crystalline ensemble makes up the fourth wall of the elevator foyer on the 32nd floor of the big glass box known as the UBS building in NYC, USA, and has the general feeling and approximate entertainment value of the Museum of Natural History's Early American Colonial Life exhibit. The Cylinder's glass is perfectly clear and absolutely spotless (owing, no doubt, to some unfortunate employee whose sole job is to make certain that it stays this way). But no matter how clear and obvious the whole set-up appears, you can't get to the other side of the structure without a security card.

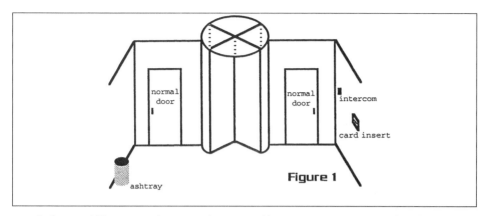

Figure 1

As fate would have it, you happen to have a nice blue temporary security card—which supposedly renders you temporarily secure. To use the card you must insert it into the Card Insertion Mechanism with a level of accuracy and care that would make workers in a virus research lab happy. If you do manage to insert the security card with the required degree of robotic precision, a small green light blinks in recognition of your achievement—validating your preapproved presence—and the glass doors of The Cylinder respond in kind by rotating with their own robotic precision.

As you are fishing around for your security card, another Secure Person enters into The Cylinder. Overwhelmed by the utter tediousness of this security process and unable to locate the blue badge of privilege bestowed upon your secure personage, you opt to sneak in behind the preceding drone and hop into a passing wedge of The Cylinder. But just as Mr. Secure Securities Man makes it through to the other side and vanishes down the hallway, The Cylinder ceases moving and you slam against the inch thick glass, smearing the surface with oil from your skin.

Trapped inside The Cylinder, you stand in stunned silence for what is probably only seven seconds, but feels like a week. You are stuck inside what is suddenly a very small space—surrounded by glass, visible to all, and unable to move. You feel more naked than if you'd come to work without clothes. You feel like a bug in a glass jar. The Museum of Natural History's taxidermy displays surface from your unconscious and you suppress the image instinctively. You wonder whether or not it would be possible to shatter the glass, and cringe at the thought of what the resulting shards might do to your body. You push, tentatively, against the immobile wall, further dirtying the glass with smudgy fingerprints. And just as the edges of panic are beginning to overtake you, a voice booms out. You jump a little at the sound and the mere fact that you jumped forces you to realize how paranoid you have become. For some reason, you are ashamed. The disembodied voice sounds out, "You have entered a security area without the proper identification. The doors will now reverse." The doors begin to rotate in the opposite direction. But they don't rotate at the same speed or with the same fluidity as they did turning in the "normal" direction. Instead, they jerk backwards (which is really now forward, considering that when a small room begins to move, you turn to face the direction it's going) and you have to shuffle along like an ancient Chinese woman with bound feet.

Now you're back where you started, in the elevator foyer. Just you, two purposeless ashtrays (remnants from an earlier era), four elevator shafts and the glass prison. From which you've just escaped. Yet the sensation of being trapped increases as you hunt frantically for your security card. B-movie images of buxom babes in high heels twisting their ankles just as King Kong reaches out his hand are relegated to the recesses of your brain right next to taxidermy. Certainly you could escape into the elevators, but escape is not the point. You have a job to do. A stupid one, albeit, but you have bills and rent to pay and food to buy. The necessity of your dire economic situation highlights the fact that you are trapped, not just in The Cylinder, or in the elevator foyer, but in a massive forty-eight-story building. You are not alone, you think. There are hundreds or maybe thousands of other people, all trapped in the big box with its steel beams and its sealed windows.

A strange, primal nervousness rises within you and you notice that the shiny brass panel displaying the floor number is reflecting your unnerved visage. Fascinated by your look of desperation, you absently note that you appear to be a smoky, sickly gold color and your skin seems tinted green. The fluorescent lights are making you look green. Or are they actually making you green? Is the very chemical makeup of your body being altered? You notice that your image is slightly blurry. It's the surface of the cheap brass. Or is it? Is your eyesight finally failing? Has staring at a computer screen begun to make you blind? Why are you trying to get back to that harmful screen, to sit under those mesmerizing artificial lights, to play dumb and act pleasant and consume toxins from a styrofoam container? You stop searching for your security card. You are made immobile once again, this time by the clamor of your mind as it screams out an endless succession of half-realized fears and desires. Each emotion occupies its own, isolated moment and they flicker by like the frames of a movie. Each tiny, temporal, emotional moment captures you as completely as did the glass cylinder. You want to scream out your frustration.

A voice emanates from the intercom: "Having trouble with your card?" Transfixed by your vague, green reflection and shocked into silence by the tumult of your mind, you nod absently in silent response. Even as you nod you realize you should be speaking into the intercom. "I'll let you in," says the voice. How did the voice know you nodded? Maybe the voice is Evelyn. She shares the coverage of your phone lines. Evelyn has to walk from her cubicle in the building's corner, down the hallway, turn right, go through a door, and then turn left. The entire journey will take her thirty seconds.

You have thirty seconds. Thirty seconds in which to do what? To escape? There is no escape. You can't escape. Your very nature as a temp dictates this you pass through these moments. What is time to a temp, if only a series of moments—fixed, fleeting, temporal, temporary? You are pinned down even as you pass through. Evelyn opens the door and you move.

ABOUT THE "THREE WOMEN IN BLACK" DRESSES

Duston Spear

ACCESSORIZING

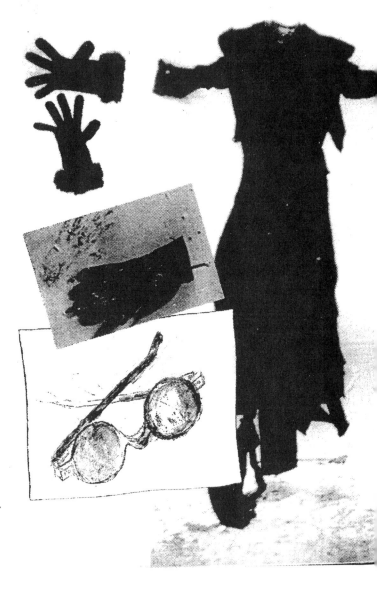

I had been using this image of a silhouetted 19th century woman 'backing away from the ruins' in my paintings. I wanted to see a battalion of women dancing—cutting through a crowd, but then the news about the former Yugoslavia came and the battlaion's job extended to bearing witness and standing in solidarity. My very loose 'plan' was to make three dress-up dresses for any three women to wear. Costumes with elaborate veils that would turn a trilogy into a force—black to silhouette them against the backdrop of the present—veiled to represent the universality of mourning.

So I 'sewed'. I bought three black pantsuits made from some slimey fake poly-something or other at a discount store and I ripped them apart below the waist. Then I dyed every piece of material I could locate black and sewed, glued and stapled these pieces onto the three hanging deconstructed rag dresses. There they were, Three Women in Black.

page designed by
Barbara Scott Goodman

FOR THE REVOLUTION

lear diary what would you know. i write and
a rite to you, you know, and what would you know
about what im going through. life is such work,
no surprise, ive been working my whole life
but i never thought workworkwork would extend
into my head the way it has, life is a mess to
be cleaned up and you know how i feel about
messes.

just looking at this room is makin g me cry.
look at it, nothing but piles of envelopes,
records, spraypaint cans, all laying around
with nowhere to go. at least i think thats
whats making me cry.
                                  who knows.

id like to tell my story if i could, but whenever i try to tell it i just get jumbled and
confused and eventually i drop it. i dont
really wanna talk about it   take a
walk if you dont mind, i dont really feel like
discussing it, the blur. a hazy white blur
and my life stretches behind it, i can just
barely make out some shapes.

i remember a lot of stuff, actually. i remember missouri and kindergarten and the pickup
truck and stepfathers and texas--there werent
as man cactusses as i expected--and i remember mens white cotton briefs. i remember a mans
cock swollen up inside of them. i remember
being underneath, and i remember dreams where
its dad. thats it. pour me a drink or get
the hell out.

so i just moved into this apartment and even
before my roommate got here it got broken into.
funny how doors come off their hinges so easy,
funny how nobody ever knocks. well at least i
get paid for it now, at least now i take my
clothes off for money and lie and lie and lie,
aint no doors that open any more without
payment in advance. the door to the VIP
champagne lounge opens for $300, starting price.

thats cash paid for services rendered.

dear diary oh how my heart aches. how it aches
and pounds and aches all the way down to my
stomach so i cant eat anymore, not to be over-
dramatic but it really does. and if only i could
keep this goddam room clean, i come home from
work and books and papers all over the floor, my
jeans and we stern shirts and dirty socks draped
across the bed and cardboard boxes still here,
stacked in the corner. i only want to go to bed,
i only want to bput this to bed between clean
sheets, smooth and untouched.

  i called dad today not tht i wanted to but
  we are chums you know ████████████████████████
  ███
  ███
  ███
  ███
  ███████. i dont know it was him anyways,
  so many stepfaters in and out x of my life,
  it could have been any one of them too.
  dont act like you dont know about mens
  facination to fuck little girls. to cram
  their cocks into the tight little hairless
  pussy. who knows what else. fingers,
  kissing, to wake up next to the smallx
  breaths hot on their face.

  the Club is the only place i feel safe with
  men, to be honest. they can touch me all
  they want as long as the cash is flowing,
  but when they cop a free feel it doesnt ka
  bother me much except in principle--no
  one will pay for something thy xx can get
  for free. but i know already. i know
  this body aint sacred, it never was a clean
  temple. well maybe once. but i have no
  illusions about bodies. i xxxx mean, its
  kinda hard to while youre trotting around
  in crotchless panties. its flesh and blood,
  who gives a shit.

still love. finger by finger, your bitter
taint is crammed down my throat like a wad
of oily rags. im disgusted with love.
i choke on it.

the memories i ~~have~~ think i have ~~i~~ of ▓▓▓.
only good. pretty pictures of me sitting
on his lap while we watched TV. his funny
whine, "candy-o, come here and scwatch my
back." card games, bickering over math
problems. what a chum. how can this one
memory be true? edged in steely terror
and clouds of disbelief, its suspicious
already. i never did see the face. i
believe that im an incest survivor, but
not that i was ever incested. i never did
see the face.

god i wish i could tell this story. i wish
somebody would tell me this story. a
scene that plays over and over again in my
head. i feel like maybe i wsnt there. i
wasnt there, who was?

im imagining a straight red ~~ladder~~ ladder, a
ladder to climb right up into nothing. deaR
diary, i dream of a crooked red ladder
slashed up the middle of my left arm. raw
holes to let out the pain inside, im full
to bursting. only to releive the pressure,
the knife is sharp, shiny, and friendly.
if only i could get u p out of bed i would
do it. i would take the knife out of the
sink where i saw it this morning and
wipe the crumbs off it with a dish towel.
id press the tip against my skin till all
the pain was only in that one spot. and
i would cut my ladder, to climb and climb
up out of the trash and broken shards.

"i want to stick it in you." the world is
dangerous and evil. his words are the
most sinister thing ive ever heard.
im at work. "you wanna try? you wanna try
baby? go ahead and i swear i!ll ~~kix~~ kick
the shit out of you." its not a very
good sales technique, i know, buti cant
help it. the anger and disgust billows
up inside. the guy takes me up on a VIP
anyways, which means i get $80 plus
whatever tip i can squeeze out of him for
hanging out in a semi-private room for an
hour. but he's scared of me now, he says.
typical. "im just a kitten, baby," i purr
at him. "now that we understand each other
im just a little kitten. a bunny." im
working hard not to laugh out loud.
in the VIP room he keeps talking about
wanting to fuck me. "all right," i say
finally. "a hand job. fifty bucks. put
the money on the table."

when the aliens stole my memories they
took my mind away too. i get drunk and
drunker all night long and score a 3-hour
VIP with some asshole. i rub my pussy sore
lapdancing for him. i jerk him off without setting a price, i let him lick my
pussy. i mean, he just did it and i couldnt
stop him. i try to stop drinking but the
bottles of champagne just keep coming. he
gives me a $60 tip, his tie, and a box of
godiva chocolates. by the end of the night
i made $400 after tip-out and the cab ride
home.

i woke up this morning and my pus was
red and swollen, caked with ~~glox~~ globs of
shame and disgust. all day all i want to do
is crawl in my bed, pull the covers up
over my head and sleep it away. knowing
i got paid is the only thing tht makes me
feel any better. except themess in my room
you wouldnt believe. Dirty Dollar Bills are

laying crumpled and wadded all over the
fucking floor. i have to kick them out
of the way to get out the door.

shes inside and she hates me. why dont you
just take care x of me! she wants to know.
shes begging, why dont i take care of her,
why cant i protect her. over and over again,
she screams, it happens over and over again.
       im knee-deep, waist-deep, chest-
high in the sewer, crawling through shit &
trash. why cant i take care of her? why
cant i protect myself?

 by Nicky Splinter (from <u>Sewer</u>)

Why I Play with My Cunt

by Lovechild (from Brat Attack)

BECAUSE I WAS NOT BREASTFED; BECAUSE MY CRIB WAS PADDED AND I LIKE THE FEEL OF STEEL; BECAUSE I WAS SPANKED BY MY BABYSITTER; BECAUSE THE KIDS USED TO CALL ME HALF-BREED; BECAUSE MY FATHER IGNORED MY MOTHER AND FUCKED THE BOTTLE; BECAUSE MY BROTHER JERKED OFF TO AUNT JAMIMA; BECAUSE MY DOG WAS KEPT IN BONDAGE TIL THE DAY HE DIED; BECAUSE A WHITE BOY TOOK MY VIRGINITY; BECAUSE I WAS NEVER TAUGHT HOMOSEXUALITY IN HEALTH CLASS; BECAUSE THE SANDMAN WAS A LESBIAN; **BECAUSE IT FEELS GOOD; BECAUSE MY CUNT IS SELFISH; BECAUSE IT'S SELF-GRATIFICATION;** BECAUSE MY PERIOD FEELS LIKE A BULLFIGHT; BECAUSE I HATE THE SMELL OF PORK; BECAUSE I LOVE THE TASTE OF PUSSY; BECAUSE I CAN'T FIST MY OWN ASSHOLE; BECAUSE I HAVE A LOT OF TIME ON MY HANDS; BECAUSE IT FEELS LIKE A BABY WHEN I SHAVE IT; BECAUSE MY PLATFORM HEEL WON'T FIT INSIDE; **BECAUSE IT FEELS GOOD; BECAUSE MY CUNT IS SELFISH; BECAUSE IT'S SELF-GRATIFICATION;** BECAUSE MY VIBRATOR ISN'T POWERFUL ENOUGH; BECAUSE TRANSSEXUALS TURN ME THE FUCK ON; BECAUSE SCENES FROM CALIGULA RUN THROUGH MY HEAD; BECAUSE CINDERELLA WASN'T MY SLAVE; BECAUSE IT THROBS LIKE A DICK; BECAUSE I SLEEP ALONE; BECAUSE OF THE QUESTION OF DEATH; **BECAUSE IT FEELS GOOD; BECAUSE MY CUNT IS SELFISH; BECAUSE IT'S SELF-GRATIFICATION;** BECAUSE FRIDAY FOSTER SAYS I'M A PERVERT; BECAUSE OF THE THOUGHT OF THREE VIRGINS IN HORSETAILS; BECAUSE MY DOUBLE-DONG WAS STOLEN; BECAUSE I SMOKED MY LAST CIGARETTE; BECAUSE I WANT TO SPIT-SHINE PRINCE'S BOOTS; BECAUSE I HATE SLOPPY BLOWJOBS; **BECAUSE IT FEELS GOOD; BECAUSE MY CUNT IS SELFISH; BECAUSE IT'S SELF-GRATIFICATION;** BECAUSE THERE ARE NO MORE VIRGINS; BECAUSE I CAN'T GIVE THE GOVERNMENT AN ENEMA; BECAUSE WHORES BECAME EXPENSIVE; BECAUSE I HATE THE THOUGHT OF CLOTHING; BECAUSE I'M THE BORDERLINE OF A DYKE AND A BOY; BE-

CAUSE I WANT TO BE SADDLED AND TRAINED LIKE A HORSE; BECAUSE SLAVERY WAS IN MY ROOTS AND I THIRST S&M; **BECAUSE IT FEELS GOOD; BECAUSE MY CUNT IS SELFISH; BECAUSE IT'S SELF-GRATIFICATION;** BECAUSE I CAN NEVER GET ENOUGH PUSSY; BECAUSE OF THE SOUND OF A WOMAN'S VOICE OVER THE PHONE; BECAUSE WHEN IT'S WET IT GLAZES MY FINGERS; BECAUSE I WANT TO BE GANG-BANGED BY FEMALE INMATES; BECAUSE I WANT TO FUCK FOR FOOD AND WATER; BECAUSE I WASN'T BORN IN A CHASTITY BELT; **BECAUSE IT FEELS GOOD; BECAUSE MY CUNT IS SELFISH; BECAUSE IT'S SELF-GRATIFICATION;** BECAUSE I LIKE TO WORK MY PUSSY; BECAUSE I WAS BORN A BITCH; BECAUSE I LIKE MORE THAN ONE ORGASM; BECAUSE I DON'T HAVE TO SAY 'I LOVE YOU' TO ANYONE; BECAUSE IN MY MIND I CAN BE FUCKING ANYONE I WANT; BECAUSE IT'S HEALTHY; BECAUSE I'M A VAIN BITCH AND ONLY I KNOW HOW TO LOVE MYSELF . . .

music

stars

idols

Fan Club

Crushes and idol worship are a basic staple in teen girl life. So many girls plaster their walls with rock groups, superstars, and pop culture icons. Initially, zines were known as "fanzines" because they so often stemmed from a zinemaker's fascination with certain cultural icons. There are still a large amount of zine pages dedicated to various heroines and heros. This section provides you with a peek at which celebrities have girls raving and which have them ranting.

A Nice

Little

Asian Girl

by Sabrina Sandata,

editor of Bamboo Girl

I started *Bamboo Girl* in early '95 because I couldn't find anything to read on girls like me, a mutt (Filipina/Spanish/Irish/Scottish/a little Chinese) who was in-your-face about issues within the hardcore/punk and/or queer communities. I also used it big time to get in touch with my anger. When I was younger, there was major fucked-up domestic violence and physical abuse going on. I was never allowed to talk back, cry, or scream. So I held it all in and never said anything even though I was getting the shit beaten out of me. I was shy and quiet all throughout my childhood, but always got into doing shit on my own because I had to (most of the time my parents either wouldn't help me or couldn't because they weren't familiar with American customs, being that I was first-generation American). Then, at the end of college, I realized that I could express myself pretty succinctly on paper, when I didn't have to open my mouth. But I could say something anyway. It was kinda like a "fuck you!" for me.

As my writing grew, so did my opinions on what was going on around me. It was then that I finally started delving into my ethnic heritage, as well as my sexual orientation (all of which started to sprout at an early age!). I also became more aware of my political viewpoints, which have now become a vital part of myself.

I've been heavily into communicating through writing, and now, also, through speaking—I've started to speak more, especially on behalf of a NYC-based, lesbian-identified, Filipina collective called Kilawin Kolektibo, as a speaker on Asian and Asian queer issues at universities. I love it! Because I've found that I really like communicating with people . . . *Bamboo Girl* gave me the push I needed to just fucking go for it already and stop wasting time doing shit that didn't please me. I've been able to be more selfish because I've started to explore certain things to find out what my limits are, instead of holding back or being overly scared to try things I've never done.

But I think the coolest thing about it is that I've met so many girls like me who are also ethnic mutts who have felt silenced, who feel like they have a place to air their issues in a really direct, "don't fuck with me" kinda way. And also, this is a *very* big also, to break the racial/ethnic/homophobic stereotypes that even *I* believed to a certain extent, even though I clearly knew what I was—a queer mutt.

Overall, it's helped me rediscover that all those times I was afraid I had permanently silenced myself, just so I could save my ass from being fucked with at home, never solidified into something that's kept me from expressing myself.

And also, to cut through the corny bullshit, it's always a great rush to see your own viewpoints and opinions in print! It's a personal validation for me on things that I've always been told were "not nice for girls to be thinking," especially for "a nice little *Asian* girl."

ROCKRGRL ♪

information and inspiration for women in the music business

SLEATER-KINNEY

conquers the world

PATRICIA KENNEALY MORRISON: goddess and rock gods
CYNDI LAUPER: a cynful retrospective • BUSH TETRAS: reunited
teen 'zines and a girl's self-esteem • HOME ALIVE: a force for safety
LAURA LOVE: her own way • FLUFFY's got the look
kickstart contest winners announced • MORE!

Roles Give You Cramp

Kim Cooper Looks at Post-Punk Proto-Feminists Au Pairs

(from scram)

Ten years on and we need Lesley Woods and the Au Pairs more than ever.

I know; Bitch bitch bitch. But it's *true!*

Seems like every time I poke my nose into a media outlet I hear that more women are playing music these days, and they're getting a new respect from (male?) critics and audiences. But the women held up as icons of this grrrl/foxcore thing are embarrassments, at least to *this* woman. "Foxcore," indeed; the very phrase sets my teeth on edge and conjures up images of Farrah Fawcett-Majors with a Japanese guitar (thanks, Thurston). Plus lots of these bands *suck,* and I mean they suck even worse than the lousy all-male acts. Hole? L7?! Don't make me fucking gag. Not merely musically lame, they're lyrically mindless as well. Where are the women who can *think* just as well as they can drink? Search me. But it wasn't always this way. When I was a

kid there was no shortage of women to look up to. Patti Smith, Chrissie Hynde, Lene Lovich, Marianne Faithfull, Debbie Harry: strong, intelligent artists who just happened to be female. There's a paucity of such role models today. Madonna and that Irish twerp are audacious, but much too dimwitted. There's truth in the cliché that women have to be stronger, smarter, better than men before people realize that they're equal. But it's difficult. There are weird barriers for women, some inside our own heads. Gina Arnold wrote an embarrassing—and very honest—piece last year about having purchased a guitar, yet being afraid to make the wretched noise required of the beginning musician. Women are "supposed" to play pretty music. Acoustic guitars, folk ballads. We need to be shown that it's okay for us to make a raging caterwaul that redefines "beauty" on our own terms. And, like it or not, that means role models are needed.

Not long ago I saw Kim Gordon and Courtney Love on MTV, and basically all they said was, "We like Hello Kitty." Kim Gordon—who writes art crit on the side, and has for a decade been an equal partner in the hugely successful "underground" business that is Sonic Youth—said nothing remotely like, "Despite what you see on MTV, you girls watching can play in a band if you want to." Which seems to me the only relevant thing she could have said. I'm not suggesting Gordon be a martyr for her sex. No one should be forced into a role they might despise. But I'm still peeved to see one of our few famous female instrumentalists behaving like a five-year-old. Kim Gordon can't afford the luxury of being a dumb rocker (Courtney Love can't help it). It's too harmful. What's the point of singing "I Believe Anita Hill," when your own actions only serve to validate every sexist attitude about women musicians? It was while watching this little travesty that a phrase popped into my mind, a phrase that's come unbidden a dozen times in the past few years. And it is simply this: "Where the hell is Lesley Woods when we need her?"

Yet Lesley Woods would have balked mightily at the notion that she might be a spokeswoman for any sexual-political agenda. She considered herself an equal member in the group that was the Au Pairs, a band she formed in Birmingham, England in 1979 with Paul Foad, Jane Munro, and Pete Hammond. In the scant four years of their existence, the Au Pairs played hundreds of gigs, recorded two dozen songs, and dissolved mysteriously in the fall of 1983. Nothing has been heard since from Woods, who, in this brief period, established herself as one of the most powerful and intriguing female musicians ever. The sexy intelligence of her cooing, sometimes snotty voice, the fact that she played guitar (not bass, *guitar!*), her fantastic lyrics and utter lack of star-vocalist pretensions made her a rare creature indeed.

If the Au Pairs were a political band it was because the band members were politically aware people. Their songs lacked any of the hollow ideology that an overtly Political (capital p) band like the Clash fell prey to, perhaps because 90% of the politics they addressed were sexual in nature. Woods' lyrics are unflinchingly honest examinations of male-female relations—never preachy. Their small songs of awkward intimacies are more affecting than a thousand cries of "Sandinista!"

Their debut single was "You" in 1979. In the next year, the band played dozens of gigs and honed their considerable talents. Fine songs were written, most going unrecorded until 1981, although two of the best appeared on their brilliant second single. "Diet," backed with "It's Obvious" embody the Au Pairs' sound and concerns: a loping, spare rock'n'roll married to smart lyrics about the trials of gender. "Diet" is, in all ways, a gem. A third-person narrative of an "average" housewife's excruciating existence, it manages to be at once sad, beautiful, and revolutionary. "It's Obvious" is a throbbing groove on the phrase "different but equal," tensely melodic and very, very good. The single was strong enough to land Woods on the cover of the NME, quite a coup for an act with only four recorded songs.

Their first album, *Playing with a Different Sex*, came out in 1981. From its distinctive sleeve—a hand-colored photo of armed Asian women running in dresses and combat boots—to the instructions for basal-temperature birth control on the lyric sheet, the record asserts the band's unique agenda. "Come Again" was banned by the BBC, with a spokesman terming the band "perverts." The irony of this censorious dinosaur calling the Au Pairs names is supreme. I know of no other song dealing with the subject matter of "Come Again": the fact that women will sometimes fake orgasms. (Lesley's goading query: "Is your finger aching?/I can feel you hesitating/Is your finger aching!?"). This song provokes thought and dialogue, plus it rocks; one of the band's finest moments.

The band was unhappy with Human Records, and switched to Kamera for 1982's *Sense and Sensuality*. The title is fitting, as it's full of songs about the power of sex upon our brains and bodies.

Graham Lock wrote a revealing story on the Au Pairs for the *NME* (11 July 1981), after joining them on a Dutch tour in support of the first album. They emerge as amiable, committed, intelligent folk, as willing to stay up all night debating whether or not the band supports the IRA as to drink themselves into a happy stupor. On the Irish question, Lesley came down hard on the side of the rebels, and felt Lock must print her volatile statements, because "if you side with Pete, you're invalidating my whole politics. Am I only allowed to have opinions on feminism? You've no right to censor me." Lock printed the exchange verbatim, an interesting window into the development of political stances within the band.

Lesley Woods was hot. Smart and daring, she had no need of stereotypically girlish wiles to come across as the sexiest thing around. And she had the power to change minds with her revolutionary lyrics, because the Au Pairs were unabashedly commercial. "We'd like to be number one, and it is feasible with the songs that we do. But it's not an aim in that everything we do is directed towards that and therefore manipulated in that way. The whole point is that what we are and what we're doing, without beliefs being sacrificed, should quite easily get to number one." (Lesley, *NME*, 11 October 1980) Their trajectory towards such success ended with a terse statement issued by the group in September 1983. Lesley, who some weeks earlier had been reported by the music press to have "disappeared," was in fact safe in the Netherlands. (Which recalls some interesting precedents of public women who needed to get away so badly that they up and vanished, but at least post-feminist Lesley didn't claim she'd been kidnapped.) The band announced their break-up, with all members heading off to new projects. Lesley's was called Schlaflose Nachte, Jane's was Apple on a Drum, Paul and Pete's was yet unnamed and featured a trumpet player. Whatever came of them, I do not know. But we should all feel the loss of the rare, exhilarating enterprise that was the Au Pairs.

cool grrl word find!

(Its probably rilly easy but I just wanted to honor these girlies somehow!)

Words!! keep doing cool stuff, ya all!!

- BJÖRK / • WOMEN ON TOP / (women's) JUSTICE BRIGADE /
- OCTANE GIRLZ / • JACKIE ROCKET (bilhgirlzme) /
- POOT (girls) / • BUST(! girls) / HORST GIRLS WHO R COOL ♥ (hi C.C.)
- KATHLEEN (hanna) / • JUANA (halfield) / TOBI (VAIL) /
- TWIZZLER (girls) / • MARY LOU (Lord) / KATHI (wilcox) /
  LESBIAN AVENGERS
- BRATMOBILE / • LORI BARBERO /
- BECCA (exaxe) / • QUEEN LATIFAH /
- CARRIE 17 / • LUCKY TIGER (girls)
- ANI (difranco) / • LTMW (usten to me whine hi chell!)
- GLADYS (all!) / BADGIRL READERS (!♥)

I ♥ You.

THE BAD GIRL CLUB

A SOLILOQUY-- *ASSERTIVE BARBIE Goes Off On Ken*

By Barbara

SO WE HAD OUR FIRST FIGHT. IT STARTED BECAUSE HE WANTED TO GO TO A PUNK ROCK SHOW, THEN HE DIDN'T. I SAID OKAY NO PROBLEM, WE'LL STAY IN. I EVEN SLAVED OVER THE EASY BAKE OVEN FOR HIM. WE ATE AND THEN COLLAPSED FOR A WHILE IN THE DREAM HOUSE. BUT AFTER GLANCING LONGINGLY AT HIS NEW SPARKLE JEANS, KEN INFORMS ME THAT HE DOES WANT TO GO OUT AFTERALL. I WAS IN NO MOOD FOR A BACK AND FORTH CONVERSATION OF I DON'T KNOW WHAT DO *YOU* WANT TO DO BECAUSE I WAS FEELING SLUGGISH FROM MY DAY TIME JOB OF FASHION MODEL SLASH PERKY STUDENT. BUT I WAS ALSO TIRED OF THIS YO-YO THING AND SAID WELL ALL RIGHT LET'S GO THEN, IN MY WEAK HALF HEARTED VOICEBOX ATTACHMENT. HE TOOK MY VAGUENESS AS EXCITEMENT AS HE BOLTED FOR THE HAIRSPRAY. AS I WAS GETTING DRESSED HE PUT ON LOUD MUSIC. JEM'S MUSIC. HE KNOWS I HATE JEM BECAUSE SHE'S THE PAT BENATAR OF THE BARBIE SET AND BARBIE GETS REALLY MAD AT ME WHEN WE LISTEN TO HER. SO, JEM IS BLASTING, AND BARBIE IS KNOCKING ON OUR CEILING WITH SOME LINCOLN LOGS BECAUSE SHE'S REALLY PISSED. KEN THEN LOOKS AT ME AND SAYS UNCONVINCINGLY LET'S JUST STAY IN THEN.

BY THIS TIME I HAD
PRIATELY AND BLURTED
GLITCH) WE MIGHT AS
WE TRUDGE TO BOTH
TRAVELING . CLUB WAS
SEEMS THAT KEN HADN'T
WHERE IT WAS. THIS WAS
HUNCH INVOLVING UGLY
WAS COLD OUTSIDE AND I
I SAID HOW UNHAPPY I WAS

ADORNED MYSELF APPRO-
OUT TWICE (VOICEBOX
WELL GO AT THIS POINT. SO
LOCATIONS OF WHERE THIS
SUPPOSED TO BE BUT IT
REALLY ACTUALLY KNOWN
ALL SOME SORT OF WILD
SPARKLE ACCESSORIES. IT
WAS GETTING A HEADACHE.
OUT LOUD BUT KEN HAD

SINCE BUMPED INTO HIS GOOFY FRIEND ALAN AND ALAN'S DRIPPY ROOMMATE POINDEXTER. THEY ALL WANTED TO GO THE "CORRAL" FOR BEERS. I DON'T DRINK BEER. KEN KNEW THAT BUT HE DIDN'T CARE. HE WAS SHOWING OFF HIS STUDDED PANTS AND GETTING READY TO MALE BOND WHETHER I LIKED IT OR NOT. HE CALLED ME A BITCH AND THEN THREW ME THAT CULTIVATED LOOK HE GETS ON HIS FACE. HE WAS WAITING FOR THE MIRACLE OF ME TO JOIN THEM IN BALLYHOOING. INSTEAD, I ANNOUNCED THAT I WAS GOING HOME. MY HARD PLASTIC BED WAS BEGINNING TO LOOK GOOD TO ME. SO THEN KEN THROWS HIS ARMS UP IN THE AIR (NOT BENDING HIS ELBOWS OR ANYTHING) AND HAILS A CAB WITH THAT SAME EVIL LOOK HE HAD ALL EVENING AND THEN TURNS TO HIS FRIENDS AND LOOKS AS IF HE IS GOING TO CRY OR SOMETHING. ANYWAY, WE GET BACK TO MY TOWNHOUSE AND KEN IMMEDIATELY STARTED GUZZLING RED WINE. MEN. WHEN HE CLIMBS INTO BED A MERE 2 HOURS LATER, HE GIVES ME THE BACK ROUTINE A LA SILENT TREATMENT. THE NEXT MORNING HE HAS TO LIKE *REMEMBER* BEING MAD AT ME (KEN'S NOT SO BRIGHT SOMETIMES). HE IS HUNG OVER AND NEEDS COFFEE. WE GO INTO TOWN AND EVERY CAFE I TAKE HIM TO IS JUST NO GOOD. TOO SMALL, TOO DARK, TOO CROWDED, TOO I-DON'T-KNOW-IT'S-JUST-NOT-RIGHT. MENSTRUATING KENS. ANYWAY, WE CLEAR EVERYTHING UP AND THAT EVENING HE GOES OVER TO SKIPPER'S HOUSE IN A LAME ATTEMPT TO TRY AND MAKE ME JEALOUS. HE SAYS WAIT UP FOR ME I WON'T BE LATE. HE GETS HOME AT 4:00 A.M. I KNOW THIS BECAUSE I AM ONLY PRETEND-SLEEPING. THE NEXT DAY HE APOLOGIZES FOR BEING SUCH AN ASSHOLE. I FELT LIKE SAYING *YEAH YOU WERE AN ASSHOLE,* BUT I SAY LET'S DROP IT, IT'S BORING.

Never Trust Any Animal Who Would Bleed for 5 Days and Live:

An Interview with Lydia Lunch

by Zoe Cliché

(from I Am a Cliché)

WHEN DID YOU FIRST START WRITING? I first started writing when I was twelve, living in a shitty hovel in New York . . . I ran away to New York City at the age of sixteen and formed my first band, Teenage Jesus, at seventeen. Ever since, I've done music, spoken word, videos, films, comics and now photography and sculpture. I use whatever medium is available/necessary to express my undying contempt for the patriarchy, corporate greed, social, sexual, and economic abuse, and the general decay of decency on all fronts, which assaults us every day at every turn. The point is not what elements/medium you use, but that the individual creates in order to release the sensation of being a walking time bomb. If you need to explode, do it with passion and creativity.

WHAT MOVIES, BOOKS, OR MUSIC HAD A REAL INFLUENCE ON YOU AS A TEENAGER? DO YOU HAVE ANY HEROES? The most important books I read as a teenager were *Last Exit to Brooklyn* by Hubert Selby, Jr., *Tropic of Cancer* and *Tropic of Capricorn* by Henry Miller, and *The 120 Days of Sodom,* by the Marquis de Sade. De Sade for the philosophical loathing of religion and the beauty of his language, as well as the fact that he was incarcerated for seventeen years, most of his writing burned, and still out-wrote/out-philosophized 98% of the population. Miller for his unrepentant sexuality and poetry, and Selby because that's as real as it gets. I have had the fortune to tour with Selby and released an album now out of print entitled *Our Fathers Who Aren't in Heaven,* which we are both featured on.

As far as music, *Berlin* by Lou Reed was my all-time favorite, because it was the most depressing, tortured LP ever produced. All the early Stooges LPs for sheer power.

My heroes are anyone that creates, even if it's seemingly into the void. Creation is the ultimate form of rebellion, because it proves that the bullshitters will not have the final word.

DOES SPIRITUALITY OR MAGIC PLAY ANY SIGNIFICANT ROLE IN YOUR LIFE? Magic is a catch phrase which I will redefine as having the knowledge to realize that energy is the driving force of nature. When one is acutely in tune with energy/nature, one can concentrate on the positive or the negative elements of that force field. One needs to be fully aware of positive/negative influence/pull in order to recognize and seek out balance or chaos in which to surround one's self. Although I deal with a multiplicity of negative factors/features/reasons/outcome in my work, I am a highly positively-charged person. At this point I can easily heed warning signs which, through instinct, illuminate the correct response to any given situation. This is simply being aware of positive/negative charges and manipulating them to your desired outcome. Magic in nutshell . . . Many people use rituals, either highly evolved or offhandedly amateur, to help them focus their "magical powers." Although rituals can be elaborate or quite simply-performed, I don't find it necessary to use them regularly, since I am already very focused.

HOW DO YOU RESPOND TO THOSE WHO CALL YOUR FILMS WITH RICHARD KERN PORNOGRAPHIC? ESPECIALLY *FINGERED*, WHICH SO EFFECTIVELY TURNS THE VIEWER OFF. HOW DO YOU FEEL ABOUT PORN IN GENERAL? Pornography has changed radically in the last five years. Better filming, higher quality, better storylines. I always enjoy a good sex-asylum/futurist slant in porno. I think porn-

ography is a useful tool, a stimulant which, when used to facilitate orgasm or arousal is no different than any mild drug or having a few drinks. The lame excuse that pornography equals violence against women forgets that men have been violent to women since the Stone Age. Religion is far more dangerous. The Catholic Church has been responsible for mass-murdering more people than all world wars combined, yet no one insists we ban that. Except for me, of course. The reason the Kern films are not related to porn, in my opinion, is that even though we depict sexually graphic material/acts/violations, it is in order to make relative points about the cause/reaction/pattern/ritual of abuse and its intoxicating stranglehold. If someone gets off on that, they need to question how guilty they are of the crimes I depict. I readily admit my guilt/repulsion/attractions, and attempt to dissect them in order to reach a more healthy conclusion in my own life, realizing also that few people have dealt with these so-called taboos, that so many women (and, as a result, men) have suffered from in the ongoing cycle of abuse, begetting abuser in an endless cycle.

HAVE YOU YET TO REACH YOUR PEAK? PEAK?? PEAK??? I have been creating for twenty years, and I assume I'll be creating for at least another twenty years. Hopefully I'll achieve many peaks and very few valleys of virolic outpourings, spanning every format conceivable.

I JUST PICKED UP A COPY OF *RUDE HYROGLYPHICS* WITH EXENE CER-

VENKA AND WAS AGAIN BLOWN AWAY. HOW DID THE TWO OF YOU HOOK UP? I met Exene in 1977 when I had Teenage Jesus. Her sister managed the band for awhile. Her brother-in-law played bass. I was living with someone Exene grew up in Florida with. She already had X, who were playing in NYC. I moved to LA in the early '80s and we wrote our book, *Adulterers Anonymous,* in 1982/83. It's being reprinted on Last Gasp now. We had done a few shows together over the years, usually on the same bill, but separate. Last year, we decided to do a tag-team spoken word world tour of which *Rude Hyroglyphics* is the outcome.

WHAT DO YOU LOOK FOR IN A PERSONAL RELATIONSHIP? I am most attracted to high-energy people like myself who harvest creative energy. Whether that means painting, photography, bike building, or martial arts. Anyone with an outlet. People who are in recovery, or learning to recover from the post-traumatic-stress-syndrome we're all burdened with as birthright. I am not referring to a "recovery program" as much as I am to self-awareness and the need to constantly strive for something greater.

WHERE DO YOU GET YOUR ENERGY? WHAT IS YOUR SOURCE OF STRENGTH? I've always been blessed/cursed with high-velocity energy. There is so much to revolt against and so much to embrace, I have a hard time sitting still. I also realize we all have a very limited time on this planet, and I do see it as a "duty" to document and catalog the afflictions we are all surrounded by. We are here and gone in (historically speaking) a fraction of a second. I have so much to get out and spit forth, too much to remain sedated for any length of time. My biggest disappointment is that I see so little *influence* being utilized. By that I mean I hope to inspire people to "do it," whatever it is . . . to create forcefully, employing a wide arsenal of mediums, with a ferocious passion; not just slacking off by picking up a guitar (the lowest common denominator), thinking they'll be the next millionaire rock star that MTV, *Spin,* and all those other corporate bullshit artists need to embrace this month in order to sell their shitty magazines. Be bold . . . use your vision wisely, forcefully, and don't give a shit about whatever anybody else thinks or doesn't think.

Fan Club
107

"I Just Met Tori Amos . . ."

by Marla

(from Rats Live on No Evil Star)

1/30/96

I just met Tori Amos . . . Oh wait, perhaps you didn't hear me . . . I JUST MET TORI AMOS!

Tori is my idol. You all know that. (Last issue was the "Tori Amos Obsessed" issue for Godsakes.) So when I heard that Tori was doing Boston radio appearances, I had to go. I just had to. And so did Kim. So Kim and I woke up *really* early, made a pit stop at Dollar a Pound, and then went and sat on the steps of WBCN. There, we met Winona and Todd, who had been there for about a half hour before.

By this time, it was about 11:30 or so and we knew Tori was *supposed* to be there by 12:30. So we sat around. Then we met Eva, the photographer (she had to leave before Tori arrived), and Larry (who knew my trivia question about "Humpty Dumpty") and his pal Derek. Scott, Justine and Melissa were hanging out too—so we all took pictures, and chatted. Then—TORI ARRIVED. The manager guy came out and basically said she was late and had to rush through us. No biggie. But I called out to her and handed her my favorite pin—it says I BELIEVE IN ELVES. Tori kinda looked at it, then realized what it said, smiled, hugged it to her brown coat and said *"Oh, Thank you!"* At that point I screamed/babbled, "I have a zine and I just want a five-minute interview with you . . . ," and she answered something like, "When you take my picture . . . just don't tell anyone . . ." Then she was gone. We all were shaking and gushing. And then we all got into Derek's car and listened to her play "Blood Roses," "Doughnut Song" (I cried), and "Losing My Religion." She said, "I realized that sad wears high heels, and she has some interesting stories too, and if you can deal with that you can be OK." Or something like that . . . anyway, special thanks to Larry who gave up his seat in the car for me.

Then I started shaking. We waited some more, and then the manager guy came out and said she wasn't going to stop, she was in a rush (to which I replied "Tori promised *me* that she was going to talk to us") . . . then another guy said we should all stand on one side—like a receiving line. She came out again . . . I *shook*. Tori got to me, and I started gushing. She signed my LE booklet, and as she did she said to me, "You have beautiful eyes, but I'm sure you've heard that before . . ." WOW! Then I gave her a big hug (she really really hugs you, pulls you in, encloses you in her aura) and got my picture taken with her. Then I asked her about her earrings—Tori is always wearing the same earrings *every time*—they are silver circles. She smiled and said they were from a woman in London—then she wrote down "Jess James," and said that was the guy to talk to about them. She said, "They make me feel good," and kinda shrugged. I then proceeded to ramble, "Oh Tori, I saw you in London. I yelled to you, but I'm sure you don't remember . . .," and the manager guys kinda moved her along (psycho fan alert?) I stood there in a daze, tried to get Kim in a picture with her (Kim hugged her too), called out, "You are so important to us Tori" and watched her get in the van and leave. . . .

Jess James

Marla &
Tori Amos

Barbies We Would Like to See

by Lala

(from *Quarter Inch Squares*)

glass, and detailed diagrams of female anatomy so that little girls can learn about their bodies in a friendly, non-threatening way. Also included: tiny Kotex, booklets on sexual responsibility. Accessories such as contraceptives, sex toys, expanding uterus with fetus at various stages of development, and breast pump are all optional, underscoring that each young woman has the right to chose what she does with her own Barbie.

Gender Fuck Barbie: He becomes she and she becomes he, and we all end up in a lovely gender limbo. Comes with interchangeable anatomy make-up, facial hair, two complete mix-and-match, gender-specific wardrobes. Barbie-sized copies of Kate Bornstein's *Gender Outlaw* and *My Gender Workbook* optional.

Blue Collar Barbie: Comes with overalls, protective goggles, lunch pail, UAW membership, pamphlet on union-organizing and pay scales for women as compared to men. Waitressing outfits and cashier's aprons may be purchased separately for Barbies who are holding down second jobs in order to make ends meet.

Oprah Barbie: Push a button on her back and this Barbie actually speaks! Hold your very own talk show with topics like how tough math class is, Ballerina Barbie's struggle with bulimia, Kens who wear Barbie's clothes.

Our Barbies, Ourselves: Anatomically correct Barbie, both inside and out, comes with spreadable legs, her own speculum, magnifying

Dinner Roll Barbie: A Barbie with multiple love-handles, double chin, a real curvy belly, generous tits and ass, and voluminous thighs to show girls that voluptuousness is also beautiful. Comes with a miniature basket of dinner rolls, tiny Entenmann's walnut ring, a t-shirt reading ONLY THE WEAK DON'T EAT, and, of course, an appetite.

Rebbe Barbie: So why not? Women rabbis are on the cutting edge in Judaism. Rebbe Barbie comes with tiny satin yarmulke, prayer shawl, tefilin, silver kaddish cup, Torah scrolls. Optional: tiny mezuzah for doorway of Barbie Townhouse.

Homegirl Barbie: Truly fly Barbie in midriff-bearing shirt and baggy jeans. Comes with gold jewelry, hip-hop accessories, and plenty of attitude. Pull cord and she says things like "I don't think so," "Dang, get outta my face," and "You go, girl." Teaches girls not to take shit from men and condescending white people.

Bisexual Barbie: Comes in a box with Midge, Ken, and a button that says I'M BISEXUAL. I'M NOT ATTRACTED TO YOU.

Birkenstock Barbie: Finally, a Barbie doll with horizontal feet and comfortable sandals. Made from recycled materials.

Single Mom Barbie: One kid to raise, insufficient child support, a job that doesn't pay enough to make ends meet. Accessories such as good child care, a support network, and a good night's sleep optional.

GlitterScum Rant

by Rachel G.

(from Quarter Inch Squares)

OK, um . . . since I was like in pre-K, I liked sex (or at least what I knew about it!). Boys and girls made me quiver when they touched me. I was like six! So anyway, I always made my Barbies and Kens fuck. Barbie would strip the other girl Barbie and then Ken would jump in. I'd make all the noises and moans and shit. Then Ken would leave and my two Barbies got crazy. My imagination ran away from when I was six years old until I finally lost my last Barbie. As I got older, Ken was less involved, except to make my two girl Barbies feel guilty (a product of my mom's teachings that being gay or bi was bad and wrong). Then, I lost interest and hid my sexual urges behind my doors.

Here's another thing, only not so great. One day, after I finally got my punk-rock Barbie, I wanted all my Barbies to be cool like her. I "shaved" their heads and dyed their long tresses purple or green or pink or whatever. I made nifty clothes, and my girl Barbies kicked ass. But one day, my mom gave them away 'cause I was "too old to be playing with them."

Pagan Kennedy Talks Marshmallows

by Zoe Zolbrod

(from <u>Maxine</u>)

When I go on vacation, I usually pack more books than pairs of underwear, but somehow I failed to do this when I went to Mexico a couple of years ago. Luckily, I was traveling with two girls who had excellent taste in reading material. Charmaine lent me Butterfly, a pseudo-feminist smut fest. Anne lent me Stripping and Other Stories by Pagan Kennedy, and when I read that book on the white sands of Playa del Carmen, it was like I was back in my preteen bedroom listening to a new album by my favorite pop star. I felt that someone was speaking to my soul!

Sure, literature had spoken to me before, but these stories of searching punk-rock teens and math-nerd tomgirls seemed to come out of a culturally specific place that I recognized to my core and had never seen manifested in fiction. Who was this Pagan Kennedy? Not only had she written these amazing stories, she had gotten them published into a book all her own. Somehow that seemed to me a huge validation of my very existence. (Is this the stuff stalkers are made of?)

More Pagan! I clamored, once back in Chicago, and Anne came though. She had a friend in Boston who sent us Xeroxed copies of Pagan's Head, a zine by the fair author herself. In 1994 came Platforms: A Microwaved Cultural Chronicle of the 1970s, then came a novel, Spinsters, and finally Zine (beautifully subtitled How I Spent Six Years of My Life in the Underground and Finally . . . Found Myself . . . I Think) which is a collection of all the Pagan's Heads interspersed with essays by the Pagan of today. This past summer, Ms. Kennedy gave a reading in Chicago, and the Maxine contingent was there in force. We asked if we could interview her, she said yes, and the following conversation (which happened months later) is the result.

Z I wanted to talk to you about ambition, and I'm coming into this with the premise that you are an ambitious person in that you've achieved so much. So I hope you're not going to ruin my whole premise by saying . . . oh no, no!

P Oh, no, I am ambitious. I think everybody is. But I'm much less so than I used to be, I think. When I was twenty-eight I began to realize that I could conceivably turn thirty. Before, it always felt like I was a promising "something." You know, like I had promise, but I hadn't realized it, but someday I would, ostensibly. But suddenly it occurred to me that this was my real life and I wasn't, um, kind of warming up for it, and so I

think in some ways that changed my ambitions to make me kind of live more in the here and now.

Z In a kind of enjoyment-of-life way or in a kind of career way or both?

P Ambition, I guess, implies that you're willing to delay present pleasure for future pleasure.

Z That's an interesting definition of it.

P Don't you think so?

Z I can see what you mean. I've been thinking of it as a consciously-considered long-term goal, so I guess the two go together.

P There was this study, one of those stupid, trendy, science studies that everybody picks up on. Something where they told kids you can either have this marshmallow now or you can have two marshmallows tomorrow. Do you remember that? Supposedly the two-marshmallow kids did way better in life. But I think I switched from being a two-marshmallow kid to a one-marshmallow kid, recently.

Z So I'm interested in that you think, because you were a two-marshmallow girl for so long, now you get to be a one-marshmallow girl . . .

P Or maybe I'm having my second marshmallow now, so I'm trying to enjoy those two marshmallows.

Z Do you think it has anything to do with the change in the cultural zeitgeist from the 80s to the 90s?

P Well, I think that the 80s was not a good period for me, personally speaking, because people weren't buying the things I did. There was a lot of interest in fiction by young peo-

ple, but they were people pretending to be young, like Tama Janowitz, pretending to be hip. It was so out of key with everything I knew about, you know, like people doing coke in their high-paying jobs in New York. Then when this whole slacker gen-X thing came along, it was like, woo woo, time to profit, you know? So, suddenly my life changed, because people were saying, hey, Pagan you can write about this. Do you want to do this? Do you want to do that? Suddenly everybody is scrambling to get a book or an article or something about slackers, gen-X. There was a market for what I did.

Z One thing I was really interested in is how you reconcile a more straightforward kind of drive or ambition within a subculture context that respects the opposite of that. I think you have a short story that sort of talks about this, where the hero of the scene is this kind of anti-success story and there's this younger girl who thinks he's the epitome of cool. And I think you said something in *Zine* about making fun of your own novel to people you were hanging out with because you were sort of embarrassed to be taking it seriously.

P To me, that's more about high culture or low culture, or pop culture and academic culture. I mean, the rock scene or the zine scene is a very anti-intellectual climate. Not the zine scene so much, but the rock scene. So, yeah, I didn't feel like very many people crossed over from the rock scene. A lot of the people don't read, which is frustrating to me. It seems pretty vapid.

Z Do you find that now that you have all your time to do your writing, your attitude towards it has changed?

P Well, actually I'm teaching too.

Z Oh, so you do have some structured time going on.

P Yeah, and the other thing I found is that I can't do fiction all the time, because it completely drives me nuts if I do it too much. I feel like I have to always do the zine stuff, too. Because I can do it at night, when I'm tired.

Z When you were working forty hours a week did you have that much energy?

P Well, I only had one full-time job in my whole life and I quit after six months. . . . I'm just temperamentally unsuited to having a full-time job.

Z Well, I don't have any more questions. Do you have any great thoughts on ambition in general, or ambition as it relates to a lifestyle thing? Do you want to talk a little bit more about the living in the moment thing, and how that relates to your ambition now?

P When I was in my twenties I would think about when I would get my novel published, because I did hate my job and I had to reward myself with thinking about when things would get better, and I was able to sacrifice a lot for that. But my father died a couple years ago and that kind of made me see . . . he was just about to retire and he worked really hard all his life. That was certainly a lesson, that you have to do whatever you want to do right now. And then I got sick, and all that kind of thing made me realize

that you may have a life plan, but it's kind of ridiculous because things are going to happen.

Z Do you feel like you missed out on anything?

P Yeah I do, although I think I kind of want an excuse to stay home and do whatever. That's why I think that I would do this even if I didn't have to, or wasn't getting paid or whatever. After a while of just going out hanging out with friends, going to movies, seeing music, I just start to feel really weird, like I'm just frittering away my time. I like to spend time alone, so I can kind of get into recluse mode. I think I use my fabulous career dreams . . .

Z It's just a shoddy excuse!

P I did slave away. I think I did sacrifice relationships. I always had a lot of good friends—but once in a while I'd go out with a rock-and-roll-guy type and not really be that interested, and not worry that much about having a relationship or whatever. I kind of didn't focus on my love life. I was so focused on my career. And I don't think I was as emotionally there for people as I am now. I mean, now, my friends and family are my first priority, the people in my life come before my work.

Z Do you think that has to do with the fact that you have achieved a certain level of success with it, or, total speculation, do you think it's something that would have happened anyway?

P It's hard to say. I think I might resent people taking my time and emotional energy if I hadn't felt satisfied in my career life.

Z Nonetheless, you worked hard and you got somewhere through it!

P So for those kids out there . . .

Z Wait for those marsh-mallows!

Hello Kitty

by Clancy

Amanda Cavnar

(from Ben Is Dead)

From H to K and back again, Hello Kitty is more than the sum of her parts. To me, she will always be the silent witness to mystery, mystic in her mouthlessness. To others, she is a friendly little girl, and still others see her in a sexual or political context. What she is does not really rely, in Kitty's case, on what she was intended to be.

The Japanese tradition of cuteness in design, rounded features, animals anthropomorphized into darling neighbors and friends, gave birth to Kitty. It is rumored that she was modeled after an English cartoon kitty, but it is not known whether that kitty had a mouth. She does not stand out as a particularly interesting character, her motives being banal and her pronouncements bland platitudes possibly chosen for the ease with which they can be translated into any of the many languages Hello Kitty merchandise is marketed in. Yet, Kitty has the power which ciphers can gain just by being mute. Kitty is much like Andy Warhol in this way, an observer, the "Sphinx without a riddle." When Kitty proclaims, "Teddy bears really are a girl's best friend," we wonder, is this really a misanthropic, sarcastic statement by a bitter, scorned kitty? Or is there something kitty knows about teddy bears that we don't? Or is it just as it seems, a statement directed at five-year-old girls which they might relate to? Like Warhol, Hello Kitty's real trip is about capitalism. She is marketed on an amazing number of products, from bubble gum to erasers, to electric toothbrushes, sleeping bags, jewelry, plastic and cloth bags of many sizes, and on and on. She is featured on an item called a "leisure mat," which is a piece of plastic with her picture on it and "can be used as 1) a picnic mat, 2) a rain cloak, 3) a wrapper, a cover, or in a variety of other ways!" The same could be said for a Hefty Bag, but any other piece of plastic lacks the special touch of Kitty, that imprint which raises it to the iconographic, which involves the owner in the world created for Hello Kitty and her friends. For a quarter, one can purchase a candy with Kitty's image, and be part of the same world that someone who spent $50.00 for the "life-size" plush doll inhabits. You can buy a piece of happiness locked into form and design which represents purity, both moral and sexual, a time before cynicism and yet purveyed with complete cynicism. In a sense, Kitty out-Warhols Warhol, because there really is no "there" there. Hello Kitty could be anyone we might want her to be. There is no secret Catholic faith, no cookie jar collection, no sexual peccadilloes to hide. Gay, straight, fascist, communist, these words have no meaning in the ultra-material world of Hello Kitty where ideas and ideology have no hold. It may be that this is the appeal of Hello Kitty; a pantheistic materialism in a world of fetishes, each new sticker and Hello Kitty pen another bridge joining us to Her.

Kitty's mouthlessness proclaims her desire to get along, to please all, and perhaps designates her as the ultimate Japanese female: subservient and opinionless. Yet there is no doubt that Kitty rules her crowd, shines as the star, and is always the favorite. She does not need words when she has the power of the marketplace behind her. Hello Kitty was created in postwar Japan, after the dropping of the atom bomb. As Japan re-entered the world community, it put on a benign face and pushed nonstop to conquer the world with consumer goods where it had failed militarily. Ever polite and concerned with "face," they did not spit at the Americans who had decimated their cities and inflicted radiation sickness on their children. They instead created the mouthless Kitty, who has nothing to say on the topic, who would only like for you to buy, and who is entirely non-threatening. Is Hello Kitty some sort of Trojan horse, sent by Japan? What is her secret? How can we ever know? Hello Kitty and her friends (KeroKeroKeroppi the frog, Pochacco, the dog, WinkiBinki, another cat, but brown and both mouthless and noseless, PickeBicke the mouse, Pekkle the duck, Mimi (Kitty's sister), Pippo the pig, Honeyfield the Bear, Tuxedo Sam the penguin, the Twin Stars, My Melody and a few lesser Sanrio characters round out the panoply of Kitty's playmates) share a realm of purity which is available in some form in almost every industrialized nation in the world. The Hello Kitty cult, with the capacity to unite nations of children in its blandly favorable outlook and extreme emphasis on the collecting of representations of the Sanrio characters, promises to spread like a benign disease until the world is saturated. Warhol never thought to appeal to children, nor to that special place in each of us which longs for a preverbal paradise where Kittens rule.

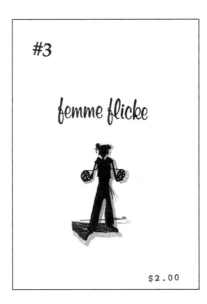

#3

femme flicke

$2.00

Trinh T. Minh-ha

by Tina Spangler

(from *Femme Flicke*)

The following is an edited interview with Trinh T. Minh-ha. I conducted this interview in the Fall of 1993 and it originally appeared in Latent Image, the Emerson College journal of film criticism. It is unfortunate in my opinion that Trinh T. Minh-ha wanted to edit her own interview, because some of the spontaneity and charm of the verbal interview is lost in the process. I think this filmmaker is concerned that she would be misunderstood in the process of the generation of her ideas from her head to the written page (i.e. her English, the transcription). In any case, what follows is about one-sixth of the entire interview, and although it is highly altered from its original state, it is, nevertheless, important for feminists and filmmakers alike. —*Tina*

Born in Vietnam, Trinh T. Minh-ha is a writer, composer and filmmaker. She has been making films for better than ten years and may be best known for her first film, *Reassemblage,* made in 1982. However, her more recent film, *Surname Viet Given Name Nam* (1989), which examines "identity and culture through the struggle of Vietnamese women" (Biographical Notes), has received much attention, including winning the Blue Ribbon Award at the American Film and Video Festival. Trinh T. Minh-ha is a professor of Women's Studies and Film at the University of California, Berkeley, and was recently a Visiting Professor at Harvard University.

TS You wrote in your book *When The Moon Waxes Red* that many independent women are rejecting the label of "feminist." Are you bothered by being called a feminist filmmaker, a feminist writer?

TM-H Depending on who's saying it. I don't have any problem with being labeled a "feminist," it all depends on what is meant and connoted. It could be just a way of narrowing down the space in which you can work authoritatively "as a feminist." This I find to be very problematic.

TS In *When The Moon Waxes Red,* you say "There is a need to make films politically," as opposed to making political films. What is the difference between the two? Do you think it is possible to make a film without political ramifications?

TM-H The answer has to do with how one sees the political. The filmmaker Jean-Luc Godard made, for example, the distinction between making films politically and making films that focus on a political subject or have a political content. Films classified as "political" usually center on authority figures, on institutions or on personalities from the body politic; or else, they focus, for example, on a strike of the workers, on a crisis that happened between suppliers and consumers or between the boss and the workers.

Such a reductive concept of the "political" has been challenged by the work carried out in the women's movement. The feminist struggle has contributed to breaking down the dichotomy between the private and the public or the personal and the societal. Is the political only something that focuses on the evident sources of authorities or institutions or of institutional values, or is the political also something that seeps in and invades every aspect of our lives?

Many contemporary theorists, like Michel Foucault, have focused their studies on power relationships in the intimate realms of our lives. Power relationships are, therefore, not just to be located in these evident sources that I have mentioned. Even if you criticize these sources, even if you eradicate them, the question remains, how is it that we continue in our daily life to be violent, to be racist, to be sexist, to be homophobic, xenophobic and so on? How is it that we continue to oppress while being oppressed? So it must be in something that is much more than these locatable evident sources of power.

We come to a situation in which to make a film politically would be to put to question your own position as filmmaker. Power relationships can be looked at from many angles. For example, you can look at how technology and the tools that define your activities are never neutral, and how they are always interpolated by ideology.

The film industry, for example, has technologies that serve their own ideology of expansion and consumption.

When you work politically, you'll have to politicize all aspects of filmmaking. So it's not just when you focus on a political subject that your film is political. The film is not yet political enough, because you can focus on a political subject and yet reproduce all the language of the mainstream ideology, reproducing thereby its oppressive mechanisms. There are no apolitical works, but some works politicize the daily realism of our lives and other works simply look at these daily realms without offering the viewer a critical space in which the tensions between the political and the personal are played out. So, sometimes a filmmaker might think that their work does not have anything to do with the political, but, as I said, there are no "apolitical" films. For someone to say "I'm apolitical" simply means "I haven't yet politicized my life or my work."

TS I think many film students and young filmmakers would be interested to know your filmic process. For example, how do you get funds together to make your films?

TM-H It is very useful to think of funding not as something that is outside of yourself. You don't wait until the budget comes to you before you start on a project, which is the kind of attitude molded after that found in the mainstream film industry. People always think that if you don't have the budget for a film, you can't work on it.

I think that there are many kinds of film-making and one need not be bound to the model that dominates the media. If you have a lot of money, you can use that money, but if you don't have money, you are still going to make films but a different kind of films. For example, I didn't have money when I was making *Reassemblage*. That film can be said to be made by myself from A–Z. The cinematography, the writing, the editing, even the conforming of the negative of the film was all done by myself. In other words, you fulfill all the functions, and like an artisan, you do the whole craft. You are not dependent on expertise and division of labor. That kind of film is, of course, something that experimental and avant-garde filmmakers always cherish because it allows them not to be dependent on any major sources of funding. They can incorporate the film process in their lives. So instead of going out to buy a package of cigarettes, you would go out and buy a can of film. And the cans of film you would get here and there would serve little-by-little to make a film. It is something that is incorporated into your daily expenses.

For me, this is an important attitude that one can also adopt when writing for grants, for example, even if the world of grant donors is not always sympathetic to it. Because if they gave me $100,000 for a film, then I would make a certain kind of film. And if I only get $30,000 for a film, then I would make another kind of film. And neither film would be more important than the other. It is not a question of quality, it is a question of difference.

Rush Limbaugh

by Jenn G. Box

(from Gogglebox)

I got a call on a Tuesday from my friend Noah. "Hey, ya wanna go see Rush Limbaugh's show on Thursday? I got some tickets." Uh, yeah. Long as it's free. "But you gotta promise me you're not gonna do anything crazy. And you have to dress normal." No problem, Noah. (Now where can I get an Uzi on this kind of short notice?) Come Thursday and I make myself look like a fucking businesswoman: suit, make-up, all that. When I get to the church (Unitel Studios) for the services (show taping), the waiting room is already filled with devotees. A few were poring over a copy of *Cigar Aficionado Magazine* on which Rush (blessed be He) graces the cover. I met a bunch of old women from Hershey, Pennsylvania in the bathroom who were in New York for their first time to see this show. Before we went into the studio, we had to all line up and go through a metal detector. Someone in line shouted out "IS THAT A *LIBERAL* DETECTOR?" and all the suits erupted in hearty laughter. We filed into our seats facing the pseudo-study set. Before the taping started, Rush came out to talk to us. He actually looks fatter in person. He made some jokes and answered questions. The old women from Hershey were totally having orgasms like crazy. Then he asked us "Who here's a liberal?" and I was the only person in the whole audience to raise my hand. Rush said, "Yep, we spotted you when you came in." (Too bad he didn't ask "Who here's a feminazi?") They started taping the show, and he spent the first half showing the clip of U2's Bono saying "Fuck the Mainstream" at the Grammy's and he ranted on and on about the situation with young people today (you know, having premarital sex, taking drugs, no morals). He ended with the declaration that "the only way for a young person to rebel nowadays is to become a **conservative.**" When the show aired that night, right after he said that there was a big close-up of me looking absolutely mortified.

imaginary FRIEND

A LIVING PERSON SHOT THROUGH SPACE WITH VIOLENT VELOCITY FROM THE MOUTH OF A MONSTER CANNON

POINTERS ON PRACTICALLY EVERYTHING

#3

April 96

Another Go-Go for Jane Wiedlin

by Denise

Sullivan

(from

ROCKRGRL)

Rolling Stone magazine did a 'women in rock' issue last year and we were one teeny postage-size stamp picture and like three words: THE GO-GO'S, 1981," said Jane Wiedlin, former singer/songwriter and guitarist of the historic, all-female band, The Go-Go's.

The Go-Go's debut, *Beauty and the Beat,* was the first album to achieve number one status by an all-female, songwriting and instrument-wielding act. But the Go-Go's have not necessarily been remembered on the public record for that unprecedented accomplishment.

"You wouldn't look at say, Hole, and claim they were influenced directly by the Go-Go's," says Gillian Gaar, author of the girl-rock herstory, *She's a Rebel,* "but the Go-Go's' influence on girls who form bands is undeniable." The Go-Go's' influence on girls in general is undeniable. Wiedlin believes she knows why young women have strong associations with the group.

"We presented ourselves as who we were and I guess a lot of young women really related to us. We weren't being presented as sex kittens—something that would make normal girls feel uncomfortable. I know that I would have related to us when I was twelve or thirteen."

It's been nearly twenty years since the Go-Go's haunted Hollywood's Canterbury apartment complex, the legendary digs of LA punk rockers that once upon a time included Belinda Carlisle and Jane Wiedlin. Inspired by their non-musician punker friends beginning to form bands, Carlisle and Wiedlin recruited Margot Olivarria and Elissa Bello to form the first incarnation of the Go-Go's in 1978. Later that year, the group's first experienced musician, Charlotte Caffey, was added to the line-up as lead guitarist, and by '79 another musical vet, Gina Schock, was exchanged for Bello on drums.

The Go-Go's gigged consistently at LA's punk rock mecca, the Masque, and at San Francisco's Mabuhay Gardens, leading to an early break—opening for English ska-gods Madness and the Specials on an English tour. A seven-inch deal with the trendy label Stiff ensued, and stateside, they were awarded a contract in 1981 with start-up label IRS. By that time, Olivarria had been replaced by bassist Kathy Valentine, also an experienced musician.

Beauty and the Beat's instant success was

difficult to match but the follow-up, *Vacation,* extended the group's profile via MTV, and a third album, *Talk Show,* turned out to be the group's swansong.

"I think what happened is we were really young when we got successful and we didn't know quite how to handle it. We were overworked and we didn't know how to say no so we did every single thing everyone told us to do. We never got away from each other and we got really sick of each other," said Wiedlin.

In addition, band members were dealing with well-publicized addiction and alcohol abuse problems, culminating in nasty in-fighting.

"In retrospect, what we should have said was, let's take a couple of years off and go recover from this experience and come and back and see how we feel about it."

The band re-formed briefly in 1990 for a show to benefit People for Ethical Treatment of Animals (PETA), but the timing wasn't right for a full reformation. "That was at the height of Belinda's career," says Weidlin. "She was incredibly busy and under a lot of pressure to be completely separate from the Go-Go's and she wasn't ready to commit to us again."

In late '94, the Go-Go's had another go at reuniting in an effort to celebrate the release of their IRS retrospective, *Return to the Valley of the Go-Go's.* "It's been almost ten years since we broke up and ten years is a pretty good amount of time to recover from these kinds of things. We joke now that we should have gotten a family counselor—which is the nineties thing to do. We've all done a lot of thinking, soul-searching, and growing up, and that's why I think it's OK now," says Wiedlin.

The Go-Go's reunion took the group on a five city run, including six nights in Las Vegas. Did Wiedlin ever imagine fifteen years ago that someday they'd be playing Vegas?

"I'm just happy that we have enough of a sense of humor about ourselves that we see it as funny or fun to be playing Vegas. Our concert is balls-to-the-wall rock. I felt really lucky that when we got together again, we didn't sound dated. I guess a good pop song is a good pop song and it can survive trends and decades. We're really aware of how the old songs might sound and we've worked on them. It's easy to change a bass part or a drum beat. Our battle cry is, 'Oh no, it's too Eighties!'" ★

(Portions of this article appeared previously in the *San Francisco Weekly.*)

A Conversation with Tribe 8's Leslie Mah!

or ... "Two sisters in hardcore nurture their inner children as they bitch about being racial mutts and other shit ..."

by Sabrina Sandata

(from Bamboo Girl)

Me Being an ethnic chick in the hardcore scene, is there anything that you want to say especially about it?

Her Well, I can talk about it for a long time, you know.

Me I know, it's a topic that I definitely can go on about forever.

Her Yeah, I really think there needs to be affirmative action in the music industry, because right now it's almost all white people, and of course they're going to sign their friends to their label, and let their friends play their clubs. They all manage their friends . . . when they make decisions they'll usually hire their friends.

Me I'm asking because *Bamboo Girl* is a zine from the standpoint of a hardcore chick on the ethnic tip.

Her Really? Well then maybe we should talk again sometime. We played with this band, Stam 66, they're really good. The singer and drummer are both Eurasian, and this has been an issue with them.

In our band, it's an issue that we talk about, but it's not so much in the lyrics. I have another project band where three of us are Chinese and the singer is African-American. And half of our practice is spent talking—one of them is Eurasian, and even the one who's all Chinese, she grew up in a southern state—we talk about being culturally Chinese. But my culture is constantly being shoved down my throat, and I don't wanna fully live my life like that.

I'm first generation Chinese-American, and I have a lot of Chinese ideas because my father's Chinese, and he's the one that raised me.

Me So you identify a lot with the Chinese aspects of yourself?

Her No, I feel really . . . kind of stuck because I go to a college in San Francisco where most of the student body is Asian. I've met a lot of friends, but they're no more culturally Asian than I am. I mean, I grew up in a small white town. And there in Colorado, I was *really* exotic, and I got a lot of shit for being Asian, like bad shit. Like "the dirty old man from China," "chinese, japanese, dirty knees, look at these."

Me But do they assume that you're Chinese just by looking at you?

Her Yeah, when I was a kid I looked a lot more Asian: my eyes were darker . . .

(At this moment, a clubster clunks her head on the hand dryer in the bathroom. [Yes, we're still in the bathroom.] Leslie is surprised by the noise and extends her sympathy:)

Me Oh, honey, are you OK?

Clubster Oh, don't worry about me . . .

(After complimenting the girl on her sequined vest, she continues:)

Me Now I live in San Francisco, and I get treated differently than my blond friends, that's for sure. I had a friend who had long blond hair, and she wasn't femme, but she got so much more harrassed than me. I don't get that very much. I live in a hispanic neighborhood, and they just think I'm hispanic. Not that often, but I think it has to do with the way that I dress.

Me Really?

Her Yeah, I think it has a *lot* to do with the way that I'm dressed. Nice Chinese girls would never talk the way I do or get tattoos. I'm not traditional. But I definitely don't get harassed as much as the white girls. I'm absolutely not an "oddity" in that racial sense, it's more in the sexual sense.

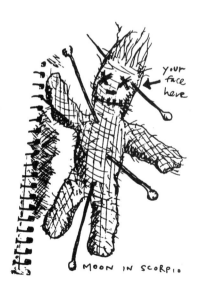

In no particular order, except for the first one...

The Gogglebox 100

1. My Mom + Dad ♥
2. Mangos
3. Ramona Quimby
4. Brooklyn
5. The Antiquarian Bookstore, Omaha, NE
6. James Todd King
7. JIMI HENDRIX
8. GIRLFIEND zine
9. JAWBREAKER (R.I.P.)
10. T.S. ELIOT
11. Chocolate milk
12. Katha Pollitt, writer for The Nation; feminist theorist; always right.
13. Fuck Guiliani.
14. The Muppet Movie
15. Gogglebox!
16. DONUT FALLS → Utah
17. Skee-Ball!!!
18. DOC HOPPER
19. LISA LIONHEART zine
20. small towns.
21. NY PRESS
22. Morning sex
23. Strawberries
24. Shout out to the COLUMBIA UNIVERSITY RAVE TEAM!
25. AVAIL

26. Corn Nuts
27. SMILE FOR ME zine
28. CITIZEN FISH
29. angstful high school kids
30. GRAND CENTRAL STATION
31. Sticky Summer Nights ☆☆☆
32. Discount (FL)
33. 7TH Floor McBain
34. ROSEANNE
35. Rolling Rock
36. Shel Silverstein
37. Bloodlink Records
38. fake haus → philly
39. CHOKING VICTIM (R.I.P.)
40. WRECKING BALL zine
41. Spinach Pie
42. museum of science + Industry, Chicago
43. BOUNCING SOULS
44. ?
45. OP. IVY
46.
47. MEG
48. Ice Cream Sandwiches
49. NEW YORK
50. JOHN from St. Louis (where are you?!)

51. YAH-MOS
52. Chicago
53. STRONGBOX zine
54. NAPS.
55.
56. E. 6th Street (Indian Food)
57. FIFTEEN
58. CUPSIZE zine
59. orgasms!
60. SURPRISE DAY
61. Noam Chomsky
62. Fear of Flying by Erica Jong
63. FOOD NOT BOMBS
64. Deee-Lite
65. Boone's Wine Product - 2 bucks!
66. Jerusalem Falafel
67. Silly Skinheads
68. R.M. RILKE
69. my beautiful red bike 11/94 - 2/95
70. Florida PUNX shout out to Mason + Rich
71. X-RAY SPEX
72. BUGOUT SOCIETY
73. "synesthesia" - look it up! -
74. GREASE THE MOVIE, DUH.
75. Lincoln, Nebraska

76. FUGAZI - forever -
77. Amigos (Mexican fast food)
78. MICHAEL Cleveland whirf Rd
79. Vintage Vinyl St. Louis
80. SCREECHING WEASEL
81. Fake Meats
82. my grandpa and grandma ♥♥
83. BIG PILES OF MAIL
84. אבני דרך
85. Too MANY Veggie Burritos
86. ♥ crushes. ♥
87. FACE TO FACE (R.I.P.)
88. STUFF zine (R.I.P.)
89. kinko's
90. W.113TH NYC
91. ΔΦ
92. TILT
93. Invisible Man by Ralph Ellison
94. Sunlight
95.
96. Ms. Dee
97. LIZ PHAIR
98. F. SCOTT FITZGERALD
99. CENTRAL PARK
100. The mag this idea was taken from... (props if you know!)

Stardom

and Fandom

(excerpt)

by Kathy

Strieder and

Kathleen Hanna

(from Princess)

The following is a conversation between Kathleen Hanna and Kathy Strieder discussing the concepts of stardom and fandom—attempting to define them and figure out what they mean socially.

S So let's start with a really basic working definition of what you think a star is . . . What role does a star play in society, why do stars exist?

H I think part of the idea of being a star involves how it separates people: stars are superhuman, or "real" people, and everyone else is supposed to be obsessed with their lives. Everyone else is supposed to be following what the "real" people do, which means that everyone else is less than real.

S Yes, there is a weird hierarchy that seems to be created. It seems that, if you've achieved some kind of stardom, people think that you've gained some kind of legitimacy or success that they don't have. This can apply even if people don't like or don't care about your work. I'm thinking, for example, of some older guy who's sitting in his house on a Sunday, opens up a magazine and sees a picture of Kim Gordon. He doesn't necessarily know anything about her or her work, but he's still going to think in some way that she has something that he doesn't, or has some kind of agency that he doesn't. You made a good point in an earlier conversation about stars being, in a way, both superhuman and "dead or cartoonish, not allowed to be real."

H Right. I mean, any form of duality is dehumanizing for those involved. In this case, there is this idea that there are "common" people in one place and "royalty" in another. Although I wouldn't say that the "royalty" is oppressed, I'd say that both sides are dehumanized, because they both work in opposition and reaction to each other. And it's not like either side is necessarily recognizing full human agency, although the "royalty" can do that to a greater degree, because they're afforded privilege and position. Both of them become inhuman, like the royalty becomes a cartoon character.

S Yes, but I think it's important to make this distinction though, that a person who becomes a star is not in reality becoming a cartoon character. They really are people who live in houses and eat food, etc. But to others they become less human, even to the point where people throw shit at them on stage, when they wouldn't

autograph assumes certain things, like that that person is valuable.

S Like you want their name written on something.

H I think a lot of people in every day life totally experience that in terms of crushes. You have a crush on somebody, you build them up in your head. Then you actually hang out with them and they're not what you thought they were or what you wanted them to be. People are really creative and imaginative. We reinvent stuff. The thing is, we have to be careful not to turn others into objects. Because you need to get some clay or pens or something like that, instead of objectifying people, why don't you just use actual things, and objectify them, rather than using Courtney Love to play out your fantasies.

S But I think there's a certain dynamic, there's a reason why people need others to do this. There's something really intense about what happens between a star and a fan, where the fan really sees something about the star (as opposed to a lump of clay) as something they can really work themselves out through.

H Yeah, well I've done that. I did that with Evan Dando.

S I think everyone does that. I know I've done it. I think it's completely normal. The thing is, I just wonder why, what is it about our society that has set up this particular structure. I just wonder how it works into the idea of capitalism, the idea of people selling their performance, and others buying it. But then, you know, when it comes time to talk to them you're unable to speak. Like there's this time when I met P.J. Har-

throw shit at people on the street. I guess what I'm asking you is, why do you think that people feel a need to have people like that in society? What kinds of responses and experiences have you had with people who you think were seeing you that way? What was going on with them?

H I guess I can talk about a common interaction that I have with people when they ask me for an autograph. I used to try to disrupt the autograph thing by being like, "Well I'm not more important than you." I talked to them about the idea of autographs, stardom, and fame. I mean, obviously that's not always practical. But then I realized it was kind of condescending, because it was assuming that they were stupid, that they might not know that already. Then I started thinking, "Wait, why are they approaching me?" Approaching someone and asking them for their

Fan Club 131

vey and I was unable to speak to her. I felt like such a nerd.

H I had that with Karen Finley, too.

S She seems really approachable, though.

H Yeah, but it's my idea, I was really afraid that she would disrupt my idea of her, and I didn't want her to. Her work changed my life, and I realized I just wanted to keep her in that context. Like there's some people you shouldn't fuck because the fantasy of fucking them is way better than actually fucking them will ever be. It takes a mature person to figure that out. Ha ha ha. Sometimes people use stars, though, to mediate relationships. The star is on stage and the audience is on the floor (because you need to be on stage so people can see you). But while people are looking up at you, they're not looking right next to them at the person they might really need to be talking to. In some instances, the stage/fan set-up prevents relationships with each other. People focus on the star and live vicariously. I think that has to do with capitalism, which dehumanizes everyone into robots. The more people get abused by their families and by sexism, racism, classism, and homophobia, and able-body-ism and stuff, the more numb people have to become. And the less we can actually deal with any real confrontation, because confrontation may remind us of all this other stuff, and that's real scary. So we avoid being healthy enough or safe enough to feel a lot of stuff.

S Yeah, I think you're very right. So it's like this safe method of exchange, and the fact that it involves someone who you make into superhuman. You project all your social needs onto this album, or something that you'll never actually deal with. That's kind of scary.

H When we perform in Olympia it's a really different situation from when we perform in New York or Los Angeles or San Francisco because people see me walking around. A lot of people have seen me in other capacities, possibly serving them food somewhere. I think it's really positive for people to see us in their community, and then in this other way on the stage. It's like, "Oh I saw that girl in the park and then I saw her on the stage," and it's not like I am Iggy Pop and I flew down in a helicopter. They're like "Oh, I could do that." That's how I started doing things. And that's why I try to, when I can, remain as accessible as possible.

S So you're saying that a star thing can work positively if the person is seen as a star as well as part of the rest of the world.

H I just hope there's some sort of suture between those two things, between being a star and being a person. I mean I've had to somewhat separate them just for me to be able to function. I had to do the same thing when I was a dancer, which is just another type of performance. It was a similar separation, in order to maintain some sort of livability in the situation. But I just hope that it doesn't always have to be a stripper/customer relationship, even in punk rock. That's what I'm trying to navigate right now.

S It seems like we're still circling around what a star really is. And I'm not thinking of a star as you, as a person, I'm thinking of it as a shell, a thing you put on, or that other people put on you. It's even separate from the performance to some degree.

H Well, I see it as analogous to focusing on a character in a novel. I think in certain ways, because of the media culture now, tabloids, etc., rock stars and movie stars and stuff have replaced characters in novels. And I think that people, including myself, follow stars as if they're characters in a novel, and their lives are unfolding in front of you.

Raw Like Sushi:
AN IN-YOUR-FACE COLLECTION ON IDENTITY BY YOUNG WOMEN OF COLOR

CALLING ALL vaginals OF COLOR!

The creator of <u>Bamboo Girl</u> (a zine by/for/but not exclusive to feisty young women of color within the hardcore/punk community) is inviting young women of color to make their mark in breaking Racist, Sexist, Homophobic, & Ethnic stereotypes by submitting their non-fictional essays for a book she will contribute to, compile, and edit, entitled: **Raw Like Sushi: AN IN-YOUR-FACE COLLECTION ON IDENTITY BY YOUNG WOMEN OF COLOR.** There will be a Foreword by Ninotchka Rosca, writer/activist extraordinnaire who fled the Philippines in self-imposed exile to escape martial law and has since furthered her work towards the Philippine-US womens' solidarity movement. This book will be an anthology of confrontational essays and works by young women of color struggling with their cultural identity, sexual orientation, and oppression of sorts by a society that pressures us to conform to what it dictates. It will look at the thoughts, ideas, and experiences of a prevalent sector within society that is seldom heard, and who, as a collective, are learning about themselves through their society and their own culture — whether it be traditional, American, anarchist, queer, asexual, straight, punk/hardcore, ethnic- or mutt-identified, patriotic, or non-patriotic. Overall, this is going to be a direct collection of works wo-manned by articulate women of color who want to focus clearly on issues that pertain to them, and are not afraid to be controversial about it. It's called "Raw" for a reason!

I AM LOOKING FOR: views expressed by women who do not fit the stereotype of "typical" young women of color (ie. are not purebreds of a certain ethnicity, are confrontational and question the injustices and mores around them, whether they be written or unsaid.) Some comics and artwork/photos will be considered, but priority will be given to **NON-FICTIONAL ESSAYS** — loud and proud ranting & raving by young women of color who <u>do not want</u> to fit the cookie cutter mold society has given them. This is going to be fearless writing on identity without giving a shit about censoring thoughts! This is your chance to go off (or get off, whichever the case may be) and get published! I am also looking for **CONTACT NAMES/NUMBERS** OF ORGANIZATIONS AND INDIVIDUALS who are working towards the visibility of fierce young women of color for the book's Resource Appendix.

GUIDELINES: All works should be no longer than 20 pages, typed, double-spaced, and be in MS Word 5.0. Please include cover letter, short bio, & copy of work on 3.5" disc. Enclose a SAS postcard for response, and SASE to have submission returned.

>> DEADLINE IS JUNE 1, 1996. <<

Submit your entries to: **Project Raw**

DESIGN BY SABRINA SANDATA, BAMBOO G

The Day I Met Oprah

by Sara

(from Sourpuss)

This summer I was able to obtain my dream of becoming part of the talk show world. I am a talk show freak now, no argument. my life's goal has been achieved. granted, if you saw the episode it was not as freakish as I would have preferred, it was actually pretty boring. But I have traveled into that world. Yes I *have* been in the green room. When I was first offered the possibility of being on the show, the first thing that I thought was that I was finally going to get a chance to say all the things that I have wanted people to know, that I was finally going to make everybody out there realize what's up. that is what I have always thought I would do if I were on a talk show. When I would watch talk shows i'd always think to myself, if I were there I would say just the right thing and everyone would realize what was right. yeah that's what I thought.

watching the episode now, I feel there was so much more I should have said. at the time when I was on that stage, thought I was glad I didn't totally make a blundering fool out of myself, so I was happy at the time. I wonder if this is a good thing, being part of this media, and I'm sure all you out there are like, "gee sara, that's a stoopid question." but the objections I have to Oprah were less important to me than getting a chance to voice my ideas. I weighed the cons of making money for Oprah with the positives of being able to let her know why what some of what she does is wrong. the main thing that is important is that I am going to continue to do what I do and support what I did before the Oprah show. Most people don't understand that they have the power to do whatever they want for and by themselves. I mean gerls out there need to see this. I mean, what would have happened if there wasn't some one supporting riot grrrl on that show? it would have been little or no talk of the things that are obstacles to us gerls. And not all gerls and women know that there is a choice, and I feel it's important to let them know. I want gerls to know, I want to help people, and Oprah gave me the advantage of having lots of people hearing me. I am upset because I didn't get to say all that I wanted to 'cause I was so freakin' nervous. but I wanted to try to convey that any gerl out there watching Oprah should go and start something. I wanted to let gerls know that there is nothing to starting a zine or a chapter of riot grrrl, that it is something we all can do. and the more gerls who do it the better.

Princess Phone

It's a common stereotype: teenage girls who are always on the phone.

Well, in this section, we see what happens when girls and women put

that energy onto paper. Zinemakers fill their pages with all kinds of

communication. Here you'll get juicy gossip and read some personal

correspondences. You'll also get a look at how girls are viewing tech-

nology and what they are intending to do with it.

gossip

letters

technology

SUZY BRENNAN

Princess Visions

by Diana Morrow, editor of Princess

The self-publishing scene, especially that of young feminist women who have developed and utilized relatively underground publication and distribution networks, is an important factor in combating the silence around issues which are pertinent to women's existences. Fanzines and independent publications challenge the myths about women's lives that are perpetuated by mainstream publications, and fill in the gaps around our differences. Fanzines provide spaces for women of different ages, from different backgrounds, and at different stages of politicalization to work out ideas and experiences, to share information and personal insights, to challenge each other. However, fanzines are sometimes limiting because they often circulate within certain scenes—specific age groups, specific cultures, and often specific racial and class groups. Therefore, they sometimes do not speak to the experiences of many women, or reach them at all.

Because I didn't see my interests or experiences, or those of my peers, reflected in any mainstream women's magazines, I decided to produce my own magazine—one that includes the aspects of fanzines that I find empowering, such as conversational, honest, personal writing, accessibility, progressive politics, underground art, etc. I wanted to bring these aspects to a larger scale in order to reach more women, to provide ways for women to reach out to one another across their differences, to further establish and maintain connections among more women, to maintain some sense of community with one another. Because communication is necessary for broader understandings of each other and our situations, a zine which provides a place for exchange and communication can be vital for such understanding.

Princess is a magazine that aims to be accessible to all women while maintaining its dyke focus, a magazine that encourages engagement with political issues on a deep level while also covering what's going on in music, art, and other scenes, and that gives coverage of and support of women who are doing amazing work, yet are not getting recognition they deserve. I want to talk to and about women and their work, which SHOULD be covered but are often marginalized or erased by mainstream media because their work is feared as "too radical," or whatever . . . What you won't find in *Princess,* what I don't support, are rigid, closed-minded attitudes (no anti-sex radical feminism) no coverage of overly publicized dyke celebrities (all three of them) or bourgie dyke events at beach resorts. What I want to do is open up feminism, to shatter stereotypes, and build new ideas of what feminism is all about, what women's lives are all about, what lesbians are all about . . .

I believe that a great source of power for many women comes from thinking and writing about their lives and talking about how they're affected by the social system of which they are a part. I also wanted to incorporate progressive political theory about feminist, queer, racial, and class issues in the editorial content. Not theory in the traditional sense, but theory that is written in non-elitist, non-academic language, that is related to personal experience, not just suspended in abstraction. I hope that the material which comprises *Princess* might encourage action. I hope its content bridges theory and practice. Being informed and inspired encourages more women to take action, and to feel that they are not alone in their work for social change. Through our actions, the violence perpetuated by interlocking structures of white supremacy, sexism, classism, and heterosexism in this society can begin to be undermined. "Action" can involve many different things, from serious organizing to making the commitment and taking the risk to be *out* about your politics, challenging and engaging whenever you see/hear/witness fucked up shit. As feminists, dykes, divas, organizers, artists, students, perverts, musicians, nerds, goddess worshippers, workers, poets, theorists, whatever, women have a lot to say to each other and a lot to learn from each other. We also have a lot of work to do, making changes within our communities, as well as within ourselves. And making changes requires talking and understanding, and working with one another. One way we can do this is through sharing what it is we do in a publication geared toward communication, awareness, and action. I hope *Princess* fulfills these visions.

#4
$2

bunny
rabbit

RUMMY BRIDE

age 10

(Closing) Comments on Zines and Whatnot

by Witknee (from Alien)

doing a zine is very egotistical. it is creating something and saying, 'here read this, i have something of value to say.' there is nothing wrong with having an ego, mind you. it is great for one's self-esteem to print up their thoughts and opinions and pass it on to others. i encourage it for everyone.

in general all art is egotistical. it is a form for the deranged, insecure population to show off. since i've been doing zines, my self-esteem has improved rapidly. before and in the beginning (of my 'zine years') i was very insecure and unconfident with my opinions, i felt i was worthless and nothing i thought had any importance. by publishing my work and making it public i began to extinguish the latter and relearn the importance of speaking out and expressing myself (this can be said for my photography as well). alien has been my tool to confidence and self-assurance. as i said before, i encourage anyone to do a zine, be in a band, show your artwork, or plainly speak out.

So... let them call you LOUD (good!) let them call you Obnoxious (fine) Just never let them excuse you as a dumb girl!

i started this zine as an outlet for my stifled emotions, and that is what i am still doing it for. my next step is to bring these emotions to my three-dimensional life. if you haven't met me, you may think i'm like the 'usual' alien-writings in person. i am far from it. for two reasons. one, this zine expresses a small part of me. as i have said before, i do not have the need to express my sarcasm and happiness, i can do that fine in person. two, i am an utter coward at expressing my real emotions in person. i rarely cry in front of people. i rarely talk about my depression in person. only one person has seen/heard me have a panic attack. it's just really hard for me to come out and talk about my feelings and why i'm depressed/suicidal/panicky/lonely. i'm stuck in this sarcastic hard-ass part of me in person that is so hard to break way from. does anyone else have this problem?

and i realize i put in a lot of writing about me, all me and my thoughts and opinions. but i do it just as much for you as for me, even more so. i hope this helps you. i hope you can learn something from this.

Princess Phone

Emelye's Computer Chronicles

by Emelye (from Cupsize)

I could write forever about my burgeoning relationship with computers. I am a reactionary/skeptic/cynic and, recently, enthusiast, rolled into one. More than anything else, as I witness this "revolution" I become a *humanist*. Here's just some random thoughts on the subject.

THEY MUSTA TIMED THIS: Come on, you can't tell me that some people at NASA and Macintosh weren't up at midnight on New Year's Eve 1995 with a stop watch, and were like, "on your mark, get set, GO! Systematically bombard America with computer hype and games and commercials." Computers, and more specifically the Internet, are descending on us uncannily just as we take the half-decade run to the fabled year 2000. I can't believe this is just some accident. What better way to suck humanity in (i.e. turn us into willing and blind consumers) than to make sci-fi predictions come true just on time and have us singing along to Prince in five years as we all celebrate the new millennium alone in our vacuum-lock chambers on some universal IRC as the ball drops, uh . . . I can't wait.

THE WORK DAY DON'T COUNT 'TIL THAT BABY IS HUMMING: Even if your job requires little work on the computer, the workday does not feel official until the computer is turned on, like it pumps some crucial energy into the room, validates the whole operation. At a job this summer, our computer wasn't even on-line. It existed to keep track of a mailing list and to do some word processing so we wouldn't be missed from some cyber community if we didn't get the Mac fired up that day. One morning, I went to work extremely hung over—demolished and woozy. I could barely get it together to turn the machine on, but once I did, I just vegged out next to it; the slight glare of the monitor, the buzz of the disc drive. I just sat there near it and somehow felt safer, or like there was . . . company. No program running. No interactive feature. Just the electricity active in the machine, my headache, and the Hudson River out the window. I tried to imag-

left

ine what it would feel like to go to work and not turn the computer on. It was a mind bender. You try it.

LEARN FOR YOURSELVES: As much as some of us might disdain the whole Internet onslaught, I advise you to swallow some of your primitive pride and learn some basics for yourself. Getting around the Net, and computers, is a social responsibility we must all take up if we don't want to be taken advantage of. This country will no longer be divided between just the have and have-nots, but the computer literates and the rest of us Windows-dependent people who won't be able to glide through cyberspace without a color-coded mouse. Learn basic terminology—how systems are set up—how your modem works. If you invest part of your life in there, learn how to take care of it. A whole class of expert troubleshooters will arise that us losers will be dependent on unless we take some responsibility for ourselves.

ONE LAST THING: I recently watched the tail end of some PBS profile of a woman whose name I could not catch. But she said something simple that made me think, akin to "in the last few years, we have progressed technologically, but not necessarily as humans." It was good to see someone separate the two. We are more than the sum of our CD-ROMs and laser printers. And, especially in a *real* world where prejudice and sexism still operate in full force, let's not be so quick to transfer to a place where gender and race are invisible if people so choose. That may sound ideal, but it seems to me a whole stage of development is being skipped over. We can't make this switch from patriarchal society to colorless, sexless society of the Internet democracy. It's a premature and dangerous jump that really only qualifies under virtual reality.

Princess Phone

"my sister is amazing . . ."

by Cindy O. (from <u>Doris</u>)

My sister is amazing. she helps me figure things out. like why i'm writing this thing. i mean, i dont have it all figured out or anything, and some of it is just because it's fun. but part of it is something else. its that i'm really interested in people's stories, you know, what their families were like and weird stages that they went through, and fucked up things that they did and thought, and crazy fun things that they did. how they got where they are, that kind of stuff. and i like to tell those things too, but it doesnt happen in my life enough. like, maybe people dont talk about it because they dont think the other person will be interested or because they don't know how to talk about it, or just how to bring it up, and i dont ask because i'm afraid they wont want to tell me, or it will make them too vulnerable or too invested in me. also because i dont know how to bring it up. like, i dont really think anyone will be interested in this *doris* thing, and i dont want it to be some stupid, weird ego thing because its not. and then there's the whole thing i have about strangers. i wrote about it a little bit later on in this *doris,* but not enough. its not quite developed, my thoughts on it, but it's something like i think theres something really subversive about giving secrets to strangers. like, look at these things that are important to me and we're not really supposed to talk about. and somehow it just makes it really apparent how alienated we are, you know, that theres so much we're not supposed to talk about and theres too few people who really know us, and we're supposed to be so shut off from each other. and here i am,  handing you this thing full of my life, and i want it to break down those barriers, and i want it to make it so people talk about their lives, and secrets aren't secret anymore, and we're not all shut off and self-conscious and scared and cool and tough and alienated and quiet. i want the range of what we talk about to be so much larger than what it is now. and i know this *doris* isn't gonna do all that, but that's what i want. part of what i want, anyway.

i started handing a zine thing we made at my old house, *this is a window this is an animal,* out to strangers on the bus. I'd get all nervous before i'd do it, like there was something very furtive about it, like i was giving them something very secret and important, like i was breaking some big taboo, giving strangers something i had helped make. i don't really know exactly why it felt like that. It seemed like a very very goofy way to feel, but it really made me want the thing to be full of secrets. any kind of secrets. maybe its because i like telling things and i havent really figured out how to do it. i have too much invested in speaking aloud—expectations and whatnot. like, i expect the person i'm talking to to listen and think about it and remember. you know, high expectations. there is something about public transportation i really like. i get kind of attached to people on buses and i really want to know about them. . . .

my biggest secrets: right now, sitting in this little grove of redwood trees, i'm not sure my secrets are so secret or scary, but last night, when I wrote the title, the title was as far as i could get. i'm all wired on coffee now, and i'm not at all sure i know how to explain. i'm not even sure i know what they are. but i'll start with the easy ones. i have herpes. this shouldnt be a secret and inside me it isn't. i mean, it's not even a big deal, but when i'm in the kind of situation where i need to tell someone, it takes on whole new weird proportions.

like i get all scared and distrustful of my body, and feel like it's my enemy, like i could really hurt someone completely by accident, and my insides start to feel really removed. and i think if i tell, that people wont want to be with me. that they'll judge my past and me in a way that is wholey new, and hateful. it's weird, i mean, i don't really have any reason to think that, and i know that isn't what will really happen, but it brings up so much of my scary past when i thought that my only worth in this women-hating world was my sex, and to have that rejected was a rejection of my entire self-worth. so i was thinking of just wearing an "i have herpes" button, but, well, i'm just not the button type.

UGH UGH UGH

(i feel stupid and dramatic and boring telling you these things) well, another secret has to do with being scared to sleep with girls. duh duh duh, i mean, the idea is great, but i get worried about what girls think of me, and worried that they won't like me and that they'll judge me a lot . . . i guess because that's how it was in my sick group of friends growing up. but i think i simplify it and that it's way more complicated than that—like, so much of the basis for friendships i have had has been sexual, and i dont really want it to be like that, but i always seem to end up kissing boys, because its comfortable and stuff . . . and lately its been pretty much fine. but still, i dont know, i deal in this sexual realm because i am comfortable there and feel secure there, but also i think it sometimes stops different kinds of friendships from emerging, like slow sneak-up-on-you kind of friendships. Like friendships founded on re-

Princess Phone
145

DORIS

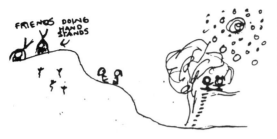

FRIENDS DOING HAND STANDS

ally common political ground. Lots of stuff, so i get worried about sleeping with girls, even though i know its a stupid way to process all this crap and a fucked-up way to deal with it, but sometimes it seems like girls are my biggest break from having to be a sexual being, and boy, do i need that fucking break.

and another one. i dont like menstruating. i don't hate it or anything, and it doesn't make me feel bad about myself or any of that creepy stuff like it used to, but it just annoys me. most of my women friends are really into their periods and i think that is so fucking cool. but i never did have the guts to say i don't like it.

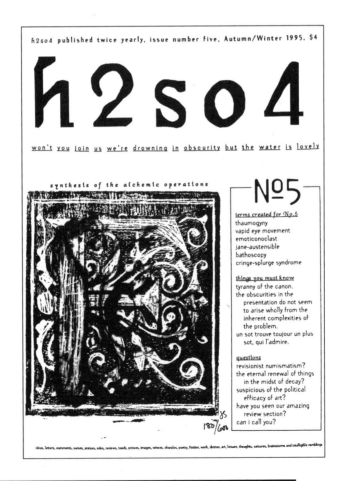

h2so4 published twice yearly, issue number five, Autumn/Winter 1995, $4

h2so4

won't you join us we're drowning in obscurity but the water is lovely

synthesis of the alchemic operations

No 5

terms created for No.5
thaumogyny
vapid eye movement
emoticonoclast
jane-austensible
bathoscopy
cringe-splurge syndrome

things you must know
tyranny of the canon.
the obscurities in the
   presentation do not seem
   to arise wholly from the
   inherent complexities of
   the problem.
un sot trouve toujour un plus
   sot, qui l'admire.

questions
revisionist numismatism?
the eternal renewal of things
   in the midst of decay?
suspicious of the political
   efficacy of art?
have you seen our amazing
   review section?
can i call you?

180/600

ideas, letters, comments, curses, praises, odes, reviews, toads, princes, images, wines, chorales, poetry, fiction, work, diction, art, leisure, thoughts, seizures, brainstorms and intelligible ramblings

top: DORIS. bottom: JILL STAUFFER, H2SO4

♥ ZINES: You should do one!

Writing a zine is simply the coolest thing ever.
WHY? because you can do whatever you want!
I started this zine about a year ago after being
pushed around by some lame-ass meathead
bouncer, I was pissed off about it, and felt
like telling the world, so I took a piece of
paper, wrote it down, doodled around it, ran
it off, put it around town w/ an address on
it, and that was the birth of the badgirl
club, now I'm getting all sorts of cool mail,
zines, I even got a little plastic purple
frog, acid and a letter from Malaysia.
So if you've got stuff to say, say it!
and say it in a zine. Its one of the
best ways to release, and if people read
your stuff and it strikes 'em as familiar
or "yeah, I know what they're talking about"
comes into their mind, you've related w/ some
one you dont even know — and thats so
cool! I could sit here and tell y'all how to do
it, but that'd be dumb, cuz you could do it
anx old way you want, and so can I,
and if people dont like it, they dont
have to read it. So hey, write a zine, and
send it to me, cuz I like trades a whole
lot better.

Having It and Eating It

by Nina Dentata (from Ben Is Dead)

ook, if you know something I don't, please tell me. I mean, is it something I say? Is it something I do? Maybe it's some bizarre unconscious vibe I'm giving off but *why why why* is it that the people I can't even imagine closer than two feet from *any* of my orifices end up liking me? Yes, yes, I know—you're right—of course it is partly because I, Nina Dentata, am irresistible. But if that's all it is, tell me this—why don't the people I want to like me, like me back? Impossible, you say? Oh please, save the flattery for when I'm in a better mood. This is real. I'm jinxed and I have to put an end to my suffering as soon as possible. Having too many people after me who I don't even like is giving me incredibly bad love karma. I'm dying of loneliness in a crowd I can't get away from. And, I have to come up with something quick before it gets any worse. I mean, I've even started having these recurring nightmares of being a contestant on that now-defunct frightening late night TV show for soft-core stalkers, *Infatuation.* You know, the one hosted by the undead Bob Eubanks.

Oh, the nightmare is so horrible. It's like I'll be minding my own business, just sleeping and dream-living the usual fantasies, and all of a sudden, Beelze-Bob appears. He looms over me as I realize I'm hanging suspended in the abysmal depths of the seventh circle of Love-Purgatory. You know, that's the one where unfulfilled promises of love float scattered here and there like so many uneaten Godiva chocolates thrown against a wall; where confessions of undying love fallen upon deaf ears echo eternally to the rhythm of Tony De Franco's "Heart Beat It's a Love Beat" in the crushed hollowness of heart-shaped cavernous walls. Oh, it scares me just thinking about it.

Anyway, there I am hovering in the seventh circle, thinking of a gentle yet witty way to turn down this suitor who is poised to bribe me for a date on national TV, when all of a sudden, I, Nina Dentata, am turned into the infatuated contestant. Pretty soon I realize I'm totally debasing myself, begging for a moment of private time with this person I thought was supposed to be shamelessly pursuing me. Then, as if that wasn't enough, I am slapped with the cold reality of a rejection I would've otherwise delivered. I scream out in shock and agony "AaaaaaAaa!!"—and hear myself whimpering to the uncannily-wrinkled countenance of the decrepit host.

"Beelze-Bob, help me. I'll do anything—sell my soul, sacrifice my unborn, handcuff myself to Penelope Spheeris until she makes a movie version of *The Newlywed Game*—anything you want, but please don't make my pathetic appearance on your show be in vain. I'm burning up in the hellfires of passion like a cheap Joan of Arc impersonation. Work your magic. Do something, anything, but make it happen for me, please!"

Then, in every nightmare without fail, the cruel Beelze-Bob seals my televised fate, cackling as only *he* can. "No, no, no. No whoopee, ah haha, no whoopee." I wake up every morning with his odious cackle stinging my ears, overcome by the humiliation, the torture . . . and that's only in my dreams. So don't go thinking I, Nina Dentata, sultress of unrequited love, don't know what it feels like to have my feelings hurt . . . cuz I do. OK?

But, despite my protracted suffering, I still don't know how someone as sincere and utterly un-flirtatious as myself can so often become the object of unwarranted infatuation. I just don't get it. Isn't love supposed to be based on some principle of reciprocity? There is even an ancient Chinese proverb about love, something like, "You can't eat hot noodles with only one chopstick." Anyway, the point is, when someone you don't like is subjecting you to unwanted attention, you want them to stop, right? Of course you do. So, if we all feel the same way, it only seems logical that you would extend the courtesy of bowing out gracefully in the reverse situation. Am I right or what? Don't bother answering—of course I'm right.

But, they say, desire is blind to right and wrong and maybe *that* is my problem. If desire is irrational, trying to logically comprehend it (let alone control it), is even more absurd. It must be absurd, cuz from the looks of the pretty mess that I call my love life, our present Generation XOXO is way over those arcane gestures of self-control. As my dear friend Kitty Leukemia would say, "it's like we have this game-show mentality toward love and its various connections propelling us to broadcast our emotions, to attain the syndicated thrill of victory." Even the agony of defeat seems to be better than retreat. Never mind whose feelings we tromp with our reckless disclosures, we feel it's our cable-accessible right to be heard.

But before you crash into yet someone else on the information superhighway of love, stop, look and listen to me, OK? When it comes to affairs of the heart, my darlings, honesty is *not* always the best policy. If you like someone who doesn't reciprocate your feelings and you just can't get over it, keep it to yourself. Of course, your feelings are your own to do with what you must, but like it or not, they do in-

Dammit Doll
When you want to climb the walls
Or just stand up and shout
Here's a little dammit doll
You just can't do without
Just grab it firmly by the legs
And find a place to slam it
And as you whack its stuffing
out - Shout -
Dammit! Dammit!
Dammit! Dammit!

Princess Phone
149

I HAVE BEEN KNOWN TO BE INDIGNANT. I HAVE ALSO BEEN KNOWN TO WEAR GINGHAM. ONCE UPON A TIME (ABOUT 3 YEARS AGO) I WAS BEING INDIGNANT AND WEARING GINGHAM AT THE SAME TIME, WHICH WAS APPARENTLY TOO MUCH FOR JESSYE AND KARA, FOR THEY FELT COMPELLED TO CREATE A SONG ABOUT IT. THUS "INDIGNANT GINGHAM" (THE SONG) WAS BORN, WHICH EVENTUALLY LED TO "INDIGNANT GINGHAM" THE ZINE, THE FIRST ISSUE OF WHICH YOU NOW HOLD IN YOUR HANDS. don't let go.

volve other people who more than likely would appreciate the consideration. Case in point: do you recall the campfire scene in *My Own Private Idaho*, River Phoenix confessing his love to a very unresponsive Keanu Reeves? Well, remember if you will, after that little episode, things went from unbearable to hellish for River in the film and now . . . Well, need I say more?

Not that I'm saying you should lie about how you feel. No no no. But why not weigh the importance of your loving feeling before you bite your tongue confessing something you will regret? Will your disclosure of desire forever strain a friendship? Be the death blow for another relationship you really value? Make *my* life miserable? Why suffer pathetically for your courtroom honesty when you could suffer poetically in silence over your precious unrequited love?

You're not buying this one, are you? OK, already, relax. It may be a thin line of argument between the poetics and pathetics of suffering, but don't go and dismiss the whole concept I'm working here. Bear with me a minute in *my* time of need. I, Nina Dentata, Venus with arms, am not going to let this misguided love nightmare I'm having continue to wreak havoc in my love life. Desperate times call for desperate actions, and if desire is irrational then maybe we all need to be a little irrational too—though admittedly it may be a stretch for me.

So what about this . . . Instead of shunning the desire of my star-crossed suitors, what if I just decided to reciprocate it? You know, end the unrequited love thing once and for all by looking for the good in these unfortunates. With a little determination, how hard can it be to turn the things you don't like about a pursuer into things you can't get enough of? Oh please, stop complaining, as if you have any better ideas.

OK, let's see, how can I work this? What if I try to see the annoying, groveling persistence of the undesired suitor as a charm point? After all, I am generally amused by a display of utter lack of self-respect. And I could let myself be caught off guard when they endlessly confess their love for me:

"What? *Me?* But I thought you already *had* a girlfriend." Remember the element of surprise is crucial since the infatuated *always* reveal more of themselves than you ever want to know. And by all means, I'll have to enjoy their awkward boldness. When they slip me the tongue in a good-night kiss, I'll just fight the urge to bite by repeating as a silent mantra, "You worship me, you worship me—how bad can you be?" I suppose, with the right amount of self-deception, I may even convince myself that I really like them. Lesser miracles have happened.

But what then? I mean, what is the possibility of a long-term love connection with these arrowless cupids? Of course, it depends on a mutual tolerance for pain, but having pursued an idealized image of me for so long, I would guess that they wouldn't take too well to the real me. (Yes, I admit it is a stretch of the imagination, but it is possible.) Then they would lose interest and, of their own accord, pack up and take their infatuation elsewhere. I'd be free of them at last, sort of.

Does this all mean that the only way you can get someone to leave you alone is to *not* want them to leave you alone? It looks like I'd be yet again unwillingly subjected to an irrational logic of desire, forever tainting my dreams of the perfect lover. Well, at least I tried. I may have been foiled by my rose-colored naiveté about the sad truth of love, but can you blame me for just wanting to make the world a better place for *me* to live in?

So, OK, it didn't work. But hey, if life were easy then all the stupid people would be smart. And since that obviously isn't the case, I, Nina Dentata, will get over it. I mean, you don't even have to read Lacan to figure out that the nature of desire sort of fucks the possibility of ever fully satisfying it anyway. And none of my insistence on the "right" thing to do is going to stop anyone from looking for love in all the wrong places or baring their soul on *Infatuation, Love Connection, Studs,* or whatever, if they really must. But at least I figured out this one thing—no matter how many chopsticks you have, 'having desire and eating it too' is no cake-walk.

Cyberscared

by Emelye (from Cupsize)

I t is the end of the twentieth century. Those in their early twenties should feel blessed (by whatever deity or lack thereof they wish) to experience the approaching millennium in the prime of youth. In an abstract, romantic sense, it truly is a wonderful event. But there are down sides. Right now, AT&T bombards America with advertisements for products we are not even sure exist yet. They blatantly admit that we do not need these products now, and only promise, as their slogan says, *"you will."* Will I? With the failure of any one religion or system of thought to prevail universally, humankind is instinctively constructing a secular medium that all can ascribe to; cyberspace [the on-line world, a word used by William Gibson in his novel, *Neuromancer*]. In the global world of multi-culturalism, relativism, and deconstruction, there can be no right and wrong, no great and bad or boring, just an accumulative mass of information being misidentified as *knowledge,* submitted piece by piece to databases through computers. Through the development of cyberspace, we are building the collective mind. Humankind's inclination to progress is not at its most fundamental about greed, accumulation, or human accomplishment, but a race for the tangible institution of collective being, an accessibility of information so complete that it provides instant omniscience to the participant in it.

In the haze of history that accompanies a liberal arts education, students are told a story of progress, change, and evolution. At our times of greatest nihilism, perhaps after having read Pynchon's *The Crying of Lot 49* and related to the self-conscious paranoia of its protagonist, we, exasperated, ask, "haven't I heard this story before?"; the story of the sense of a generation encroaching on doom. Has Generation X a right to fear the technological age that awaits it? Is their seeming laziness a rightful conservative reaction to the whirlwind of their first twenty years? In the span of their mean twenty years, the 8-track tape player has stayed around just long enough to be mocked, the cassette has been overrun by the compact disc, CD challenged by DAT systems, and all along vinyl has been loved the most. The generation approaching the millennium should distinguish their precise, distinct, and unique fears. In effect, learn to build an argument against progress—that not everything can be entered into cyberspace as data and retain its "essence."

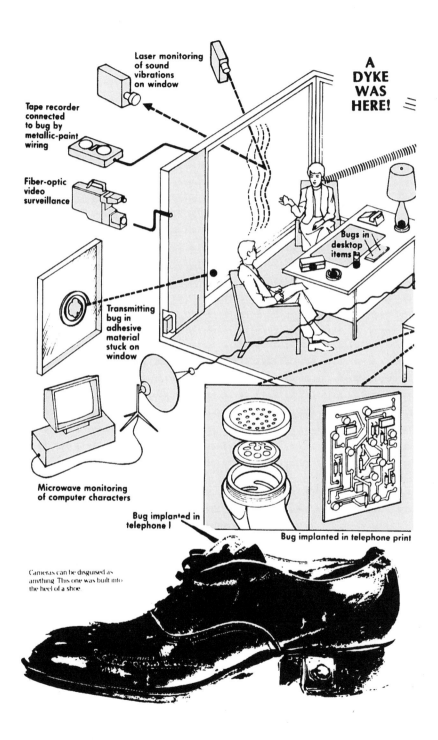

Laser monitoring of sound vibrations on window

Tape recorder connected to bug by metallic-paint wiring

Fiber-optic video surveillance

Transmitting bug in adhesive material stuck on window

Microwave monitoring of computer characters

Bugs in desktop items

A DYKE WAS HERE!

Bug implanted in telephone I

Bug implanted in telephone print

Cameras can be disguised as anything. This one was built into the heel of a shoe

J.T.O.

In a recent AT&T commercial, a child sits in front of a computer terminal. She is smiling. On the screen are graphics of a book. An encyclopedia. In this case, not only is the information of the book entered as data, but the form itself. With a click of the mouse, the pages turn before her. Graphically-produced images of pages turning. Setting aside obvious environmental advantages of on-line encyclopedias (less paper, less trees slaughtered, more forests) we must examine the urge to make this transition. Or how it is being sold to America. There is a seemingly instinctive drive to immediately turn all of life into an image of itself. Weddings are staged so that they look more real in the videotape than when they are actually taking place. This is more than a universal increase in vanity; we are building things to produce images, to represent the real objects and happenings of our lives. In cyberspace, rather than being the mere spectators of images, like in the local movie house, we are participants—creating the images, changing them, shaping them, interacting with them. Are we moving swiftly to a time when real actions and events and objects will be kept around merely for their anachronistic appeal? If this is the instinctive drive of humankind, is it ultimately a doomed process—can we distinguish when cyberspace has enveloped too many aspects of our physical and sensible world? If a series of generations only viewed books on cyberspace, would the graphics eventually just represent random blocks of color, no longer attached to the original object?

The vastness of the super highway scares me and does not intrigue me. I e-mail and that's it. I don't even use the PHONE function of most e-mail lines. It just all seems so ephemeral to me. When people try to teach me the rules to use MUDS and other databases, my brain shuts off, because I know the rules will probably be revised tomorrow or the whole "world" may be deleted in an hour. If a piece of information has a life-span of a day, I may just as well bypass it. Why do I want to go cruising through an arena of graphically produced sensations, "getting to know" cyberspace, when I haven't even been to Europe yet for real.

I am scared that the job market will insist that I exist in cyberspace. My humanity screams out against it. Am I a conservative, a reactionary? If I were around when the printing press was developed, would I have protested against that too, saying handwriting dictates nature's natural text reproduction rate and we shouldn't tamper with it? It's all changing so fast that I just can't get the energy to learn today what may be obsolete tomorrow. I don't want to spend my free-time existing bodiless in cyberspace. I could spend my whole life walking the streets of New York and not know everything. I'd rather start there than at a computer prompt.

I admit that I like limits. I like books with a beginning and an end. Is being able to remix Todd Rudgren's new album on CD-ROM really progress? Our forthcoming technological age overcomes boundaries like time, place, location. By global communication linkage, we can all be present all places at once. All information is accessible at all times. Time is not lost in tracking down books in libraries. Projected into a perfect future, all history and human discourse would be downloadable. The role of chance and limitation in shaping human life becomes less, or becomes limited to the function of technology. I had a hard enough time carving an existence for myself in my high school, learning the quirks of my peers, where I fit in. The prospect of existing with meaning in the infinite world of cyberspace makes me yearn for the simple days when my Commodore 64 was hot news on the block, but my neighbor's new BMX ruled over all.

ALIENATED

AND PROUD

Do you Believe in God?

by Collette (from <u>Looks Yellow, Tastes Red</u>)

These are the results from the religion question on the first twenty Reader's Poll thingies I got back:

Yes—25%

No—25% ("many reasons"/"I'm very confused about religion at this time in my life"/"I've never seen him and he never hears my cries"/"there are more important things to worry about").

Other answers—50% ("I believe in animism—God in everything everywhere"/"I believe in the Light"/"This isn't enough space"/"People should find something spiritual, it doesn't matter what"/"I don't like God very much *if* he exists"/"I believe there may be positive and negative energy floating around . . . religion is a pacifier for the masses"/"There is someone up there—I don't know who."/"I do believe in a higher power"/"I don't know"/"I'm a UU so it doesn't really matter")

A lot of people complained about the lack of space on the survey. If you want to write about your religious beliefs, I would be more than happy to print your thoughts in here.

I am, personally, by birth half Jewish (Russian) and half Roman-Catholic (Irish/Scottish). However, I don't believe that religion can be passed down like nationality can. I am neither Jewish nor Roman-Catholic, I have not personally accepted either religion. My family does not attend church or formally recite prayers.

When I was seven, I told some kids that I did not believe in God. There was a pure and simple statement—I did not know that there were other people who did not believe in God, I had only been thinking about it and had come to the conclusion that I did not believe in him. The other kids were mortified. I alternately told people I was an agnostic or an atheist as I got older. I don't know now. I *am* a spiritual person. I believe in balance—like Yin and Yang, etc. I like to think about reincarnation, though I really have no definite opinions about what happens when you die. I believe that all life is connected. I don't believe in God in the sense of an all-powerful creator who sits up in the sky somewhere pulling strings to direct our lives. Why would anyone want to waste their time doing that? And why would he want to punish us so brutally for things that he gave us the capability to do?

"DO YOU BELIEVE IN GOD?"

"YES, I HATE HIM!"

I like to talk about Satan. Satan is a joke to me. I do not believe he exists, literally or metaphorically. I do not believe that people possess "evil." I do not like the concept of "sin," I think it was contrived to control people's behavior. I feel bad when I say sacreligious things. I don't like to insult other people's beliefs. I admit that I think it's funny to talk about Jesus and the Antichrist. I do it all the time. I used to go around telling people that I was the Antichrist. In eighth grade my friend and I wanted to start a cult based on me being the Antichrist. I never wanted to offend anyone though.

I think that many religions are based on the concept of controlling their followers. It is important to many people to be spiritual in their own way, be it through a major religion or their own personal system of beliefs. There is nothing wrong with this, some religions *do* help people make sense of the world around them and help them lead more meaningful lives.

fondling the present
here & now
grabbing with both hands
mouth open
no scruples, no morals,
immediately
no time to wait, no time to waste
desperately.
the season is here
for bedroom talk
& naked conversation
passionate raging
ocean storm
of desire and lust
suck my nipples
grab my ass
firm, let's ride each other
throbbing between
the cheeks
waves of heat
tingling electrical
power
fantasy embodied,
no inhibitions
mono on mono
clitoris caress
enter, thrusting, gasping
muy caliente,
obscene words yes,
awesome, yes,
quiver, shudder, horn
no bullshit,
just fuck

Princess Phone

157

Sexists on the 'Net

by Sara Marcus (from Kusp)

his is about my experience with the now-famous e-mail list by four cornell freshmen entitled "75 reasons women (bitches) should not have freedom of speech." i believe i received
it maliciously—it arrived from an unfamiliar address at the university of
maryland, and since over half of my high school goes there, and

she doesn't need to talk to get me a beer.

since everyone at my high school knew me as a big-time feminist, i think
some random classmate of mine sent it to mess me up. it worked. i sat frozen in the overheated
basement computing center, my stomach boiling. the list was full of more woman-hating than i had
ever seen—more than i had believed really existed.

for the rest of the day i couldn't be around boys. even those who were my friends, i kept think-

nothing should come out of a woman's mouth—SWALLOW BITCH!!

ing "he might have laughed at this, he might have agreed
with even one of the items." one boy said hi to me on the
sidewalk and i snarled, half in tears, "just say the word
'bitch' to me. i dare you, just say it." i was hostile and nau-
seous all day, reflecting on the absolute hatred of women that would prompt men to write such
things and other people to pass them on.

luck was on my side, though: it was the eve of the "young ♀'s day of action." late that night, i
met with members of my guerrilla theater group and other feminist organizations, and we set off to
transform the campus. "end male domination and misogyny," i chalked in front of the main library
buildings and sidewalks, hung pictures of women on top of the oil portraits of white men that grace
most dining halls, and clothed the statues of men on the old campus quad with dresses and bras.
nathan hale in a miniskirt. it was rich. we laughed and shrieked and dashed all over campus until well

**this is my dick. i'm go-
ing to fuck you with it.**

past midnight, cathartic and healing.
a week or so later, i received the hateful list again, this time with
the e-mail addresses of the self-titled "four players of cornell"
and an exhortation to flood their mailboxes with outraged letters of con-
demnation. if this had been my first experience with the list, i would have

**if she can't speak,
she can't cry rape.**

blasted these kids, but now i couldn't muster the fierceness to do it. i had already exorcised this list and its effects from my life, and i had no desire to deal with it any more. i also couldn't justify writing to them. my letter wouldn't show them not to hate women, but only not to put it out on the internet where people could get a hold of it. what would have been better, i think, would have been to forward the list to every woman at cornell, so the jerks would never have a date again. outraged students everywhere flamed the "four players;" bryn mawr's computer system shut down under the strain of all the e-mail going out. cornell's administration figured out what was going on, but determined that the boys were just exercising free speech when they sent the list out to twenty of their

 personal friends (i agree). the boys did publish an apology in the cornell paper, but i bet they didn't mean it. they've probably concluded from this experience that women are controlling bitches who deserve every bit of hatred we get and then some.

one of the "four players" is from a town near me. he went to the best public school in my county, and my county is near the top when it comes to public education. the question nobody is asking is, where were these boys taught to view women as fuck toys and punching bags? how can we prevent the attitudes instead of trying to silence expression of these attitudes? the expression definitely needs *not* to be silenced. i learned a lot about misogyny from reading that list, and witnessing other people's reactions to it. people had been asking me all week why a "young ♀'s day of action" was still needed, now that women had equal rights and all, and i actually had a hard time answering. the list was a powerful reminder for me of how far we have to go before we change the structure of this rape culture. we all need wake-up calls like this sometimes. ♀

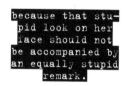

Princess Charming

by Lauren Martin (from Princess Charming)

January, 1996

ecome the princess charming of your dreams." *Princess Charming* is about self-reliance. It's about not waiting to be rescued because you can rescue yourself. It's about self-empower-ment and self-love. At the same time it recognizes the importance of self, *Princess Charming* also recognizes the importance of friendships. It recognizes that girl-love and support can help women to become strong enough to be their own saviors. *Princess Charming* is about me, *Princess Charming* is about you. We all have the capability inside of us to become our very own *Princess Charmings*.

Princess Charming began as a side project of mine in May of 1995. I always discuss feminist issues in my other zines, but this has become a forum where I can completely devote myself to the topic of girl empowerment. At the time, I thought it would just be a one-shot zine. But I've decided to put out another issue. I see a need for this and maybe even for future issues. As with the last issue, *Princess Charming* is free (but stamps are nice) to help make this available to anyone who wishes to read it. If you'd like to contribute in spreading the word, please feel free to copy and distribute this. Either make copies of the one you have in your hand, or else write me and I'll send you a flat copy or a couple of issues. *Princess Charming* needs your support.

I am not a spokesperson. These are *my* definitions. They may not be "right," and you may not agree with them. But that's OK, cuz I know what *I* believe in and I'll try my hardest to fight for it.

This time I'd like to talk more about girl love. Cuz there's a lot more that needs to be said about it. Like the misconceptions surrounding it.

Girl love ≠ man hate

Do you hear me? It does not. Why should it? The two have nothing at all to do with each other. Why do some people assume it does? It's yet another example of how male-centered this society is. Just because I support my "sisters," it should not follow that I am trying to put down my "brothers."

So what is girl love? To me, it doesn't necessarily mean loving all women just because they are women. I still believe that people need to reciprocate love and respect to maintain it, girls included. That's what some girls have problems with in this "girl love" discussion. They don't want to be forced into forgiving all the shitty things that girls do to each other. But that's not what girl love is about. If *anyone* fucks me over, I'm not going to love them, no matter what their anatomy is.

Girl love is supporting each other. Girl love is giving other girls the benefit of the doubt. Girl love is helping other girls. Girl love is not sitting back when your sisters are being raped, abused, harassed, laughed at, or discriminated against. Girl love is recognizing the fact that a boy on your arm is not necessarily the key to happiness. Girl love is not tearing down other girls.

You do not have to be Ms. Supreme Alternakiddie to practice girl love. You do not have to be a riot grrrl. You do not have to be punk as fuck. Girl love is not limited to those of us in "the scene." Girl love should spread to the masses. That's where it's needed the most. The thing about *Princess Charming*, about zines like this, is that most of those who read them are already familiar with the subject. We're not the ones who need to be "enlightened."

But, I think there's still a lot more we have to learn and realize. There needs to be clarification. Even from those of us who call ourselves feminists, riot grrrls, proponents of girl love and "the revolution." I'm talking about the way *we* treat other girls, the words *we* use to disparage one another.

As women, we know how much emphasis is put on our appearances. We know how it affects our daily lives. Yet we still judge other women on the basis of their appearance, we still use the way a woman looks to put her down. Have you heard yourself utter the following words? Be honest. Most of us have. I admit it. I've done it:

"I hate her; she's too skinny."
"Do you think she's pretty? I don't think she's even that pretty."
"Why is *he* with *her*? He could do better."
"She should *not* be wearing that outfit!"
"Fat bitch."

I've been trying to stop myself before I say any of these or other harmful things. And, though not as often, although I know I should, sometimes I point it out to other girls when they do it. When I told

Princess Phone
161

one friend that, "I don't believe in putting down other women because of their appearance," it was such a foreign concept to her, and she didn't understand why. Face it, we've been bred and trained to notice these things, to pick each other apart by the way we look. It all comes down to this: *girl competition.*

We are still competing with each other for the attention of boys. We are still competing with each other because of our own insecurities and jealousies. Why are we still competing? Girl competition = girl hate.

There's also a lot of self-girl-hate going on. Too often do I hear girls complaining about their weight, about their lack of boyfriends. One of the most disturbing things I have been hearing is girls wishing that they hadn't done sports because it caused their legs to develop muscle. *Muscle!!* Women should be proud of their muscle, which symbolizes their *strength,* hard work, and activity.

And then there's the whole model thing (just *model*—are they any more "super" than you or me?). I do not hate models. I know that a lot of you may, but I refuse to. Why? Because I don't know those models, and they have done nothing to me. I *don't* respect them or what they do, but I don't agree with *hating* Kate Moss because she is skinny. Is it her fault that some corporate assholes picked her body type as an ideal for us all to follow, and heralded the waif? Models are not the ones to blame for setting up unrealistic beauty ideals. Instead of hating the women in the pictures and on the runways, we can turn around and focus that energy on the system *behind* those models and on the people who put them there. Don't buy the magazines that feature models of unrealistic standards and proportions. Don't buy clothes or products of designers and companies who use these models on their runways or in their advertisements. Most importantly, *don't let them get to you;* don't let them make you feel any less perfect or beautiful than you really are. Let's change the society in which a few "elite" women's appearances can determine how we are all looked at and judged, how we all feel about our own bodies.

Oh, and concerning the previous issue, where I discussed the way women are affected by the myths of fairy tales and fashion mags? I neglected to mention the unique take it has on women of color (which was doubly lame of me, considering *I* am a woman of color); how the ideal of the tall, emaciated yet voluptuous woman is an ideal mostly of *White women.* I've read books and essays by women who were disappointed by Kate Wolf's *The Beauty Myth* because the book concerned itself mostly with the way *White* women are affected by the myth. bell hooks discusses this in *Outlaw Culture—Resisting Representations,* as do several young women in *Listen Up!: Voices from the Next Feminist Generation,* edited by Barbara Findlen.

I saw some show on ABC hosted by John Stossel a couple of months ago. In one segment of it, he discussed the subject of women's body size and image. He asked several women how much of an issue it was to them. There were differences across racial lines, according to the women he interviewed. White and Asian women were very preoccupied with their weight. Young White women are more likely than anyone to develop eating disorders. It was different for Latinas and African American women. Body size was less of an issue to them.

An article I read in the Winter 1996 issue of *Hues* magazine (a new mag aimed at young women—I highly recommend you pick yourself up a copy) entitled "The Big Picture—Do Black Women Have Better Body Image Than White Women?" backs this up. They cite a study done by the University of Arizona that found that 90% of White junior high school girls don't like their bodies, while 70% of African American girls of the same age do. They cite the fact that having the ability to *choose* to starve is viewed almost as a privilege, and is none too appealing to many Black women who have seen so much poverty in their history.

Women of color are increasingly becoming more and more affected by White images of beauty in the popular media, and more and more of them are developing eating disorders and getting plastic surgery to fit into that ideal. Women of color *are* affected by the White beauty myth. It is no coincidence that many of the top African American models have "typically" White features. *All* women are affected by beauty/body image, and we cannot forget that.

As a side note, men are also becoming more and more affected by body image too, as some of my male readers have pointed out to me. Being "buff" and "fit" has gained increasing importance as the sexual objectification of men has become all the more popular in the media.

Princess Charming needs dialogue. I need you to write to me and tell me what you think, to point out any inaccuracies, to share information, to bring to the light other issues that are important to you and that you think need discussion.

Thank you for listening.

men? I thought I'd let them speak for themselves
by Jennifer

"All that came from your pretty little head?"
-Randy, ex-boyfriend

"What do you think of implants?"
–My ex-doctor during a breast examination

"You'd be pretty if you wore some makeup"
-Stranger at the county fair

"DON'T WORRY, IF YOU GET PREGNANT I'LL MARRY YOU."
-BOB, EX-BOYFRIEND

"Are you serious about a career? Or do you just want to pay off your car?"
-Executive during a job interview

YOU SHOULD WEAR PINK."
-JEFF, EX-BOYFRIEND

"Spread your legs and pretend I'm not here."
–My ex-gynecologist

"I thought you were attractive, until you stuck that cigarette in your mouth."
-Stranger at a mall

"Do you pump your own gas?"
-Executive at job interview

LOOSAH

"You'll make some man a nice little secretary."
–Grandpa

"YOU GET TO LAY AROUND ALL DAY AND READ NOVELS—I WISH I WAS AN ENGLISH MAJOR."
-BRIAN, EX-HUSBAND

"I KNOW I'M NOT SUPPOSED TO ASK, BUT ARE YOU ON BIRTH CONTROL?"
-EXECUTIVE AT JOB INTERVIEW

"THINK OF IT AS A POWER TRIP—AS LONG AS YOU'RE SUCKING MY DICK, YOU'RE CONTROL-LING ME."
-FRED, EX-BOYFRIEND

"We can't let you accompany your husband to our country, you'll distract him from his studies."
-Japanese ambassador

Runaway Daughters and Rebel Girls

No zine book would be complete without tackling some of the more difficult issues in the lives of girls and women. We must not forget that a lot of women create zines to break the silence against taboo topics like incest and rape. Zines are also used as a rallying tool to make people aware of the injustices in this society. This section discusses tough issues like race, class, and violence against women. But these girls don't just discuss things; they are motivated and are finding ways of fighting back.

DIANA MORROW

Fall/Winter 1996   ADULTS ONLY

P U C K E R U P

The Gender Issue

Kate Bornstein
Loren Cameron
Chloe of the Transisters
Leslie Feinberg
Sandra Lee Golvin
Marga Gomez
Gerry Gomez Pearlberg
Della Grace
Karen Green
Kate Lambert
Laure Leber
Alvin Alfred Orloff
Rachel Pepper
Carol Queen
Dennis Rodman
Camille Roy
D. Travers Scott
Michele Serchuk
Linda Smukler
Christopher Stahl
Marc Swan
Tristan Taormino
Alison Tyler
Riki Anne Wilchins

Gender Icons:

Lily
Mo B. Dick
Mildréd "Dréd" Gerestant
Hopey
Buster Hymen
Lovechild & Erotica
Michelley Queen of Queens
Glennda Orgasm
Nicole Zaray

$5US, $6CAN   Volume 1, Issue 4

What was your first exposure to zines? The first zine I remember seeing was in the early eighties—it was a zine called *No Worries,* and it was done by a girl and her friends. This was long before there was any kind of girl zine culture, but maybe it's why I never thought that zines were a "boy thing." Not long after that, I actually started helping a guy that I knew do his zine. And then a few years later, I ended up working on this punk zine, *No Idea.* I hadn't founded the zine, so I didn't consider it "my" zine, but I co-edited and co-published three issues. This was my first real experience with the response to girls doing zines. Even though I always did half the work—and for one issue, I did more than half the work—people would still always assume that it was my male co-publisher's zine. People assumed I must be just his girlfriend or I just helped out. I was surprised that people didn't believe that I actually could have that much of a contribution to the zine. We were also putting on shows locally, and the same kind of thing was happening. I would do all this work for the show, and then a guy who showed up when the band got there would get thanked by the band and they wouldn't mention me. I was really starting to get angry. So, I started my first zine (which I did by myself)—*Mad Planet,* a music zine. I figured if I did the entire zine myself and no one else's name was on it except for mine, people

An Interview With Action Girl's Sarah Dyer
by Tristan Taormino

would have to realize that I did the work. And still, I got three reviews that said it was someone else's zine. One reviewer listed a guy who had done one comic strip in the entire zine as the editor!

I started reading a lot of zines, and I started really wanting to find other girls who were doing zines. And I would look and look and look for zines that were edited by girls, and I could not find them. I had found maybe three or four, just a few, in 1990, and it was really frustrating me. At that time, *Factsheet Five* wasn't coming out—it was on hiatus for a couple years. I went to the UK for a comic convention and found this zine called *Girl Frenzy* with all women contributors. It had a list of all these zines, and there were eight zines listed from the United States that were by women that I had never heard about. I couldn't believe that this stuff existed and I couldn't find out about it. So that was why I started the *Action Girl Newsletter* because I figured if *I* want to find other girls doing zines, *they* probably want to find other girls, too. The first issue of the newsletter was one side of one page—that was literally every zine in the United States and Britain that I could find being done by a girl. That was all of them!

So, it started out as just one page—give me a brief history of

the *Action Girl Newsletter.* I placed classified ads in other zines for the one-page newsletter, and I sent the newsletter out to people who were doing zines. It happened coincidentally that I did that right as the Riot Grrrl movement was starting, so a lot of girls were just starting to do zines. Every time I did an issue, the number of new zines I got back would double or triple! Also, a lot of the letters I've gotten were from girls who found out about zines from *Sassy* or *Seventeen.* They didn't know anything about zine culture; they just heard about this idea. I was getting mail from young girls—as young as twelve years old—who totally were not clued in to zine culture, but wanted to do their own zine. So, I started getting all these zines from all different kinds of girls. None of the zines I had originally listed in that first issue of the newsletter were really like "girl zines"— they were all zines that happened to be done by girls.

As we have put together this book, we define girl zines as zines done primarily by and for girls and women. What do you consider a girl zine? Riot Grrrls got so much press and hype that people thought that all girl zines were Riot Grrrl zines. I tried to let people know that Riot Grrrl zines are part of a larger movement of girl zines, which are zines by girls which are specifically about being a girl and the "female experience." I started *Action Girl* in 1992, and it wasn't until the next year that I really started seeing what you might call girl zines. Up until that, it was mainly zines about music, literature,

art, etc. that happened to be by women. But women always include stuff that is in specifically girl zines, stuff about things happening to girls.

So how many issues of the *Action Girl Newsletter* have you produced, and what's happening now with it? There are thirteen regular issues, two special issues and an on-line edition which has only been up for a few months. I got up to thirteen issues last year and that's when I put it on hiatus because I was getting ten to twenty new zines every day on top of dozens of letters, orders, and mail about my comics. I got to a point where I couldn't even look at another zine. And, at that point, I felt like the network of girl zines had grown strong enough that if I stepped back, it wouldn't collapse. I mean, for the first couple of years, the *Action Girl Newsletter* was really a hub for girls to network with each other. But last year, I felt that if I went away for a while, everyone would be fine. I had completely sacrificed everything else in my life to do this, and I just had to take a break.

Zines have been getting a lot of press and there are a bunch of different zine books in the works that are all getting lumped together. But I think that girls making zines is a very specific thing. What do you think? Coming from originally doing punk zines and then watching this whole girl zine culture develop, I find that the girls doing zines are coming from a really different place. Traditionally, zines have been done by people already involved in a subculture—whether it's science fiction or poetry or punk rock or whatever. But girl zines are a form of expression for girls, regardless of what subculture they may belong to. I did a project with *Seventeen* magazine which was actually a positive experience. I had done a special edition of *Action Girl* for the CMJ Music Festival with a woman who was involved with this women-in-music group. Someone from *Seventeen* saw it and contacted me. They were getting all these letters from girls who heard about zines but didn't know anything about them. I did a special edition and they ran a little plug, and I stopped counting at 1,000 orders. It ran two and a half years ago, and I still must get one order a day from a girl who read that back issue of *Seventeen*. These girls were all from the middle of nowhere who don't have access to lots of publications. I've gotten letters and zines back from a lot of people from that *Seventeen* piece. I know that girls from New York City and Berkeley can find out about this stuff, but I'm concerned about the girls in other places; these are the girls who really make girl zine culture different. They are not from a subculture; they are completely traditional American girls who've discovered this way of expressing themselves that they weren't getting anywhere else. That was a real crowning moment for me—that all these girls who had no access to stuff were able to get into zines.

Where do you think we are in the girl zine movement? I think it's difficult for girls to do zines as they get older or go to college or leave home, because it's an expensive endeavor. I think that a lot of girls who did zines have since quit because it's so much work and they don't really have the money. I've noticed that a lot of girls that I am still in touch with who don't do a zine anymore have gone into other kinds of publishing work. And a lot of them are doing writing which they may not have done, if they hadn't done a zine. They've learned a lot of skills, and they know these other girls around the country who are doing different things, and I think that's really important.

We are at a very tumultuous moment in feminist history, full of volatility, confusion, and division, as well as progress and change, but feminism is on shaky ground at best with mainstream media. There are a lot of girls and women who don't want to identify themselves as feminists; there's all this debate about what a feminist is and what a feminist issue is. To me, a lot of girl zines are very clearly feminist—although they won't necessarily call themselves that. I'm wondering what connections you see between girl zines and feminism. That is one of the most common things that girls write to me about. They are completely into what most people would consider "feminist" ideas—body issues, equality, choice—but they'll write to me and say, "I really believe in these ideas, but I can't be a feminist or a riot grrrl because I like to wear makeup or I have a boyfriend." Feminists of the original Women's Movement of the seventies don't understand that young women of today grew up with the things that feminism was trying to achieve for women. So, adolescence is completely different today. Certainly, it was the strides they made that have made our lives easier, but I think that older feminists don't understand that younger feminists' lives are different than theirs. For example, many don't understand why my friends and I prefer the term "girl" over "woman." They think girl is a horrible insult. To us, well, we actually prefer it.

One of the most important results of the girl-zine movement seems to be a general interest in empowerment for girls—do you agree? I always thought that self-empowerment was the most important part of zine-making. That ability to express yourself and learn about yourself is so important, and there aren't that many opportunities for girls to empower themselves. Doing zines, or in fact accomplishing anything, can really affect your life. One of the most important things about my *Action Girl* projects, to me, is to constantly emphasize my philosophy of ACTION. I totally believe that doing things for yourself is the key to taking control of your life and becoming empowered. And I don't think it has to be anything as obvious as doing a

zine or playing guitar—anything can be empowering! Learning to sew, or cook, helping someone else on their zine, doing a web page, volunteering . . . one of my most empowering experiences was when I moved up to New York City after I finished college. I had rented a small truck, and when I went to pick it up they said, "Oh, sorry, all out, here's a 24′ truck at no extra charge!" I just about lost it—not only did my stuff only take up about one corner of this monster truck, but I was terrified of driving it! But I drove it by myself all the way up the East coast, and I learned that I could handle a huge truck just fine. I got total respect from all the guys at all the truck stops I filled the tank at. Things like that give you confidence, and that confidence spills over into the other areas of your life. That's why I think it's so important to continually learn to do new things and to always be the person in control of your life by being active, and never passive.

And the great thing about girl zines, and other girl-power-related acts (putting on shows, making cool shirts, writing for zines, doing comics, you name it!) is that anyone can do them—it's a road to empowerment that is available to everyone. You don't have to join a club so that you can be validated by other people. You don't have to follow anyone else's rules; you just do what's right for you, and you *are* girl power!

I have proudly aligned myself with feminism for over eleven of my brief twenty-two years. Even in the rocky years of junior high, when such ideas didn't win me any friends or popularity, I hooked an abortion rights pin to my shirt for my class picture. For years, throughout high school and most of college, it's been at the bedrock of my values, suspicions, analysis, snap judgments, and total worldview.

Three years ago, I transferred to Barnard College, a Seven Sisters school affiliated with Columbia University, having narrowly escaped from Amherst, a claustrophobic old boys' club in Massachusetts. But when I graduated from Barnard this May, I left another school with a sour taste in my mouth, not only about the College, but also about liberal feminism in general, the philosophy that informs the outlook of my school, its leaders, and most of its students.

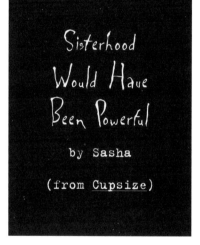

Sisterhood Would Have Been Powerful

by Sasha

(from Cupsize)

In the months before I donned my slate blue cap and gown, a bitter labor strike unfolded a few feet from the buildings where I took my seminars, and as I watched, I became older, wiser and decidedly more skeptical of liberal feminism. It was a strike with a statistically unusual and incredibly revealing twist: on the one side was my school, a place that sells itself as a feminist institution. On the other was a union of predominantly women. They are the lowest-paid group on campus: secretaries, desk attendants, and clerical workers.

For over four months, this was the scene outside of Barnard's serene, leafy oasis in Manhattan: an exhausted picket line of mainly female workers of different races, fenced in by blue police barricades. As backpack-wearing Barnard and Columbia students scurried past them every day, they picketed in a circle in front of a banner reading BARNARD CUTS WOMEN AND CHILDREN FIRST, and sometimes ceaselessly chanted, "2-4-6-8; Barnard discriminates." After the novelty of such a noisy campus conflict wore off, few students paid attention and the strikers became strangely invisible. But to me, the raucous, and then as months wore on, increasingly subdued picket line was an image that should have made the enduring fault lines of liberal feminism—race and class—starkly visible to everyone who walked onto Barnard's tiny campus in Morningside Heights.

In the first few days after the initial walk-out in February, a group of sympathetic students formed the Student Strike Committee, which organized student support for the union and pressured the administration to settle a contract. By May, the administration had told seven seniors on the Committee, including me, that our diplomas would be delayed because of our participation in a four-hour sit-in. At this point, the press took an inordinate amount of interest in our diplomas, after ignoring the strike for months, revealing at once the inanities and biases of the mainstream press.

The delay was really just a thinly disguised way to intimidate students and quell protest at graduation. But as it turned out, the Student Strike Committee had voted on silent protest for commencement anyway, where, for the better part of two hours, I sat in the crowd, slumped in my alphabetically assigned seat, unmoved by the pomp and circumstance. As I listened to speaker after speaker tell the Class of '96 that nowadays, women can do anything, I became restless and impatient for the president to begin her address. At that moment, if no security guards were the wiser, three underclasswomen who had been hiding for hours would drop a banner reading ANTI-WORKER = ANTI-WOMAN from the roof of the library, directly above the podium where the president would give her speech. At that cue, forty students and I, out of a class of 530, would rise to face her holding placards of mute protest.

Please consider this article the commencement address I so sorely wished someone had made.

Many of the people who were picketing outside graduation are Black and Latino, many sole breadwinners for their families. The salaries of this predominantly female union are modest, averaging $24,000 a year, less than what their counterparts earn at the other schools in the University. They consider employer-paid health-care benefits the main reason to work for Barnard.

In an effort to control what they see as "spiraling health-care costs," the college has insisted that workers contribute to health-care premiums and switch to the health plan used by faculty and administrators. In their one substantial concession since February, Barnard has asked that only new workers pay for health care. Local 2110 of United Auto Workers opposes this proposal, maintaining that a two-tiered system would divide new and old workers, weaken their ability to negotiate as a group, and open the door to health-care contributions for everyone in the near future, which was Barnard's original objective anyway. Both union members and the administration acknowledge that this standoff is really about power and safeguarding for the future. But in my opinion, one group—a school with a multimillion-dollar endowment—has far more financial flexibility than the other. Barnard has spent far more on scabs, lawyers, mediation, PR, and other sundry costs than they hoped to save in the beginning, and as of July, the strike is still unresolved.

This is the longest strike in the history of Columbia University. The directive comes from the freshly inaugurated President Judith R. Shapiro, an anthropologist who did her work on transsexualism. When she arrived last year, so many in the "Barnard community" gushed about her, delighted that the college had a self-identified feminist as president.

Moments before the most significant women's event of the year, I was standing with my feet planted solidly on the sidewalk, outside the gates to Barnard at eight o'clock on a warm April night. It was the Take Back the Night march through Morningside Heights, the one night of the year when women formally reclaim to streets. As hundreds of women pour out of campus onto Broadway, I separate myself and cluster with the women union members who have been leafleting the crowd. Streams of women rush past me, triumphant, some arm in arm, and I listen to the chants, "Women Unite, Take Back the Night." They ring sickeningly hollow and false to my ears. This year, I will not join the march, as I have done in the two years past. I have found that most of the women before me tend to see "women's issues" as a preordained set of concerns in a vacuum, divorced from politics in general, and consequently fail to make the obvious connections to issues unmention-ed in Women's Studies 101. Most of them have ignored the strike, which seemed to me like the most pressing "women's issue" on campus.

Perhaps most maddening of all was the myopia of the "feminist" students in allegedly political groups. So few of them challenged Barnard on what seemed to me like an obvious contradiction: the gap between what Barnard practices and what they teach. With their noses buried in Judith Butler and other pomo theorists of the moment, those girls didn't even see it themselves.

I had hoped that more students at a women's college would appreciate that feminism is about more than networking and dressing for success. But instead, Barnard produces graduates who think that becoming a woman CEO is a feminist act. They are resume-obsessive, grade-driven, and soon to be power feminists in power suits.

They are, after all, coming of age at an elite school in a reactionary time. It should be no surprise that most Barnard students are in step with the majority of White, middle to upper-class America. They share the peculiar belief that they live in a classless, casteless society.

With the benefit of hindsight, I wouldn't expect that many would be actively supportive of the union: we live at a time when particularly on campuses, identity politics trumps class-consciousness, when union membership has been declining in recent years and labor has become vilified. At the same time, surprising numbers of people have absorbed Republican rhetoric and accept the idea that everyone should "take responsibility," regardless of how little money you make. And of course, Barnard is also a school that costs more than the average salary of the striking workers, and half of the students don't receive any financial aid.

The Barnard library is full of promise in other places, like the third floor stacks, housing books by more visionary feminists. Throughout all of the draining, acrimonious debate on campus, when students would tell me that the strike was *not* a feminist issue, I held on to this deceptively simple definition: "Feminism is the political theory and practice to free *all* women: women of color, working-class women, poor women," said Barbara Smith, at the 1979 National Women's Studies Association convention. "Anything less than this is not feminism, but merely female self-aggrandizement."

Twenty years after Barbara Smith made those remarks about self-aggrandizement and feminism, some historians have observed that in a bitter irony, the classes of women who never had a choice about working and stood to gain the most from the women's movement have arguably seen the least meaningful changes in their lives.

The second wave of feminism has brought many wonderful things, among them, a momentous influx of women into the professions. But, by 1990, 80 percent of working women were still clustered in undervalued sex-segregated jobs, like clerical work. In these kinds of jobs, women earn 70 cents on the male dollar because of structural sexism: the logic that women's work is less skilled than men's, and the enduring idea that men, and not women, should earn enough to support an entire family. Women's lower wages are also a result of female exclusion from labor unions in the thirties, forties, and fifties.

When sociologists talk about the "feminization of poverty," they are talking about these women. In the last twenty years, more and more mothers are unpartnered and stuck in the pink collar ghetto, which pays them barely enough to feed, clothe, and house their children. If current trends continue, some scholars estimate that by the year 2000, the poverty population will be composed entirely of women and their children.

That background, against which we see a minority of women incorporated into the power structure, should tell us that dismantling barriers to female advancement is not enough. I saw this acutely, every day this past semester at Barnard. Such liberal strategies that ignore structural inequality generally benefit only women who can take advantage of resulting opportunities, girls (like me) who can go to fancy schools and have "careers." Consequently, liberalism winds up leaving the rest of the sex in the dust, doing pink collar work for unfairly low wages, possibly without health insurance, child care, or any hopes of breaking out.

Liberal feminism is also atomizing: it privileges individual female achievement (like a Barnard grad becoming a CEO) over collective struggle. Individualism works fine for women who have profited from reforms and have something to show for it, but does little for the women who are floors below the glass ceiling and need the power of their numbers. Liberalism offers nothing to those on the losing side of the class war, whose only real means to seek redress is collective action as a group.

In addition, the essentially conservative nature of classical liberalism prevents feminism from engaging with the possibility of serious structural change. Without that kind of change, sisters will remain unequal.

The interests of labor and the interests of capital are inherently in conflict, and any gains that working women and men win, indeed, any gains that any group wins, are inevitably wrested in the context of that dialectic. Feminists need to start to grapple with their alliances in the very real, but largely unreported class war continuing in this country and throughout the world. A liberal women's movement that ignores the question of restraining or dismantling capitalism is doomed to become purely bourgeois. Which side are feminists on?

I t is true, and somewhat disturbing, that many modern independent women not only will not call themselves feminists, but will deny the name if given it and speak badly of those who would claim the name. And there are those who claim the name who then take it upon themselves to dictate to others the "acceptable" forms of *dogma, vocabulary,* and *political orientation.* There is a misunderstanding afoot with regards to what feminism is.

Feminism has become a branch of academia, and, like any other branch (say, philosophy . . .), contains many different schools of thought within its supposed whole. And, like philosophy, no human being could possibly, nor would one want to, agree with each and every school of thought contained within feminism, especially considering that many of them contradict one another. If one wants to include the concept of "freedom" within one's worldview, one has to allow for the fact that *not everyone will agree* about what the steps are on the path to attaining "freedom," and that such disagreement has to be "OK."

I am a feminist, and I do not like what a lot of feminists do or say. I do not like being told

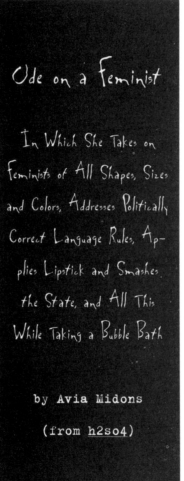

Ode on a Feminist

In Which She Takes on Feminists of All Shapes, Sizes and Colors, Addresses Politically Correct Language Rules, Applies Lipstick and Smashes the State, and All This While Taking a Bubble Bath

by Avia Midons

(from h2so4)

that there is a party line to which I must kowtow; I do not like being handed a tray of dictates that are just as restricting as the patriarchal role structure that feminism supposedly desires to *smash or subvert.* But I am a feminist and I will say so, and I would go so far as to assert that any feminist who tries to place limitations on what can be included under the rubric of "feminism" has betrayed the original intention and meaning of the word. There can be no inherent contradiction in this: I can read Mary Daly and wear Chanel lipstick, I can wear Betsy Johnson and smash the state. I can love men, women, eat meat, be a vegetarian, prefer activism or dance clubs, be straight-edge or use drugs. I can be a lawyer, a mother, a writer or an astronaut. . . . Contradiction enters into the picture only when I am told by my feminist sisters or mothers (or brothers) that my choices must be constrained, *that I must change, alter to someone else's design,* in order for me to be "free."

Of course, change *is* what we want. But I don't want the new roads chosen for me.

Feminism, if it is to have any viable meaning at all, must mean that women make their own choices, live their lives according to their own definitions. That is the only true path to "freedom," power, or self-determination. I suppose we're seeking "equality," but what that means in this world I don't know. I am always wary of slippery-slope words that are so easily defined by *those who write dictionaries* . . . equal to what? For whom? On whose terms? Ending up where? Let's just say we're seeking to *live*.

Of course we all need to work together on whatever common ground we can find to call attention to the issues that matter to us. Splintered interest groups tread water and go nowhere. *This is the history of liberalism.* But you can hold your own and help others at the same time. It has to be possible to do this, we must make room for these efforts, or we are doomed. Think about how we have had a feminist "movement" for decades, and still, affordable child care for mothers who must work is not available, men are, for the most part, paid more than women for the same jobs, and gynecological exams are often not "covered" under health insurance policies. What the hell is that? And on and on with the real world stuff. We are debating over whether or not we as feminists are allowed to think that pornography is "OK," whether or not we can like men or *have sex with men,* whether White women have anything of value to say that does not oppress their culturally diverse sisters. Silencing each other, passing judgment on lifestyle choices. Sound familiar? These debates are important, but we are allowing them, or the media's attention to them, to rob value from *the here, the now, the what-must-be-done,* the day-to-day lives of women.

One problem with the model of intellectual political correctness is that no one is allowed to excel to such a degree that it makes anyone else feel uncomfortable, "oppressed." There is simply a new look for oppression on the runway this season, à la the high school cafeteria. *You may not stand out*—in idea, ideology, opinion, certainly intellect, maybe even attire. You must conform to expectations or you are out of our clique.

Susan Sontag summed it up well in her book, *The Volcano Lover,* a favorite in certain sectors of the *h2so4* editorial office: "We feel oppressed by the call to greatness. We regard an interest in glory or perfection as a sign of mental unhealthiness, and have decided that high achievers, who are called overachievers, owe their surplus of ambition to a defect in *mothering* (either too little or too much). We want to admire but think we have a right not to be intimidated. We dislike feeling inferior to an ideal. So away with ideals. . . ." [*emphasis added*—blaming the mother is the ultimate responsibility-shift].

So away with ideals. And thus we have gone too far. There is a line on which we should keep our eyes at all times. Respect others, but recognize the *line,* which is your *self,* your ideals. Allow your views to be open to outside input, but not force fed by dogma. Because, as Queen Latifah might say, *no respect is given to one who cannot respect self.* And who wants to go forth from this point, raising a "movement" or "discipline" full of judgmental, self-involved and closed-minded "feminists" who dictate to others in the name of *"what's best for women"*? Not I, sister, not I.

I do not feel oppressed by the call to greatness (which is far removed from believing I've attained it, by the way)—it may be the only thing that keeps me going. The only thing worthy of me and mine that I have to look forward to in life is what I might do, what I might accomplish, how I might succeed, if I put my mind and body to the task—if I risk the exposure involved in seeking greatness, if I do not allow myself to fall prey to the mindset of oppression, and *disallow progress* before trying action. This is all there is—along with those who have the courage to accompany me, to join and cheer me in the process.

I must allow everyone the freedom to seek greatness in their own way, even if they are, in my opinion, idiots, like Camille "*the Ross Perot of feminism*" Paglia and Katie "too bad no one bought the book" Roiphe, or "anyone else trying to gain fame by stating what should be obvious from a position of limited vision but with a controversial market-aware self-serving twist," to quote Anne Senhal's infamous fiction, "Letters to Potential" from *h2so4 №2.* I have my ideas about what entails a noble or worthy pursuit in this world, and certainly not everyone in the public eye adheres to this Aviascheme-of-things, but that's the cost (as opposed to the price) of *freedom.* And I tell you it's worth it.

The channels of communication are blocked and thereby they are opened. The grease on the squeaky wheel sends us slip-sliding 'cross the glossy satin pulp sheets of tyrannical tycoons' wet dreams, where we leave an oil stain. The shortest distance between us is a four-lane highway with no speed limits so we put up a (phony) detour sign, hock our cars to gridlock, and throw a block party on the cloverleaf exchange. Told to "do it yourself" (what do they think we've been doing?), we did—see? We've been conducted . . . we've been conducting . . . our conduct has been so good for so long, that when we now, on the downbeat, arch our backs up out of the jet stream, the electrical energy is ours, flowing still through our spines, the paths of most resistance. I want you all to hear me, but I don't want to drown out your voices. Are we listening?

Resist Stance

by Evelyn

McDonnell

(from resister)

Welcome to the premiere issue of resister. Borrowing willy-nilly the best aspects of both mainstream and marginal publishing while respecting none of their conventions, resister is a scholarly arts and literary journal for the masses, a fanzine of the mainstream, a magazine that's raw and sticky, not slick and glossy, a nuts and bolts guide to thought and expression. At a time when the increasing concentration of information-resources into a few conglomerate hands has paralleled the widespread availability of the tools of dissemination—i.e., when for every Time Warner there's a hundred Xeroxed fanzines, punk rock record labels, and queer websites—resister is stepping into the breach of faith between the omissions of the mass media and the myopia of the subculture set. Our sights may be high, but hey, our aim is truth.

Specifically, resister was born out of my frustrations after a decade as a critic writing for various magazines and "alternative" newspapers. Media-bashing has become one of America's favorite pastimes, but we journalists have brought it upon ourselves. Screened off from actually being of the world by objectionable objectivity, reporters reduce cultural developments to passing trends as TV crews stick their cameras into the crying faces of our exploding inevitable, and pundits package it all into tidy clichés, indistinguishable from the ads. The no-nonsense cynicism of the media watchdog has become the no-conscience jadedness of Murdoch stooges looking out on the world from their Central Park West windows, champions of the expensive press. Even among so-called advocacy journalists, the sense of a democratic imperative has been twisted and betrayed, as the sons of Yale at your favorite lefty paper look out on the public not with a feeling of commonality, but with a pitch of bitter divisiveness.

That divisiveness is unfortunately echoed in the fractious, fragmented world of the underground press, where identity niches are often reinforced rather than resisted, where there's very little cross-cultural communication. One of my goals with *resister* is to bring some of those voices together and let them dialogue. Many of our contributors are people I've met during my travels as a journalist: Nuyorican poets, feminist performance artists from the Pacific Northwest, queer punks from San Francisco, Lovecraft channelers from Providence, street artists and jazz divas from New York City. Some of them step outside the fields for which they're best known: Tribe 8 singer Lynn Breedlove contributes fiction and a letter to Kevin Costner, poet and novelist Paul Beatty weighs in with his friend Chloe Chung on the New York Film Festival, and poet and bandleader Tracie Morris debuts her TV column.

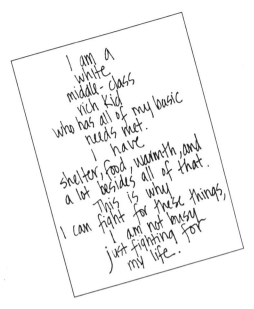

As the title of one of my other favorite journals, *A Gathering of the Tribes,* makes clear, our world's divided into nation-states that too often are at war. I've given *resister*'s first issue the theme "Inside Your Heart" because I think a recognition of shared blood-base is essential to any mutual human endeavor—and because maybe not all we need is love, but love is something we all need. As an unapologetic feminist who's embedded the word sister in the title of her zine, I'm fully aware of the ways in which love has been a euphemism for women's forced dependence on men. The theme's actually an abbreviation of the title of a song by the Vancouver band Mecca Normal, "Trapped Inside Your Heart," in which singer Jean Smith describes romantic love as "a publicly manufactured code." Mecca Normal are inside the heart of *resister,* dialoguing with Slim Moon and Lee Foust—the first of many artists on whom we plan to focus in ways you won't find in your usual celebrity profiles.

Every time I go to a bookstore and see the stands full of magazines, I wonder what the hell I'm doing adding to this glut. But if I often feel overwhelmed by the information overload of our millennial times, I also feel we suffer from an idea deficit: Everyone's talking but no one's making sense. Of course I know that's not true; there are publications that inspired me to start *resister*. They're put out by people who realized that their interests weren't being covered in other magazines and knew that that didn't mean that they weren't interesting, but that maybe there was something wrong with the available media.

Welcome to the resisterhood.

I wrote this article originally for Hues maga-zine (sans title), which is, overall, a cool mag-azine in content, but sucks when it comes to free speech and censorship. When you give an arti-cle to somebody and they say "Go Crazy!", and then say they want you to take out parts that might be "taken the wrong way," revise you many times over, change the whole topic of your article, and have you do all of it for free, you can say it is a bit of a piss-off.

So I withdrew the article and ran it in Bamboo Girl. Like it or lump it! . . .

Asian FUCKING Stereotypes

by Sabrina Sandata

(from Bamboo Girl)

Take your average white male fantasy: "Oh, yes!! Then she'll slap my behind and tell me that if I don't suck her boots, she'll shove the end of her whip up my—"

Fuck dat shit! . . .

Have you wondered what the Asian female stereotypes are but were afraid to ask? 'Well, today class, I will be extrapolating on the sicken-ing yet very real phenomena of Asian Stereotyp-ing. For the non-subliminal, here's the lineup— as it is perpetuated in pop culture and common misconceptions:

1. Asian Dominatrix or Slut-Diva Extra-ordinaire All she has to do is walk into the room to get attention. She wears moderate makeup that accentuates her curvaceous lips or fuck-me eyes. The Slut-Diva Extraordinaire oozes sex, and every white male or lesbian will give up his/her right breast to spend the night with her.

2a. The Submissive Step-All-Over-Me-Thank-You Asian Most often than not, she will wear glasses that will cover up her almond eyes, wear no makeup, and will not care that her clothes don't match. But she *will* care if some-one tells her that her job performance is not up to par. This Asian stereo-type is very concerned with the issue of approval, and will do *anything* (ex-cept lick your boots clean) to have it from her boss and elders.

2b. The Submissive Beat-Me-Again Sex-Slave This variation of the Submissive Asian again deals with the popular no-tion that all Asian girls are natural receptacles for sperm. She is different from the Slut-Diva Extraordinaire in that she would rather be the one to receive the end of the whip. She finds whiplash marks on her back exciting.

3. Miss Saigon Please-Save-My-Child Viet-cong She is more of a look than a personality. Usually she has long straight black hair, and wears no makeup. She dresses simply and looks like she just left her country in search for the American dream. She has a lost look in her eyes, and guys who like being martyrs are naturally drawn to her.

4a. The Don't Pull My Big-Ass Earrings or Baggy Pants or They'll Fall Down Flygirl The flygirl type, with the baggy pants almost falling off the ass, Pumas, gigantic tee (preferably with the face of Tupac on it), big gold earrings that make the lobes bleed, and hair that's pulled back so tightly the hair follicles stand up. They either identify with Black culture or think they *are* African-American.

4b. The Don't Use My Chopsticks or I Kill You Gangsta Chick Don't mess with her! She bleaches her hair into light auburn streaks, spikes the top, and leaves the rest long. She could be the bad little sister counterpart of Lilly in *Vanishing Son.* The guys in the gang are her posse and they protect her from other gangstas. The updated version of this stereotype may have ethnocentric tattoos on her arm and butt.

5. The Studious The-Computer-Is-My-Life Nerd This hopeless anti-social possesses natural tendencies towards being President of the *Star Trek* Club or a Dungeons and Dragons fanatic. She has become unnaturally attached to her computer and caresses it at night. She doesn't care for people, but loves the Sci-Fi Channel.

6. The GOTTA SING! Asian The elegant Lea Salonga type, complete with long flowy pants, sleeveless vest (on sale from the Limited), high-heeled black shoes/boots, and well kept, never-shorn hair, and, usually, a big mouth. She practices pieces from *The Little Mermaid* and *Aladdin,* and believes that she will someday have her own talk show.

7. The I Am But a Lotus Blossom Girl-Child This Asian female plays up the fact that most Asians look very young—she may/may not have breasts, but what is important is her childlike outlook on the world. She loves getting teddy bears from her boyfriend and would never think about living in the city. She plays peek-a-boo with her pets at home and sits on her bay window dreaming about Prince Charming.

8. The Sensei's Most Honorable Daughter This unfortunate Asian has the responsibility of perpetuating the *Karate Kid* image: she is usually the daughter of a very well-respected martial arts teacher, and falls in love with one of her father's young white male students. She teaches him 'the ways' of her country, and he teaches her how to be 'American.' Whether or not she has her father's permission does not matter, although it makes it more exciting if she doesn't. Her boyfriend then takes much pride in having her show up at martial arts tournaments to spur him on to victory. It is usually a bittersweet relationship.

Well, that's a crash course for ya. Just so you know, not all Asian females fit the stereotypes. On the other hand, some Asians may fit more than one at the same time.

As a Filipina mestiza who grew up in the boonies of Southwestern Pennsylvania, I dealt with a lot of rednecks who were ignorant about minorities. They always assumed that I was Chinese, because Chinese people are the only Asians that existed for them.

When I came to New York, I found that people had many different perceptions of what they thought I was, and had me mixed up with other ethnicities. I guessed it was partly because of the makeup I wore, or because I didn't wear typical Filipina youth gear (See above, especially 1, 2a, 4a, and 6).

Of course, I'm sounding like a cynical bitch about the whole stereotypical thing—I'll be the first to admit that I can't stand it! And that's why when I come across ads that are listed under "Pen Pals," reading "Asian ladies waiting to please you" or "Abiding Asian ladies seeking caring men to correspond with," I get ballistic. It should probably read something more like, "Asian ladies desperate to get hitched to get out of economic devastation," or "Abiding domestic violence reps seeking housing outside of the Philippines."

It's the same deal on the tube, our sistas (meaning your typical Asian representation) are shown either as sensei daughters, bar girls, exchange students with black-rimmed glasses, or more often than not, sluts . . . Hel-lo!!

That's what helps give life to publications like *Asian Girls Are Rad,* which is a zine put out by a desperately-needs-to-get-laid David who dedicates his thoughts year-in-year-out to Asian women. In a way it's kinda cute to know that people like him find us so endearing. But I'll let you in on a secret: (whisper) knockin' boots with an Asian chick is not going to lead you to a secret pathway of Oriental enlightenment like Ralph Macchio in *The Karate Kid*, OK? I swear, sometimes that dojo/geisha complex just gets way out of hand. Can we *please* find some movies that are not set in Chinatown, and have us doing normal things like driving well, hitting our computer in frustration, or leading lesbian lifestyles?

There's also a zine on sex and relationships with S.E. Asian women called *Asia File.* Of course, the purpose of mentioning these publications is not to spur you to go out and get them, but more to educate you on the factoids. So I don't wanna see any educated fake trying to cop a look at these kind of things. Then again, if people were educated in the first place, I wouldn't be writing about it.

As I was saying, *Asia File* gives you the inside scoop on bars, brothels, and the entire sex industry in S.E. Asia. As it's described in the blurb, it's "forty-three pages packed full of tips on the best 'pay for play' in the Philippines, India, Vietnam, Japan, Cambodia, and especially Thailand." I know that at the moment they were reading this, many repressed men were grabbing their crotches, salivating at the prospect of exercising their control complex.

Do I have to say it? . . . It's just NOT GOOD!

When I got annoyed at the dick-pushing people on the street who'd harrass me (verbally and physically), I'd start slowly circling my arms in front of me and make Bruce Lee noises. It actually works! At that time, I knew shit about the Martial Arts, but whatever I did sure wigged out the perpetrators. I bring that whole Martial Arts thing up because most people assume that because you have pseudo-slanted eyes, you can chuck a roundkick like nothing. For once, a stereotype ended up working for me. And now I am learning the Martial Arts for real.

Much of my anger growing up stemmed from being pissed off about the stereotypes/fetishes people had of me because I had Oriental blood—strangers in the street found it easier to touch me without asking, call me names pertaining to my Asian heritage, interrupt me while I'm speaking, and step into my personal space without giving a shit. Before, I used to punch people in the street who did this. Seriously! I used to. The anger used to build inside of me until I just whacked the unassuming assholes. With much medication, true friendships, Martial Arts classes (and must I say, some lovely therapy), I've been able to use my energy more constructively. Now I channel those frustrations elsewhere, or take people up on the invitation to speak about it. *Hues* let me go off on this whole Asian Stereotype thang, and Ophira is quite a gal for letting me do so.

Like many other Asian chick-adees, I've turned to my roots—initially to get a sense of identity as a mixed blood, but ultimately to see myself, the little girl everyone thought was a gawky "chink," develop into her own radical ethnic Pinay-mestiza mama self.

As much as there are numerous stereotypes of the Asian female, there are numerous blockheads out there who act on these assumptions. It would be great to separate the "chaff from the wheat" by wishing that all of the ignorant chicos and chicas were wiped off the face of the earth with a gigantic spray of Bug Off; but it is more possible, and realistic, to combat those stereotypes by standing up for yourself when one of those losers attempts to lay one of them on you.

As a woman, it is even more important. It's like we have a double-whammy: we're minorities *and* we're women. By standing up for your culture(s), you also say something about being a chick who knows what's goin' down. Whether you write about it, talk with your closest girlfriend about it, or straight up confront the jerk on the street, it's important to let it out—and to be loud about it. Yeah, you'll be noticed. But it's better to be noticed as an individual who sticks out instead of an unattractive mass with no voice. Stand up and be counted sistahs!

iot Grrrl is an underground, non-commercial womyn's support/action group here to open people's eyes and promote womyn in society. Riot Grrrl is not a bunch of angry man-hating lesbians wanting to take over the world. Let me explain:

1. We ARE angry! We are pissed off how we as grrrls (females) are treated in society. We are angry that patriarchy rules our lives from birth to death. We are angry that the media continues to promote and condone the abuse and rape of womyn. Womyn are seen as the lesser gender: the one to be dominated, owned, ruled. We are angry that more people don't stand up and tell patriarchy: "FUCK OFF AND LET ME BE!"

What is Riot Grrrl?

by R. G.

(from Mons of Venus)

2. We do not hate men. We promote grrrl love. That's one reason the meetings are womyn only. We want a pro-female community of support. The act of loving yourself as you were created (female) has been devalued. We promote loving yourself as you are. We meet with guys once a month to keep communication flowing.

3. We are not a lesbian group. We have grrrls who are lesbian, bi, and straight. We don't care what sexual orientation you are. You are a grrrl. We all bleed the same, we have the same struggles. Together we can make it.

4. We DO want to take over the world. PAD POWER—LET THE BLOOD FLOW!

What Does RG Do?

We discuss topics relevant to womyn and how to deal with them; we volunteer with the NOW escorts at the reproductive health clinic and ACT UP to educate people about HIV; we come together, create our own positive space and build strong female friendships; and we create our own zine, *Mons of Venus,* a collection of our feelings and opinions.

We can do anything else you want . . . this is your group. You can do as much or as little as you want. Our group ranges in age from fifteen to twenty-nine, but all ages are welcome. All womyn are welcome, regardless of age, ethnicity, religion, political thought, shoe size . . . Variety adds spice to life!

i am your nanny. i am your —

gardener. i am your housekeeper

DO YOU KNOW ME? I make my living off of loving blue-eyed babies. Yes, I am underpaid but since I'm the only legal employee and don't require work papers, I enjoy the _priviledge_ of leaving out the front door instead of the side door. like the rest of the help. Sure, I'm brown ~~too~~ but Spanish is not my first language and I don't even have an accent. And someday, if I'm lucky, I'll work in a big house with a swimming pool and my own little maid's quarters. YIPPY! Oh, of course it won't be much — just four Spartan walls and the obligatory Frida print hung just for me. But it's my own little patch of heaven. Tucked away like a secret in that big house in the hills. Near a golf course. Safe at night with the well-heeled circular footsteps of my fat cat master, [oopsImeanboss] methodically lulling me to sleep from the room above me.

My money is clean, bloodless, white-collar money and I earned every cent of it. like a good little Spic.

I AM

THE PILLAR THAT SUPPORTS YOUR WHOLE FUCKING LIFESTYLE.

i am your cook. i am your concubine. i am

C all me crazy, but I just have this thing for guns—or gurlz with guns. Quite simply, I think it's hot. I don't know if it's the power that I find so seductive, or what. But I'm definitely sold on the image.

However, reckless girls with guns is a real put-off. You gotta be smart-n-slick if you're gonna play with the "I'm a girl whose got a gun down her pants" image. And that's why I'm writing this article. More and more girls are playing with the "girl/gun" image, and I'm thinking that many of these girls know little to nothing about guns. If this is the case, read on.

I'm afraid I can't offer an in-depth gun safety course within the confines of this article, but I do have some basic safety tips that I'd like to share with those who are interested. And for those of you who are further interested, I suggest taking a gun safety class, or having a knowledgeable friend show you the ropes. (I was lucky enough to have some guy friends of mine take me blasting . . . yes it's true, I learned what I know from penis holdin' humans, and I love em for it—thanks guys!)

1. Okay, so you find a gun, or want to check out a gun. What's the first thing you do? You check to make sure the safety is on, and then you check to see if it's loaded or unloaded. If it's loaded, you unload it.

Girly Gun Safety

by Christine Johnson

(from Not Your

Bitch)

2. So now you got this unloaded gun in your hands, what next? That's simple, you check it out. Feel it's curves, caress it's metal, and realize it is a killing machine—be careful, notice everything. If it's a semi-automatic rifle or hand gun, check out the slide, see how it loads bullets. If it's a handgun, cock that hammer back, twirl the barrel . . . feel it's essence. Most girls have never *really* held a gun, now's your time.

3. Alright, now you are at your target shooting area. Set your targets (cans work good) against a hill. (If you shoot through an open field, you risk shooting something—someone—that's in the path.) Now that your targets are set, put your ear plugs in, load your gun, take your safety off, aim, and shoot.

4. Never ever point your gun at anyone! This is how accidents happen. Even if your gun is unloaded, it's stupid to aim it at a friend, or yourself, as a joke.

5. Very important: DO NOT mix guns, drinkin', or drugs! You should have a clear head when you shoot.

6. Clean guns after every target practice. A clean gun is a reliable gun. Also, try to pick up most of your spent shells if you are shooting in nature—polluting sucks.

7. If you own a gun, always keep it unloaded in your house, and make sure the safety is on. Also, keep all guns out of reach from children, or those who act like children.

8. Not everyone needs to know that you have a gun if you have one. Tell those who need to know, but the fewer people who know, the less likely it will get stolen, or used against you.

9. Never fucking bluff! If you are in a threatening situation and feel you need to use your gun, only pull it out if you are DEAD serious! My motto is, "someone can rob me or beat the fuck out of me, but if they try to rape me, or threaten my life, I'll *think* about shooting them." In reality, I hope I'm **never** in that situation.

10. Taking a gun safety class is a good idea because they can teach you how to aim. What good are you if you can't hit the target! And target shooting is really good practice.

11. If you find guns to be a turn on . . . just please, please, please make sure the gun is unloaded and the safety is on during foreplay and sex . . . have safe sex!

So that's about it for my tips. Guns may be an extension of the patriarchies; but so long as rape exists—the rape of women and of the earth—so will women who are ready to turn the patriarchies' fire-power against them. Make it more than a myth, become a *smart*-n-sexy girl with a gun!

1. asserting my knowledge of it with non-white people. as if it's not already obvious enough.

2. accommodate other white peoples' racism, cuz i think i can explain racism in a disconnected, calm, rational way.

3. think i'm disconnected from racism cuz i'm white; the ways in which racism affects me are often invisible to me because i benefit from it.

4. map out oppression, giving out "X marks yer spots" on *my* fucken diagrams.

5. ever think because i'm white it means i'm not qualified to recognize racism and call people on their shit.

6. act as though WHITE-GIRL is an absolute. all white girls are not the same; class and background are very important roles in a person's behavior and attitudes.

7. thinking i can just SIT THIS ONE OUT and wait for a non-white person to point out racism. i should trust my own instincts.

8. i'm gonna stop thinking all i can do about my undeserved and unearned privileges is THINK ABOUT how shitty capitalistic patriarchal society is. wallowing in my own self-pity is lame cuz I know at the same time i could be using the en-

ergy to be actively confronting myself and other white people on our racism.

9. think my privileges somehow negate the ways in which i'm marginalized. this whole scorecard crap is weird. I AM A WHOLE PERSON (HOLE) NOT A MATHEMATICAL EQUATION . . .

10. think cuz of my experiences as a white girl i have *total* frame of reference to understand racism cuz of my head on experiences with sexism and classism, racism and sexism, as do all forms of oppression, work similarly, but they are NOT the same thing and affect white and non-white people differently.

11. ACT LIKE I WORK ALONE. typical white girl style to make like i act alone. my work is part of a whole that is bigger than i can ever imagine, deeply connected to the work of hundreds of other people working on their shit. and i may not be saying it all right but i am saying that i am partly whole cuz i am in this process and i am WORKING, not fixing it by noon tomorrow. this is a constant.

12. theres no such thing as letting a situation work itself out (ain't that the fucken truth). i know well enough from my friendships with other people (and from fucken growing up eco-

things i'm gonna stop doing with my white privilege

by Mary (from Wrecking Ball)

nomically disadvantaged) THINGS (money or comfort) DON'T APPEAR OUT OF NO-WHERE (unless stolen or gambled) and i am working towards confronting racism not just when its convenient for me or only when i'm around all white people.

13. feel safe or comfortable at the expense of the safety or comfort of non-white people.

14. martyr myself.

15. expect my work to be appreciated by non-white people. its a matter of fact, it is my *responsibility* as a white girl to confront racism inside this fucked up world inside my community inside ME.

Real feMeNiNe protection

MACE →

BLACKJACK

38 SPECIAL
(also the name of a cheesy redneck band)

THE BRAIN — filled with juicy self protective tidbits - hone in on them.

I've been thinking a lot about how my class background has informed different aspects of my life, specifically my sexuality and my body image. [Note—I grew up in a family on welfare, the women in my family remain on welfare. I'm not going to bother with a detailed account of deprivation.]

I've been trying to uncover stereotypes that are created in the conflation of sexuality and class. Most female-specific stereotypes are based in the universal fear of an unbridled and autonomous female sexuality. For women on welfare, this is complicated by their assumed undesirability and dependency on a patriarchal *state* economic system as well as the physical and material ways that poverty and working class lifestyles are visible on the body. Women on welfare are perceived and discriminated against in terms of their sexual activity and their body image. It is assumed that loose sexual morals or deviant desires placed them in the shameful status of poor; but not just poor—poor women that no man wants or that men only want for one thing.

As a teenage girl from a welfare family I automatically was labeled as SLUT, actually long before I was a teenager, by the time I was nine. *There's two kinds of girls, those you marry and those*

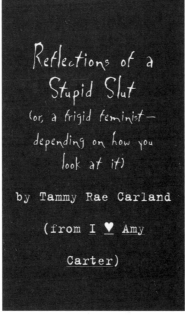

Reflections of a Stupid Slut (or, a frigid feminist— depending on how you look at it)

by Tammy Rae Carland

(from I ♥ Amy Carter)

you don't—if you are poor you are a don't. My sexuality was named and positioned before I was sexual. Adults were constantly deciding that their sons and daughters were not allowed to be around me and especially not allowed in my house/apartment (whatever it happened to be that month).

Being on welfare also places women and children under constant public surveillance, within a *state* system that equates sexual activity with criminality. By this I mean that women who are receiving AFDC are monitored to make sure they don't have a live-in-boyfriend/lover or are not receiving monetary support from a boyfriend/lover. When I was a child, an unannounced social worker would visit our apartment and question my mom about her personal life, like if she was dating—and the social worker would take note of any new purchases and inquire about how they were paid for. Anything out of the ordinary was suspect and assumed to be connected to a man and not an off-the-books job. We were taught to keep secrets and tell lies in order to stay together. I was taught that my mother's sexuality was to remain invisible and non-existent.

Women on welfare are pretty much expected to be single and not sexually active. Welfare women (particularly African-American and Latina) are experimented on with birth control and sterilization. An enormous amount of women on the welfare dole go through sterilization in order to maintain their so called "benefits." I've yet to hear of a man who has fathered numerous children with a woman (or women) on welfare being forced by a *state* agency to get a vasectomy.

Welfare recipients who are in a situation of domestic violence are less likely to seek help because they stand the chance of losing their children, their financial assistance, or their living situation, which is almost always tenuous and temporary.

Lesbians with children on welfare stand an even greater chance of losing their children, especially if they are found to have a lover or lovers. I saw this happen when I was a child. This one particular woman gave up her lover and retreated to the closet, but still lost her children to the father despite the fact that there was proof he had raped her during their marriage—that was legal in the state at the time and maybe still is. I've begun to track how all this informed my desires as a girl and shaped my insistent separation between my class and sexuality. A separation that kept me silent and ashamed about my class history and my community affiliations.

Another complication occurs when there is physical/sexual/emotional abuse in the home. Of course, this is always traumatic for a child despite her or his class status, and every situation has its own separate issues. However, as a child on welfare, you learn that sometimes the threat of being taken away from your family is almost more scary than staying, partly because there is a big emphasis on beating the odds and assumptions by staying together, alive, and out of prisons and "homes." I know so many horror stories about children, teens and/or moms that got taken "away." And you're always battling the stereotypes of what's expected to take place in your home. I've actually had friends say to me that it's easier for me to deal with my abuse history and the effects it's had on my family than it is for them to deal with their issues. In other words, my family is supposed to be drunk, abusive, and violent but their upper middle class families are not supposed to—so therefore I have less of a stigma to overcome, because I am "less than" to begin with. Fucked up.

I have also been noting how the assumptions of ignorance particularly diminish poor women and the incredible brilliance they operate in. *Stupid girls make easy girls.* As I write this I am half watching "The Beverly Hillbillies" on TV. And I'm thinking about what my role models (as far as TV goes) were as a child. No one on television (or in the movies I saw or the books I read) was on welfare. I never saw an image of someone going to the store with food stamps and being humiliated by other kids and sometimes adults. I never saw a mom begging some social worker for a medical voucher to take her child to the dentist. The closest thing I had to my reality was "Good Times," but they still weren't as poor as us. All the shows and movies I can think of had daughters that were sexy and stupid. More accurately, this stupidity was presented as a childlike naiveté.

When I was a senior in high school I was (academically) third in my class, and in the Fall, when people were being prodded and guided into looking at colleges, I was being ignored. When I finally got the courage to go to my guidance counselor and ask how to apply to college, she just sat there dumfounded, and remarked that she didn't think I had wanted to go to college. As if I was taking all those college prep classes for nothing. Basically, I was expected to drop out, and when I didn't, they were at a loss as to what to do with me.

So when I finally began to be more honest about my class background (which isn't behind me by any means), I was confused by the resistance some people had in confronting what I was saying. It seems that people have this vision of a romantic working-class pride that has nothing to do with growing up on welfare in this country. (I value my friendships with my younger sisters for so many reasons, one of which is that there is never this confusion.) People weren't able to have an image for what I was saying because they've never been fed that image. Except maybe in human interest news stories which almost always represent the welfare class as urban African-Americans. And I think that this is a perpetuation of racist stereotypes.

The fact of the matter is that there are more White women (per capita) on welfare than any other race, and a large population of the welfare class live in rural areas (I got this statistic from an Ishmael Reed essay). I am not by any means denying or trying to diminish the level of poverty that far too many African-American, Latina/os, Asian-American and American-Indian people live in, I am trying to complicate the image and idea that so many people have of poverty. An image that is often either racist, romantic, invisible, violent . . . all of the above. In so much of the work that is being done about social- and personal-identity politics, it seems as though class is the final frontier. People conflate class with race as if to talk about one you are automatically covering the other, another racist assumption. And if class does get discussed and the "lower class" is initiated, it is the working class that is being referred to. I did not grow up "working class"—there is a certain pride that is afforded to the working class that the "non-working class" doesn't have access to. The working class position themselves far outside of the welfare and homeless class.

I never know how to "out" my class because in so many ways it feels as though I am outing my family. According to others, I am not

the same class as my family. Because I went to college and had the self-serving audacity to pursue my work as an artist (how elitist—huh?), I've been told I am now middle class. And this isn't about financial security, because I have none. This is about notions of assimilation. Just because I know some big words and don't have the same accent I grew up with and I am "so different" than the rest of my family, I have apparently breezed into civilized respect and personal integrity. By the (questionable if not absolutely untrue) fact that I am surrounded by no one who shares my class history—I have no history, unspoken = unheard.

My body doesn't believe this message, a message articulated by others but not always voiced aloud. The message says "you escaped, you survived, you are better." I'm sometimes grateful that my body rejects this. My skin that has never looked youthful, my back that inherited my mother's work history, my hands that started manual labor at the age of eight, my teeth that have generations of bad nutrition behind them, and my reflection—yeah, it's all there in my reflection.

I never look in the mirror and simply see myself, it's always a third-person consciousness. A reflection that has been talking back to me since I left my mom's home when I was fifteen. It says, "what are you doing here?—who do you think you're fooling?—they see through you—you can't get away with this—they know who you are—you are not one of them." I used to think I had to get rid of this self-produced antagonism until I realized it was one of the ways I stayed connected to the women in my family. This internal critic doesn't overpower my productivity or my sense of self-worth. It does, however, keep me on my toes as far as the place in the life I've made and the place in life that was made for me. I experience these things simultaneously, daily in my bank of memories.

I truly don't want to think I've "made it," or that I'm any better, smarter, or safer than I was when I was fifteen. Because I'm not. Recently, one of my sisters told me about how a certain male member of our family (yes, I am going to protect his identity—I don't know why) sat drunk at a kitchen table and called a woman in my family a "welfare slut." This happened in front of at least three other women in my family who receive state aid. Nobody said anything to him. She said it was silent. I can hear this silence because it is a typical experience in my family. It's a silence that is fueled by all this outside world shame and this inside family pride. It's a very loud silence that I'm sure one day will combust and blow the roof off the entire fucking charade. I'm waiting.

arly this summer, Leyla, a high school grrrl, joined up with her friend and fellow grrrl, Sam, to put on the Los Angeles Riot Grrrl Convention. They started with a successful riot grrrl benefit at Macondo Cultural Center. I got to work the Revolution Rising table there. Four of the members of Revolution Rising (Sisi, Tye, Debbie L., and Danielle) are original LA Riot Grrrls from the first meeting.

No one was more surprised than Leyla and Sam when the *LA Weekly,* KROQ, KXLU, and MTV called for more information. The *LA Times'* Calendar Section featured a color picture of Lois from the Free to Fight tour, and an article by Lorraine Ali contrasting Free to Fight's openness to the mainstream media and Leyla and Sam's unwillingness to co-operate.

On July 29 at Jabberjaw, friends were turned away because it was too crowded. Grrrls walked through the crowd giving away zines. There was a Riot Grrrl Press zine table and T-shirts on the wall in back where a little cool air from the street slipped through the locked iron grill door. This night was an *LA Weekly* Pick and more than half the people there were boys. Some were familiar from grrrl shows but most were old-school, standing around like zoologists on unfamiliar turf. A crusty boy with liberty spikes and a couple of his friends got into a fight and

were kicked down the alley by members of Free to Fight. It was hot, crowded, and sweaty inside. Sue P. Fox paced and poeticized with tears and sweat streaming from her face. Riot Grrrl Press band Diamonds Into Coal were awesome. C.B. Barnes and Sleater-Kinney were inspired and inspiring.

On July 30 the Riot Grrrl Convention was held in Pomona. We had a long drive in major hot sunshine. We cruised up to a new business park, more like warehouses. One nearest the railroad tracks was an AA center for local kids. They wound up having their meeting outside in the parking lot. As soon as the doors opened a small group of gray-haired women went in, bought one of every zine, and left. There were tables by Riot Grrrl Press, Rock for Choice, Women's Action Committee and Revolution Rising. It was a great turn-out—two hundred or more, most not in riot grrrl costume, mostly high-school-aged, with some college aged. Moms in station wagons dropped off kids. A few outnumbered boys attended. Free to Fight kicked the boys out for a grrrl-only self-defense workshop. Most of the boys, including the Revolution Rising boys, just left, but Danny of the band Mine demanded an explanation and was dragged out by the hair. He looked pretty tragic standing outside in his Crown for Athena shirt with his Wonder

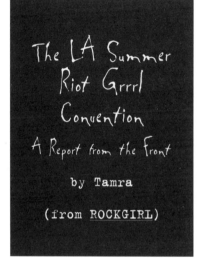

The LA Summer
Riot Grrrl
Convention

A Report from the Front

by Tamra

(from ROCKGIRL)

Woman Pez dispenser. He later confronted everyone and was ejected again. A small line of solemn girls out back stopped to tell him they didn't agree with what happened.

Lucid Nation's drummer, Debbie, faced the confusion and led a really inspiring workshop on body image with help from Sara of Revolution Rising. Sisi of Revolution Rising read her essay on race and Riot Grrrl as experienced by a Mexican-American Grrrl. Free to Fight performed to a rapt audience. Lois played and sang her lilting melodies. 151's booming bass and African samples underscored precise Rap—they were solid. Nikki Maclure moved through the kids using her sternum as a drum and sang nursery rhyme melodies with reality lyrics. Although the bands were supposed to begin at 5:00 PM the first one didn't start until eight.

I believe the exclusion of boys is our right and was a necessity for the self-defense workshop, but it should have been made clear on the fliers and at the door that boys would have to sit on the asphalt for a couple of hot August hours, and prior provisions should have been made for the PA.

10:00 PM or later, the Free To Fight people piled into their touring van and departed. Revolution Rising packed up because they had to go to work the next day. A boy band, Los Cincos, refused to leave the stage after their allotted three songs. They had driven a very long way and waited in hundred degree weather, having been told they would get a half hour, possibly a forty-five minute set. Their boy fans circled stage manager, Chelsea Starr, chanting, and the grrrls all backed away. Chelsea yanked the guitarist's chord to silence him and shouted down both he and his fans, clearing the stage for the next band. Los Cincos took offense to being excluded without warning, especially in light of their reputation as one of the most respected indie bands in LA and as supporters of riot grrrl.

At 2:00 AM, the sound man, who had run three stages at the Irvine Indie Fest the day before, spent two hours dismantling his equipment. He said he hadn't been asked to leave so many times since getting sober! The boss at the venue said he'd never been dealt with so rudely.

Although I didn't attend the July 31 convention at Jabberjaw, I heard it was great.

I found it all inspiring, infuriating, boring, hostile, exhilarating, occasionally transcendent, and often rad, like Phranc's brief but great impromptu set in the Pomona parking lot, and the trains passing by every few minutes. The fighting and hostility and rudeness and self-righteousness suck, but in a way it's great to see so many powerful and angry women! And it worked! A bunch of grrrls showed up. All the bands played, were recorded, and the essential information was shared. ★

THE SUMMER FROM HELL/CANADA ISSUE

BAMBOO GIRL #2

Things to gawk at:

» *Interviews with*
Selena of Lucy Stoners
Melora of Rasputina
Joan of Dambuilders
NYC Pinay-dyke chicks
Kilawin Kolektibo!

» *Canada's* Femzine *Contributes*
Their Stuff!

» More *Angst!*

» More *Weird Filipino Shit!*

KARANG!!

$2

I've been thinking a lot about the decision of whether or not to own a gun. I've been thinking about how things might be if there was this widespread assumption that girls and women were walking around armed with weapons for self-defense. I've been thinking about how, when I was a child, I lived in a house with guns and I learned how to use them, not for sport or fun. Simply because I knew I was living with people who used them recklessly and manipulatively. I felt a tad bit safer knowing that if need be I could defend myself. I'm talking about a ten-year-old girl. A girl who had guns held on her and demands made of her. I feel unable to make a political decision as far as gun control legislation goes. Lately it seems like an issue of practicality that I can't reckon with on the terms of an either/or choice. There has been a media blitz of female aggression lately, everything from made-for-TV movies to info-tainment shows to so called "hard news." Historically speaking, there has also been a resistance within feminist agendas to outwardly address issues of female aggression. And more specifically, the resistance has been focused on not dealing with the fact that there are women and girls who murder. There are a disproportionate amount of lesbians on death row in this country, seventeen out of the forty-one. Being a lesbian is also considered an "aggravated circumstance," when a lesbian-identified woman commits homicide. A woman's sexuality is a criminal offense when she is a dyke who kills someone but not when she is a hetero who kills someone. Sounds fishy to me. I'm not sure where I'm going with all this but I've been doing a lot of research and work about women murderers, and I'm curious if anyone has any opinions or information that they would be willing to share with me. I've received more than a helpful portion of warnings about dealing with a "sensationalist" subject such as this. It certainly isn't as though I have separated my work in, and about, violence against women from this work about women who commit violant acts. I'm mostly interested in the sutures and fissures of what usually gets lumped together as contradiction or as cause and effect. And besides, if I avoided working through everything about women that the media turned into a carnival (and turned a buck on), I would be sitting here with my thumb up my butt, now wouldn't I.

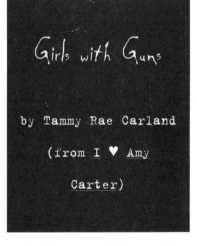

Girls with Guns

by Tammy Rae Carland

(from I ♥ Amy Carter)

The current war in Bosnia is not a war we can understand. All the homes in the villages I visited in November had military uniforms on the clotheslines because all men over the age of nineteen belong to the militia and fight every ten days. Refugees hide in abandoned cars in the forest for only one night until the villagers take them in, whether Muslim or Catholic. A Croat ran home from a prison camp four miles outside Mostar because his Muslim guard was a childhood friend and looked the other way. You don't see rage that rape was used as the Serbian weapon in this war, because everybody wants to bury that fact, fearing that, otherwise, there will never be an end to the destruction.

I went to Bosnia in November to try to understand what was going on and to figure out my own justice position. I marched at the Pentagon protesting US involvement in Vietnam in 1967 and I protested outside the Democratic Convention in 1968 because Vietnam was my war. The only member of my family to get his name on a United States monument was my cousin Michael John Coleman, who is on Wall 33 East of the Vietnam Memorial. It took a week to ship his body home because Khe Sanh was many thousands of miles away from his Chicago home. That war was a different type of war.

Rape is used in Bosnia as an instrument of

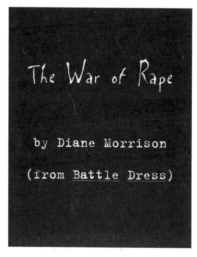

The War of Rape

by Diane Morrison

(from Battle Dress)

war and not only an incident of war. The reports last winter made me wonder what the US government could do. I wavered like so many in the peace movement as my anti-war self fought with my woman's heart. My trained lawyer mind also remembered that I studied at the same Georgetown School of Foreign Service as President Clinton, where we learned that foreign policy was similar to dealing with the Mafia—you had to be as tough as they are. I was confused. Visiting Bosnia straightened me out again. At this point it's a war in which the US government has no role, but we women do. This is our war.

Rape as a tool of the Serbian policy of ethnic cleansing is well documented, especially in an innovative lawsuit brought against the Serbian government by victims of that policy in a US Federal District Court. That policy of the use of rape in ethnic cleansing was widely talked about in the US press a year ago, and by the people I visited in Bosnia this November. Now it is being considered only "allegations" in the US press since a peace settlement is near which is favored by the US government. The awfulness of crimes against women is to be buried under a settlement of land seizures won through the use of this inhumane tool of war. Susans Brownmiller and Sontag are quoted as our feminist spokespersons, quoted as saying they don't think that rape was the issue. Once again, the tragedies we know as women are being shoved under a rug and woven into the fabric of the lies about this war.

This further crime against the humanity of woman is what makes this our war. We cannot and must not let that happen. This is our Vietnam to fight and it is for us to maintain our own memorials. We must not forget or let the world forget. Our role is profoundly simple. We must not let this happen again. Never again shall rape be used as a tool of war.

Never again.

Contributors

Sarah Dyer *Action Girl*

Sarah grew up in Gainsville, Florida, the "Berkeley of the South" (or so they say), where she first became involved in zine culture. After moving to New York, she began the *Action Girl* project series with the *Action Girl Newsletter,* which eventually blossomed into all sorts of things, including the quarterly *Action Girl Comics.* She loves pink, glitter, and cats ("so sue me") and hopes her work will help empower girls and boys everywhere. You can find her on-line at http://www.houseoffun.com.

Witknee *Alien*

Witknee started *Alien* in the summer of 1994 as a feminist-oriented zine to vent frustration and to meet people. Then, she started including more personal writing that was about her mental illness. As a result, the zine came to focus more on mental health and the personal struggles, stereotypes, and political aspects she deals with being mentally "ill." Through her zine, she hopes that other members of her community will become more aware of mental health issues. And she hopes to provide a safe space for others who would like to talk about their mental illness.

Amy Hixon *The Badgirl Club*

Amy loves to write and to walk around and look at people. She's a fan of grrrlbands and grrrl related things.

Sabrina Sandata *Bamboo Girl*

Sabrina lives in New York City where she creates *Bamboo Girl.*

Clancy Amanda Cavnar *Ben Is Dead*

Clancy is 36, and a graduate student at San Francisco State. She is majoring in counseling and is doing an internship as a therapist at a home for severely emotionally disturbed children. She has an MFA in painting from San Francisco Art Institute. She is currently working on a book of her own illustrations and poems about a stuffed animal named "Wyat." She is a lesbian, and she is from New Jersey.

Darby *Ben Is Dead*

Darby lives in LA and edits and publishes *Ben Is Dead*.

Destiny Itano *Ben Is Dead*

Destiny is a really cool chick living in Los Angeles.

Erika Langley *Blue Stocking*

Erika grew up in Arlington, Virginia and graduated from The Rhode Island School of Design in 1989. *Lusty Lady*, a book of photographs and text, is published by Scalo.

Judy Smith *Blue Stocking*

Judy started *Blue Stocking* on a temporary secretary's salary and ran up a massive credit card debt. She made a lot of friends and some enemies by publishing a free feminist newspaper. (Most of the enemies were made inside the feminist community. Friends were made all over.) Currently, Judy is expecting her first child (a girl) and wondering how it's all going to work out.

Michelley Queen of Queens *Boji for the Mentally Ill*

Michelley, Queen of Queens is a work in progress and guerl about town. She has survived a somewhat troubled adolescence, received a BFA in Illustration from Parson's School of Design, and given birth to a future fashion model. On any given night in NYC, Michelley can be seen singing her guts out, hurling bloody panties at her bewildered but adoring audience, doing goofy-sexy interpretive gogo dances, wooing the ladies as her male persona Brad Clit, or simply destroying people's hearing and blowing their minds with her seminal rock band, Mother Jugs and Speed.

Lovechild *Brat Attack*

Lovechild is a writer and performer who currently resides in New York City. She is author of the book *GAG (Hardcore Erotica and Anti-Hate Propaganda)*. Lovechild's pleasures include paying with her two sex kittens Erotica and Cleopatra and doing male drag. Lovechild's goal is to hit the American society so hard in the groin that they have no choice but to unshackle their warped beliefs and ignorance towards one another which one day shall lead them to ultimate freedom.

Melissa Iwai *Bust*

Melissa has recently been transplanted to New York, where she works as a web designer for an advertising firm by day, and as a freelance illustrator by night. She graduated from the Art Center College of Design in Pasadena in 1996 with a BFA in Illustration. She did not smash her dolls' heads as a child, but she can relate to those emotions.

Lotta Gal *Bust*

Lotta Gal is a contributing writer and interviewer for *Bust*. She also writes and directs for television and film under her government-sanctioned name. She lives in Manhattan next door to a stuggling opera singer, and, not unlike everyone else, is writing a feature screenplay. She owns her own couch.

Jennifer Wagley *Bust*

Jennifer Wagley lives in Dayton, Ohio, and is currently looking for a new gynecologist, family doctor, and job. Her significant other is "Little Fattie," a Shepherd/Husky mix who loves her just the way she is.

Fran Willing (aka *"girl"*) *Bust*

Much to her fury, Fran Willing's dad once told her she ought to be a writer. (She was in art school at the time and had been proclaiming her desire to be a painter, just like mom, ever since she could talk.) Now she is an artist who also happens to write. She has been a regular contributor to *Bust* since the first issue.

Sara Zoe Mondt *The Charm Booklette*

Sara lives in LA, squeaking by writing music videos and animated movies for a living; living by writing short stories which have been published twice in the *Santa Monica Review;* and working on a nearly finished novel-in-progress. In addition to doing her zine, *The Charm Booklette,* she wrote two short movies that were produced by Rock the Vote and aired on MTV in 1995.

Tara Emelye *Cupsize*

Tara was raised in Suburbia and spent her teens listening to rain and new wave. She has a BA in Philosophy from SUNY Stonybrook. She started *Cupsize* while a diner waitress and gallery intern, bassist, and vocalist for her band, The Mad Planets.

Sasha *Cupsize*

Sasha was raised in suburban Rhode Island, and is responsible for countless yearbook layouts. She has an American Studies degree from Barnard. Sasha was published in *The Village Voice* for her involvement and support with the striking workers union at Barnard in Spring 1996. She's an active proponent of bi-visibility and issues.

Sandra Lee Golvin *Diabolical Clits*

Sandra is a Jew born at The Queen of the Angels Hospital in LA. She is a published author and pre-menopausal genderfucker who looks as good in a suit as she does in a dress.

Cindy Gretchen Ovenrack *Doris*

Cindy Gretchen Ovenrack lives in California, where she likes to trade her zine *Doris*.

J-Me *Easy!*

J-me is an east Pennsylvania born and raised twenty-year-old snooty art-school girl studying graphic arts and design, film, women's studies, and art history in Philadelphia. She will be studying in Italy for a semester. She digs Nickelodeon, caffeine, books, and Xerox machines. She is also sympathetic to "high school experience."

Queen Itchie *Everything I Touch Turns to Shit and Garbage*

Quenn Itchie grew up a Navy brat, which instilled in her a certain wanderlust. She's lived all over and is now trying to settle down. Her interests are still all over the place. She's obsessed with glamour, comic books, nookie, animals, and Scorpio women. She has red hair and a temperament to match. She's also obnoxious.

Max Airborne *FaT GiRL*

Max Airborne is an artist, musician, writer, tattoist-in-training, clown, and all around creative dyke.

Tina Spangler *Femme Flicke*

Tina was born in Wisconsin in 1970 in a little farm town. She went to college in Milwaukee in the late eighties before moving to Boston in 1991. In 1994 she received a degree in film and writing from Emerson College. Currently, in addition to publishing *Femme Flicke*, Tina has been putting on film shows to screen the types of movies covered in the zine. She also works as an editor for *Natural Health* magazine,

Zoe Miller *Girlie Jones*

Zoe, a graduate of Bates College, now lives in Portland, Oregon, where she works two jobs. She continues to work on *Girlie Jones* with Colleen Summer, as well as various other projects.

Jenn G. Box *Gogglebox*

Jennifer just got back from a year of traveling alone in Africa and the Middle East. She is working on a degree at Columbia. She's still fucking shit up, but in subtler ways these days.

Barbara *Hey There, Barbie Girl* and *Plotz*

Barbara lives in New York City, where she works on *Plotz*.

Ariel Gore *hip Mama*

Ariel Gore started *hip Mama* as a senior project at Mills College in 1993. As a teen mom on welfare, Ariel was sick of drowning in family values. She just got her MA, got off welfare, got a book deal, and got her period on the publisher's chair.

Jennifer Kosta *hip Mama*

Jennifer just got married to the dude. They live in Media, PA, with their son Jesse.

Kathy Sloan *hip Mama*

Kathy has been a freelance photographer in the Bay Area for almost twenty years, photographing wherever there's a story to be told about the diversity of the area and the struggles for social justice and change. Kathy is the mother of 26-year-old Ayisha Knight, a feisty, beautiful poet, actress, and artist. A portfolio of some of her jazz images appeared in the December 1996 issue of *Jazz Times* and was shown in New York at the Fiterman Gallery in December of 1995. This body of work is currently showing at the San Francisco City Hall.

Elissa Nelson *Hope*

Elissa is a twenty-year-old writer and playwright who has been editing or co-editing a zine since she was sixteen. She grew up in Minneapolis and is currently a student at Bard College in New York State, where she is majoring in creative writing and literature. She likes to dance, read, and get good mail. When she is at home in Minneapolis, she is a regular at Balls, a weekly cabaret at the Southern Theater, hosted by Leslie Ball. Her first story was published in *Seventeen* magazine in July, 1996.

Jill Stauffer *h2so4*

Jill Stauffer edits *h2so4*, a politicoliterary journal based in San Francisco that has been nominated for an Alternative Press Award and been voted best zine by the readers of the *SF Weekly*. *h2so4* aims to combine the serious and the silly, the arcane and the mundane, each without making excuses for the other.

Zoe Cliché *I-Am-a-Cliché*

Zoe is never a social butterfly; in fact, her adolescent personality leans more toward sheer introversion than anything else. Zoe writes, "when book, music, movies, and the four walls of your bedroom become your closest companions, you're exposed to a hell of a lot more info/experience than your peers." You notice the difference. The whole point of Zoe's zine or anything else she creatively produces is to communicate this difference, frustration, awareness, whatever you want to call it.

Tammy Rae Carland *I ❤ Amy Carter* and *J.T.O.*

Tammy Rae is an artist, filmmaker, and writer who currently teaches photography in Indiana. After finishing five issues if *I ❤ Amy Carter*, she's moved on to her new zine project, *Jailhouse Turn Out*.

Sara Marcus *Kusp*

Some of Sara's favorite things are: queer theory, noisy picket lines, green tea, city streets at dawn, homemade vegan sushi, and underground culture. She plays drums and bass in a band and has not yet lost all hope in the potential of punk rock. She is currently an undergraduate at Yale, where she is learning how the System works so she can help destroy it.

Colette *Looks Yellow, Tastes Red*

Colette is the creator of *Looks Yellow, Tastes Red*. She's 16 years old and lives in Massachusetts.

Martha Bayne *Maxine*

Martha gave up a promising career in New York as a loading dock foreman to move to Chicago and start anew in the fast-paced world of scholarly publishing. She is a pointlessly competitive croquet player, but remains appalled at her poor aptitude for Scrabble.

Anne Bruns *Maxine*

Anne Bruns, art director for *Maxine*, designs during the day for a Chicago university. She hopes to someday create luscious lamps without duct tape and finish her novel about her previous sitcom place of employment where she met Ms. Zoe.

Zoe Zolbrod *Maxine*

For money, Zoe has been writing educational material. She fears that one day some parent will discover that his kid's social studies book was worked on by the publisher of a wild feminazi zine, and the gig will be up. Her short fiction has been published in *Fish Stories Collectives I* and *II*.

Christine E. Johnston *Not Your Bitch*

Christine is twenty-three years old and is currently enrolled in Women's Studies at the Metropolitan State College of Denver. Through an Antioch College Women's Studies course held in Europe, she did research on the girl zine scene in England. When she returned to the US, she started a zine catalog called *Twat*, which listed both English and American girl zines. She is now living in Olympia, Washington, and will be attending Evergreen State College to study "The Politics of Revolution" in the fall.

Sarah-Katherine *Pasty*

Sarah-Katherine was born in Prague and came to the US in 1973. After inventing the leisure suit, she decided to turn her immense talent towards the production of a small, independent publication. Now she divides her time between whipping slave boys, giving out free phone sex on the local chat-line, and doing missionary work with Our Sisters of the Holy Stigmata.

Sarah F. *Pisces Ladybug*

Sarah Pisces Ladybug is a senior at a public high school in Bethesda, MD. Though she doesn't like school and has a hard time relating to the kids there, she is very active: she is President of the NOW Chapter, editor of the literary magazine, and captain of the debate and forensics team. In addition to her zine, she loves to paint, make magazine collages and drive with all the windows down. She plans to attend college in the Fall of '97 and study Sociology and Women's Studies.

Diana Morrow *Princess*

Diana has a B.F.A. in Photography and a B.A. in Women's Studies from Parsons School of Design and Eugene Lang College, respectively. Diana was active in Riot Grrrl NYC in college, where she worked on *Riot grrrl* and her own fanzines. *Princess* came out of the desire to synthesize and express all her interests and insights. Now she works as graphic designer at a publishing company in New York City, but photography and *Princess* are her first loves. She hopes to eventually make *Princess* a full-time job.

Goddess of Mars *Provo-CAT-ive*

Goddess of Mars is 18 and a sophomore at Auburn University (a state college in Alabama). She likes writing, painting, writing songs, playing keyboard and guitar, and reading.

Goddess of Venus *Provo-CAT-ive*

Goddess of Venus is 19 and a sophomore at Chatham College (an all-women's college in Pittsburgh). She likes writing her zine, booking shows, buying records, attending rallies, and taking pictures. She plans to be an environmental lobbyist and to open a club for indie bands.

Lala *Quarter Inch Squares*

Lala lives and creates chaos in Minneapolis, MN, where she writes, performs, paints, and turns heads every chance she gets.

Marla *Rats Live on No Evil Star*

Marla does the zine *Rats Live on No Evil Star*, and goes to college in Massachusetts.

Evelyn McDonnell *resister*

Evelyn McDonnell is the author of the official history of *Rent*, (Weisbach books, June 1997). She is co-editor of *Rock She Wrote: Women Write about Rock, Pop, and Rap.* Evelyn has contributed to *The New Rolling Stone Encyclopedia of Rock and Roll, Trouble Girls,* and *The Spin Guide to Alternative Music.* She also served as Senior Music Editor at the *Village Voice.* Evelyn's work has been published in the following: *Rolling Stone, Interview, The New York Times, Artforum, h2so4, Bust, Girljock,* and *Billboard.*

Carla DeSantis *ROCKRGRL*

Carla is a publisher/editor-in-chief of *ROCKRGRL.* She had many years experience as a bass player, publicist, and journalist before conceiving the idea for *ROCKRGRL* in the summer of '95.

Tamra Spivey *ROCKRGRL*

Tamra has helped organize several Riot Grrrl Conventions, beginning with the LA convention in 1995. Her band, Lucid Nation, played all of the West Coast conventions in 1996. She writes for the zines *Revolution Rising, TV1, Lucid Nation, Eracism,* and *Girl's Guide to Making a Band and Record.* She has shown her freestanding assemblages, autopsy stamp mandalas, and other art in undergroud art shows in LA.

Denise Sullivan *ROCKRGRL*

Denise Sullivan is the San Francisco–based author of *R.E.M.—Talk about the Passion, an Oral History,* and the senior editor of *Speak* magazine. Shonen Knife, Patti Smith, and Exene rock her world.

Lisa Crystal Carver *Rollerderby*

Lisa was born in 1968, and the rest of her life story can be found in *Rollerderby: The Book,* published by Feral Press.

Kim Cooper *Scram*

Kim is a loner bookworm with neo-sociable tendencies. She is a Hollywood native raised by hippies. She earned an MA in art history and is currently using it in a major West Coast museum. Kim is married to a swell fella she met after he disagreed with one of her *Scram* articles and wrote her to say so. Her cats are called Evel and Tallulah.

Nicky Splinter *Sewer*

Nicky Splinter is a pseudonym for Christine Doza. She's from Nashville, TN, but she currently lives, works, and loves in New York City.

Sara Sourpuss *Sourpuss*

Sara was born and raised in Pittsburgh. She attended Catholic school until third grade, which made her the psycho gerl that she is. She had always felt ugly and a dork until her involvement in the riot grrrl movement made her feel strong and empowered.

Leah Lilith Albrecht-Samarasinha *Sticks and Stones* and *Patti Smith*

Leah is a twenty-one-year-old, mixed-race Tamil Sri Lankan, bi-queer-femme-slut, abuse survivor, very tired, very cynical, and cranky woman who is committed to fighting for an anti-colonial revolution within her lifetime. She is trying like hell not to kill all her *companeras* in the process. Right now, Leah is finishing school and working at the Lesbian AIDS Project and within the student and prisoner support movements.

Lauren Martin *You Might as Well Live* and *Princess Charming*

Lauren is a Sociology/Gender Studies Major at Bard College and has a New York City middle-class Chinese/Hungarian/Jewish background. She does several zines and is involved with way too many projects.

Suzanne Rush *youtalkintame?*

Suzanne is a writer and graphic designer who's worked mostly in alternative publishing at the *LA Weekly,* the *SF Weekly* (in San Francisco) and the *Santa Fe Reporter,* with a stint at *Movieline* magazine as well. She wrote a column at the *LA Weekly* called "Valley Talk" a shopping column for *Movieline.* Mostly, Suzanne writes brooding, dark stories about betrayal and love lost. She's working on web design now, trying to get out of print publishing, unless she can own it. She's a Gemini and she can't make up her mind what to do next.

Additional Contribtors

Diane Morrison *Battle Dress* **Jennie Boddy** *Ben Is Dead* **Nina Dentata** *Ben Is Dead* **Missy Bean** *Easy* **Rachel G.** *Glitterscum* and *Quarter Inch Squares* **Lauren Barack** *hip Mama* **Avia Midons** *h2sO4* **Heidi Pollock** *h2sO4* **Marissa Walsh** *Indignant Gingham* **R.G.** *Mons of Venus* **Leora Wien** *My Life and My Sex Thrive in the J. Crew Catalogue* **Kathleen Hanna** *Princess* **Kathy Strieder** *Princess* **Jean** *Scrawl* **Julene Snyder** *youtalkintame?*

Girl Zine Reference Guide

How to use this guide:

We have compiled a list of girl zines from all over the country (plus a few from Canada and elsewhere). Please keep in mind that, at press time, we had verified all the contact information; however, addresses frequently change, so always use your return address in case your correspondence must be forwarded or returned. We have included the price of each zine, the price of a subscription if one is available, "pv" if the price varies, and "T" if the editor likes to trade. Your best bet is to send cash. Many girls do not have special checking accounts for their zines or checking accounts at all, so send them cash, wrap it carefully, and give them some time to get back to you.

100% Acrylic an optimistic pro-girl zine often dealing with women's issues, communication, and personal happenings in Wendy's life. Wendy, P.O. Box 15524, Gainesville, FL 32604 ($1 + 2 stamps/T).

The Action Girl Newsletter listings, reviews, and the ultimate guide to everything you need to know about girl zines. Sarah also does *Action Girl Comics*. Sarah Dyer, P.O. Box 060456, Staten Island, NY 10306 (pv).

The Adventures of Baby Dyke a comic zine that follows the adventures of Baby Dyke and Rocky—two dykes, one-track mind. Terry Sapp, 2215-R Market Street #437, San Francisco, CA 94114 ($4.50/T).

Alien well written, honest, super-personal zine exploring mental illness. Witknee's healing process, acceptance of being "crazy" by herself and others (or non-acceptance) and just about everything it encompasses. Witknee also does *Subway Sissy Zine Distro*. Witknee, P.O. Box 12262, Berkeley, CA 94712-2262 ($1.50 or 4 stamps).

Angry Young Woman collection of personal rants, social commentary, and general opinions on a variety of things. Gloria, P.O. Box 50167, Fort Wayne, IN 46805 (pv).

Aunt Franne a punk rock zine with a queer slant for everyone. frAnne, P.O. Box 523, Stratford, NJ 08084 ($1 + 1 stamp/T).

Babykins "a zine full of kitty cats, laughs and a slice of my kooky teeny bopper life." Amykins, 25 Wilner Road, Somers, NY 10589 ($1 + 1 stamp).

The Bad Girl Club grrrl related issues, fun, quirky rants, happy, silly girlie things, and lots more. Amy Hixon, 2100 Grand Ave. S. #2, Minneapolis, MN 55405 ($1/T).

Bamboo Girl a zine by/for/but not exclusive to young girls of color, dealing with issues faced in the hardcore/punk, queer and "ethnic" communities with a non-apologetic slant. Sabrina Sandata, P.O. Box 507, New York, NY 10159–0507 ($2/$6 sub).

The Barber Shop News it isn't a feminist zine—but it definitely appeals to any rebel girls who are into things that are eclectic, weird, funny, and personable. Theresa Meire, 2085 Burlington-Columbus Rd., Bordentown, NJ 08505 ($1.50/T).

Battle Dress—3 Women in Black published in 1994 by the Women's Action Coalition, this zine was created by a band of artist-activists; the only zine with an instant-action rape sticker inside. Duston Spear & Teri Slotkin, 463 Broome Street, New York, NY 10013 ($2).

Ben Is Dead (see Darby's essay for details). Darby, P.O. Box 3166, Hollywood, CA 90028 ($5).

Bi-Girl World fiction, poetry, rants and raves, historical info, all about being a Bi Girl a.k.a. bisexual woman in this either/or world. Fun, sometimes steamy stuff. (No longer publishing, 6 back issues available). Karen Friedland, 99 Newtonville Avenue, Newton, MA 02158 ($2/T).

Billy's Mitten a silly, cute girly zine by a teen girl who wants to start a teen revolution . . . go teen go! Theresa Mitten, 6255 E. Via De La Yerba, Tuscon, AZ 85750 ($1 + 2 stamps/T).

Blue Stocking currently focusing on being a national publication, and continuing to push the envelope on feminist topics. Judy Smith, P.O. Box 4525, Portland, OR 97208 ($3/T).

Boji for the Mentally Ill a bubbling cauldron overflowing with disturbing childhood memories, mental illness, pop culture, potty humor, anger, and music. A very tasty brew. Michelley Queen Of Queens & Julia Seizure, P.O. Box 1876, Hoboken, NJ 07030 ($2/T)

Bombscare personal zine about coming out and staying out. Tyrant, P.O. Box 8131, Pittsburgh, PA 15217 ($1/T).

Boredom Sucks to celebrate her high school graduation in 1995, Lauren put together a large compilation zine by lots of kids all about how high school is one fucked up institution. Lauren Martin, Bard College, Annandale-on-Hudson, NY 12504 ($2 + 1 stamp).

bunny rabbit Amy's world in many mediums—writing, drawing, and singing. C'mon in and sit a spell! Amy Fusselman, 51 MacDougal Street, Box 319, New York, NY 10012 ($3).

Bust Marcelle Karp, P.O. Box 319, New York, NY 10023 ($2.50).

Butterknife Junior Hilary Small, 129 Sugarplum Lane, Benton, KY 42025.

Calico a no-holds-barred zine for all people with poetry, fiction, non-fiction, and reviews. Rachel Johnson, 44 Manomet St., Brockton, MA 02401 ($1-$2 w/stamps).

The Charm Booklette a baby pink and blue stingeroo stuffed fat with girl wit and wisdom. Sara Zoe Mondt, 929 E. 2nd St. #206, Los Angeles, CA 90012 ($2/T).

Cheese a zine devoted to exposing the ubiquitousness of cheese and the preponderance of cheesy culture. Each issue has a different "culture" theme. Mary Brandt, P.O. Box 55211, Portland, OR 97238 ($1-2).

Cheshire an aqueous blend of comix, humor, and scandal! Jackie Sarratt, 4401 Dartmoor Lane, Alexandria, VA 22310 (2 stamps).

Chickfactor 245 East 19th Street, New York, NY 10003 ($3).

Coming Out Party a zine I make to talk about creating revolution in our everyday life and bringing it to the outside world. Personal and totally honest, I talk about racism and prejudice, sexual identity, being a kid, being a girl, and fat hatred. (Rori also did the zine *Mimi's Revenge*). Rori, 78 Prospect Park West #5F, Brooklyn, NY 11215 ($1/T).

Crush pocket-sized cut and paste number with a bad girl sensibility. Kristyn Samok & Kathe Izzo, P.O. Box 1559, Provincetown, MA 02657 (T).

Cunt a radical dyke zine covering sexuality, clubbing, and cynical witticism (no longer publishing). Rachel Pepper, 401 Cortland Avenue, San Francisco, CA 94110 (pv).

Cupcake a zine concerned with feminism, personal strength and healing, art, and fun. Jocelyn, 4225 Glenmuir Avenue, Los Angeles, CA 90065 (50 cents/T).

Cupsize inherently feminist, intentionally hilarious, there is no topic too great or too small, from grape soda taste tests to a consideration of the ways in which liberalism retards feminism. We mine the mundane for the magnificent and give it back to you in written form. Sasha & Tara Emelye, P.O. Box 4326, Stony Brook, NY 11790-4326 ($2/T).

Diabolical Clits a panoply of LA perv pornographers of all proclivities—het, lez, gay, bi, and other. Our mottos: "Good writing makes us wet" and "If it's sexy, it's sacred." Sandra Lee Golvin (co-editor: Hannah Bleier), 2219 Grand Canal, Venice, CA 90291 ($6).

Disgruntl T.V. zine on politics, people, and music. Judas, P.O. Box 394, Chatham College, Woodland Road, Pittsburgh, PA 15232-2826 (pv/T).

Dog Star Girl a homosexual mutt shrine incorporating amusing and not-so-amusing newspaper-clippings, quotations, original writings and images, "found" material, star worship stuff, erotic musings, poems and dogs, dogs, dogs. For dykes, fags, and dog fanatics everywhere. Gerry Gomez Pearlberg c/o T. Taormino, P.O. Box 4108 Grand Central Station, New York, NY 10163 (pv).

Doris stories about umbrellas and cornfields, cities and bugs, bikes, dogs, strangers, and some crazy kind of hope. Cindy Gretchen Ovenrack, P.O. Box 4279, Berkeley, CA 94704 ($1.50).

Easy a motivational and support guide for girls infiltrating the boy-dominated punk scene. J-Me, P.O. Box 185, Northampton, PA 18067-9998 ($1/T).

Ectoderm female empowerment for girls who have good intentions but can still giggle at the idiosyncrasies of the world. Kristin Campbell and Shannon Babcock, 188 Country Club Drive, Kingston, Ontario, K7M 7B6 Canada ($1/T).

Everything I Touch Turns to Shit and Garbage walking the voluptuous line between glamour and seediness. Firecracker smart, obsessed with childhood, and really, really bossy! Queen Itchie, P.O. Box 770, Sherburne, NY 13460 ($2.50).

Face First a sort of personal fanzine with design bits as well. Julie, Mount Holyoke College, 1284 Blanchard Student Center, South Hadley, MA 01075-6002 ($1 or 2 stamps/T).

FaT GiRL started in Spring 1994 from the loins of several creative and fed-up fat dykes in San Francisco, *FaT GiRL* is dedicated to providing space for fat dykes (and the women who want them) to express the gritty truths in all areas of our lives. FaT GiRL Collective, 2215-R Market St., San Francisco, CA 94114 ($5).

Fat! So? P.O. Box 423464, San Francisco, CA 94142.

Femme Flicke a filmzine written mostly by, for, and about women in underground film, with interviews with young female film directors, articles on how to get your films shown, reviews, a comprehensive list of women directors, and much more. Tina Spangler, 99 Hancock Street #4, Cambridge, MA 02139 ($2).

Get What You Want a fully illustrated B&W comic book. A wild ride through the bedrooms and backstreets of San Francisco freaky dykes. Big girls, safer sex, sex work, flaming cootchies, and a turtle. Mary Anderson & Youme, 418 Duboce Street, San Francisco, CA 94117 ($4).

Girlie Jones art, politics, and popular culture in the lives of young women. Zoe Miller, Colleen Sumner, Aimee Gagnon, P.O. Box 67, Springvale, ME 04083 (free in Portland, ME/$15 sub).

Girljock Roxxie, P.O. Box 882723, San Francisco, CA 94188-2723 (pv).

GlitterScum Rachel G., P.O. Box 760, Groveton, TX 75845 ($2).

Global Mail a resource directory of current mail art projects, exchanges, zines requesting contributions of art and text, network news, and more. Generally 600–800 listings from over 40 countries. Ashley Parker Owens, P.O. Box 410837, San Francisco, CA 94141-0837 ($3/$9 sub/T).

Gogglebox now dead, this zine was once a kicking baby in the collective stomach of all wild girl soul adventuresses. Jenn G. Box, P.O. Box 250402, New York, NY 10025 ($2).

h2so4 aims to combine the serious and the silly, the arcane and the mundane, each without making excuses for the other. Jill Stauffer, P.O. Box 423354, San Francisco, CA 94142 ($4).

hip Mama the parenting zine. Ariel Gore, P.O. Box 9097, Oakland, CA 94613 ($4/$12–20 sliding scale sub).

Hey There, Barbie Girl! now produced as *Plotz*.

Hope a small zine consisting mostly of the editor's stories, poems, the occasional rant, zine reviews, and work by other writers. *Hope* may be small, but it's dense, and each issue is made with much love and trepidation. Elissa Nelson, Bard College, Annandale-On-Hudson, NY 12504 ($1 or 4 stamps/T).

Hot Snot Pot chock full of funny-ass shit with no holds barred. Lauren Fury, P.O. Box 1194, Blue Bell, PA 19422 ($2/T).

I-Am-a-Cliché celebrates the feminine force in the underground. The cut and paste pages contain estrogen-fueled rants, raves, and verse. Zoe Cliché, 2315 Green St., Harrisburg, PA 17110 ($3/T).

I ♥ Amy Carter (see Tammy's essay for details). Tammy Rae Carland, 509 E. Anderson #4, Greencastle, IN, 46135 ($2–3).

Imaginary Friend "a crazy cut-up visual mess of words and images to alleviate the author's profound sense of alienation and loneliness and angst-o-rama and to satisfy her incredible urge to relate the strange and wonderful and disturbing life she lives." Zelinda McSeven, 94 Atwater Street, West Haven, CT 06516 ($1 + 2 stamps/T).

I'm So Fuckin' Beautiful Nomy Lamm, 120 State NE #1510, Olympia, WA 98501.

Indignant Gingham a girl zine about life in NYC's pop culture, and things that make me indignant. Marissa Walsh, P.O. Box 1239, New York, NY 10185-1239 ($1 + 2 stamps/T).

J.T.O.: Jailhouse Turn Out (see Tammy's essay for details). Tammy Rae Carland, 509 E. Anderson #4, Greencastle, IN, 46135 ($2–3).

Kusp and **Out of the Vortex** the accumulated broodings of a politically opinionated nerd dyke who doesn't see the sun enough—sexuality, gender, activism, privilege, feminism, and relationships. Sara Marcus, P.O. Box 203258, Yale Station, New Haven, CT 06520. ($1 + 2 stamps).

Kye an eclectic assortment of fiction, plays, poetry, up-n-coming band interviews, author interviews, book reviews, and anything else musically and worldly related. Robyn Pickering, c/o co-editor: Eric Zass, P.O. Box 3351 Vassar College, Poughkeepsie, NY 12601 ($2 + stamps).

Lezzie Smut a lesbian sex magazine which attempts to be provocative, enticing, and seductive. Completely created and run by women, we hope to give lesbian sexuality an outlet in Canada and the rest of the world. Hey Grrrlz Productions/Robin Hand, P.O. Box 364, 1027 Davie St., Vancouver, V6E 4L2, Canada ($6/sub $28 US/sub $22 Canada).

Looks Yellow, Tastes Red personal zine that includes things like work, school, relationships, music, comics. Collette, P.O. Box 1275, Wellfleet, MA 02667 ($1 + 1 stamp/$3 sub).

Madwoman angry women fight back with a great graphic sense, biting humor, and a vengeance! Helena Perkins, 30 S. 4th Street, Madison, WI 53704 ($2/T).

Maxine a literate companion for churlish girls and rakish women. Loosely explores a topic of the season through the rants, revelations, manifestos, critical inquiry and personal disclosure, and marginalia of a host of contributors. Editors Zoe Zolbrod, Martha Bayne & Anne Bruns, 2025 West Augusta, Chicago, IL 60622 ($3).

Ms .45 ostensibly a feminist zine—not "riot grrrl," not "power feminist," not "pro-sex," not "netchic(k)"—just feminist. P.O. Box 2063, Fitzroy Mail Delivery Centre 3065, Victoria Australia ($2).

Ms. Stucco Girl a homemade girl zine; personal writings, poetry, and cut-n-paste style art. Heidi Annalieze Boruff, 1805 Virginia Park Drive, Valparaiso, IN 46383 ($1 or 4 stamps/T).

Mudflaps queerpore comix for bratty gurlz . . . from bruised hymen to broken noses, *Mudflaps* is a cure-all for any raging dollface. Nytsirk Noinnud, 189 Main Street West, Kingsville, Ontario, N9Y 1H7 Canada ($2 or $1 w/SASE/T).

Muffin Bones "an autobiographical art-lit-truth-fiction-fun-comic sort of thing" Emily K. Larned, Wesleyan Station Box 4724, Middletown, CT 06459-4724 ($1 + 2 stamps/$5 sub/T).

My Last Nerve "it's been called angry (usually by men), but we think it's just real—stuff on music, anarchy, tarot, abortion and anything else on our minds." Carol Petrucci and Cheri Haines, P.O. Box 3054, Madison, WI 53704-0054. ($1.50 or 6 stamps).

My Life and My Sex Thrive in the J. Crew Catalogue a collection of personal cartoons, poems, and essays, sometimes inspired by my identification with the Crew as a parallel universe. Leora Wien, 12941 Otsego Street, Sherman Oaks, CA 91423 ($1/T).

Mystery Date "a zine dedicated to my obsession with used books, particularly old home economics texts, sex and dating manuals, and etiquette guides." Lynn Peril, P.O. Box 641592, San Francisco, CA 94164-1592 ($1.50).

Nothing a zine to be happy about—fun drawings, ska adventures, Naked Tuna comics, tributes to friends and fashion—that will make you want to ride your scooter all day and play dress up all night. Marissa, 349 Ash St., Willimantic, CT 06226 ($1 + 2 stamps/T).

Not Your Bitch an ever-evolving zine that maintains a queer feminist anarchist tune. Mostly political rants, but some funny stories, poetry, and music stuff. Christine Johnston, P.O. Box 11843, Olympia, WA 98508-1843 ($1).

Ocho y Media a collaborative work from the San Diego Women's Discussion Circle & Action Group—life perspectives from thirty-two eyes. Ocho y Media Women's Group, P.O. Box 81332, San Diego, CA 92138 ($1/T).

Pasty spewing hatred and vitriol since 1994, Pasty gleefully mocks the handicapped, the ignorant, the pc, and customers unfortunate enough to shop at the author's condom store. Chock full of hostility! A mostly unpleasant read. Sarah-Katherine, 6201 15th Ave NW #P-549, Seattle, WA 98107 ($2).

Pawholes an eclectic mélange of satire, sanguine cynicism, sexuality, and pop culture produced primary by a randy troupe of Steel City chix. Deborah, P.O. Box 81202, Pittsburgh, PA 15217 ($4/T).

Pisces Ladybug a feminist zine with a creative edge, includes pieces on homophobia in high school, body image, pre-teen literature, menstruation, and other topics taboo in suburban high schools. Sarah, P.O. Box 341122, West Bethesda, MD 20827 ($1/T).

Plotz (formerly produced as *Hey There, Barbie Girl!*): a Jewish pop culture zine that dares ask the question, "What's your favorite kosher food?" Barbara, P.O. Box 819 Stuyvesant Station, New York, NY 10009 ($1 + 2 stamps).

Porn Free a free, internationally distributed sex zine that focuses on a different theme in each issue. Abby Hoffman, P.O. Box 1365, New York, NY 10009 ($2 for postage).

Pornorama polysexual porn fiction, comics, pix; with reviews of bands, books, and zines. Geared to dykes and bisexual women, but anyone is welcome to enjoy. Nairne Holtz, 386 Concord Avenue, Toronto, Ontario, M6H 2P8 CANADA ($3).

Princess a dyke-centered women's magazine which covers art, music, sex, politics, whatever women do. The purpose is to give recognition to women who do important work to make a difference in women's lives, especially through creativity and political engagement. Diana Morrow, P.O. Box 20370, New York, NY 10009 ($3).

Princess for girls who know what they need. 175 Fifth Avenue #2416, New York, NY 10010 ($4).

Princess Charming Feminist zine about girl love, beauty/body image, and self-reliance. Lauren Martin, Bard College, Annandale-on-Hudson, NY 12504 (2 stamps/T).

Provo-CAT-ive Venus and Mars, coming from different avenues of life (and different planets), speak about: feminism, masturbation, discrimination, flight sickness, run-ins with the law, road trips, Chinese zodiacs, first date advice, tributes to women, and interviews. Goddess of Venus & Goddess of Mars, P.O. Box 1636, Auburn, AL 36831–1636 ($1 + 2 stamps/T).

Pucker Up pansexual erotic zine that's brainy, daring, sharp, sexy, off-beat and sassy; fiction, essays, poetry, photography, art, interviews, reviews, crushes, and more. Tristan Taormino & Karen Green, P.O. Box 4108 Grand Central Station, New York, NY 10163. ($5/$18 sub).

Pussycat Rag the vision is simple—women need to hear other women's voices. Exploratory, insightful, high-quality writing by women. Naomi Graychase, 640 Anderson, San Francisco, CA 94110 ($1).

Quarter Inch Squares a venue for Lala and her friends (both real and imaginary) to record their adventures in the world with poetry, essays, rants, art, propaganda. Lala, P.O. Box 80606, Minneapolis, MN 55408-8606 ($2/T).

Ramona the Infamous Toothpaste Queen a very personal, cute zine containing photos, silliness, Ramona Quimby tributes, recipes, zine reviews, doodles, writings, butterflies, and more. Scilla, 154 Railroad Ave., Hamilton, MA 01982 ($1 + 1 stamp/T).

Rats Live On No Evil Star Marla, P.O. Box 333, B.U. Station, Boston, MA 02215-9991 ($1 + 2 stamps).

Rebel Fux! a "cut-up" zine which attempts to interweave texts of various adventurous/infamous individuals with images which are related or completely unrelated. It explores the use of collage and "cut-up" poetry as an anarchist tool. Kate Huh, 18 First Avenue #15, New York, NY 10009 (free/T).

resister a fanzine of the mainstream, a nuts and bolts guide to thought and expression, with poetry, photos, essays, satire, reviews, art, and fiction. "The resister increases electrical flow by disrupting dominant pathways, whose qualities of conductivity have been eroded by oversaturation, and diverting signals into new channels for transmission." Evelyn McDonnell, P.O. Box 1479, New York, NY 10276-1479 ($4).

Riot Grrrl Press publishes a ton of zines, including *Riot Grrrl, Fantastic Fanzine, Cross My Heart, Discharge, Wrecking Ball, Fix Me, Marika,* and distribute plenty more. Mary & Erica, P.O. Box 12801, Olympia, WA 98508 (pv).

Rock Candy "a zine about being an eighteen-year-old girl, sexual-abuse survivor, and general badass, and all the hope and beauty I see in myself, my friends, and everyday life." Marie, 717 Davis, Kalamazoo, MI 49007 ($1).

ROCKRGRL for and about women in the music industry, primarily rock; includes profiles of women rockers as well as women working behind the scenes, legal tips, new equipment, concert reviews and much more! Carla DeSantis, 7683 SE 27th St. #317, Mercer Island, WA 98040-2826 ($5/$24 sub).

Rollerderby (see Lisa's essay for details). Lisa Carver, P.O. Box 474, Dover, NH 03821 ($3).

Sappho's Scribblers the lesbian publication at Hunter College, published from Fall '94 – Spring '96. Ilsa Jule, 129 East 7th Street, New York, NY 10009 ($3).

The Scaredy-Cat Stalker a zine about obsessions (and hates), celebrity and otherwise. Krista Garcia, 5535 NE Glisan #5, Portland, OR 97213 ($1 + 2 stamps/T).

Scram the only place where you can read about the secret history of rodents in rock, Walt Disney Corp's sinister new planned community in Florida, the recorded work of Burt Reynolds, the sexual subtext of bubblegum music, or the ultra-theatrical Thai sex industry. Kim Cooper, P.O. Box 461626, Hollywood, CA 90046 ($4/$16 sub).

Sewer from the creator of *Construction Paper* and *UpSlut* comes a zine about healing from the continuing effects of sexual abuse and the steamy underworld of strip clubs. Nicky Splinter, P.O. Box 20513, New York, NY, 10009 ($1).

Skew writings that explore the sexual politics of class, privilege, violence, language, religion, and other engendered institutions. Recognizes the stagnation in naming an almighty Enemy and considers our personal part in feeding the mutually sustained gender conflict. Britton Neubacher, P.O. Box 81332, San Diego, CA 92138(50 cents + stamp/T).

Skin on Skin lesbian porn for the daring. Sorel Husbands, 639 14th Street, San Francisco, CA 94114 ($3).

Slug and Lettuce a free punk zine emphasizing contacts, networking, and communication within the underground punk scene. Total supporting the DIY (Do It Yourself) ethic of underground punk. Contains band photos, punk art, free classifieds, reviews of music and zines, and more. Christine Boarts, P.O. Box 2067, New York, NY 10009 (55 cents/T).

Slumber personal, low budget victim of teenage copy-shop workers full of great writing and venting. Spence, P.O. Box 139, Cazadero, CA 95421–0139 (pv).

Sourpuss a small zine about fat girl power and revolution, this zine is a fat positive, sad, psycho-gerlie gerl zine. Sara Sourpuss, 330 Ophelia Street, Pittsburgh, PA 15213 (50 cents or 2 stamps/T).

Spilt Milk a collection of poetry, prose, thoughts, and drawings reflecting the experiences and feelings of the contributors, with individual handmade covers. Anna Gosselin & Sarah Frankfurth, P.O. Box 33442, San Diego, CA 92163 ($2/T).

Spinsterwitch a personal zine on rantings, body image, rape, books, and films (#4 split with the zine *Alien*). Jenni, 3354 Palm Aire Court, Rochester Hills, MI 48309 ($1 + 2 stamps/T).

Squealworm "a girl-produced zine by me—a young bi-dyke who loves her bicycle, various girlfriends, turtles, and eating well." From the genius who brought us *Mons of Venus*. Freda, P.O. Box 7581, Ft. Lauderdale, FL 33338-7581 ($1).

Starache "personal writings with rants on feminism, race, music and whatever else I decide to print." Amy Funaro, 9902 Hampton Woods, Kansas City, MO 64152 ($1).

Sticks and Stones and **Patti Smith** two personal zines on surviving familial abuse (especially emotional) by a queer, mutt-raced, South Asian feminist. Leah Lilith Albrecht Samarasinha, 1011 Landsdowne Avenue #508, Toronto, Ontario M6H-4G1, Canada.

Tazewell's Favorite Eccentric a grrrl, queer, personal zine that the author created as an outlet for her creatively repressed self, to share with the rest of the world. Sarah, P.O. Box 1010, N. Tazewell, VA 24630 ($1/trade).

Thrift Score the zine about thrifting for cool stuff you don't need—not about tightwadding. Al Hoff, P.O. Box 90282, Pittsburgh, PA 15224 ($1).

Tobi's Veil sometimes silly, sometimes serious ramblings of a music-worshipping riot grrrl and feminist activist complete with aesthetically pleasing pictures. Elizabeth Velic, Room 3304C Bevier Hall, SUNY New Paltz, New Paltz, NY 12561 ($1/T).

Twat! A Grrrl Zine Catalog Christine Johnston, P.O. Box 11843, Olympia, WA 98508-1843 ($1).

two girls review a culture crashing, art, and literature zine. Lydia Yukman, Kelly Vie, Paige Price, Devin Crowe, 3331 NE 36th Avenue, Portland, OR 97212 ($6.99/$12 sub/T).

Wild Honey Pie and **Riot Grrrl Review** Kristy Chan, 1732 Fowler #G, Ft. Meyers, FL 33901 ($2).

Wives Tales a do-it-yourself guide to gynecological self-help and natural healing. Alternatives to patriarchal medicine through self-cervical exam, menstrual anarchy, natural birth control, home remedies, herbal abortion, and more. Britton Neubacher, P.O. Box 81332, San Diego, CA 92138 ($3/T).

Yawp "I had to do a zine (for therapy my own way) but I discovered my intensely honest and often painful writings helped others too—this zine is about connections, overcoming pain, sisterhood." Johanna Novales, Box 752723, Dallas, TX 75275-2723 ($1 + 2 stamps).

YOB C. Garrett, 2 Cedar Lane, Orinda, CA 94563 ($1).

You Might as Well Live After doing zines for a number of years as outlets for her depression and anger, Lauren went to college and created this zine for a fresh start. Taking the personal as political, this is emotional, feminist, and kid-powered. Lauren Martin, Bard College, Annandale-on-Hudson, NY 12504 ($1 + 2 stamps).

youtalkintame? is a literary zine showcasing new short fiction produced by a disturbing group of women writers in San Francisco, CA, and Santa Fe, NM. Suzanne Rush (Co-editors: Julene Snyder, Annette Weathers, Patricia Good, Noria Jablonski), 369 Montezuma Avenue, Santa Fe, NM 87501 ($4).